MAVIS BATEY

MAVIS BATEY

Bletchley Codebreaker, Writer, Garden Historian, Conservationist

JEAN STONE

Matador
9 Priory Business Park,
Wistow Road, Kibworth Beauchamp,
Leicestershire, LE8 0RX
Tel: 0116 279 2299
Email: books@troubador.co.uk
Web: www.troubador.co.uk/matador
Twitter: @matadorbooks

ISBN 978 1838591 496

British Library Cataloguing in Publication Data.
A catalogue record for this book is available from the British Library.

Printed and bound by CPI Group (UK) Ltd, Croydon, CR0 4YY
Typeset in 12pt Minion Pro by Troubador Publishing Ltd, Leicester, UK

Matador is an imprint of Troubador Publishing Ltd

Mavis Batey
(1921–2013)

For Elizabeth, Christopher and Deborah

CONTENTS

LIST OF ILLUSTRATIONS

ACKNOWLEDGEMENTS

I first came to know Mavis Batey several years ago, and when I later met her daughters, they were so pleasant and helpful that I felt I had also known them for many years. I would like to give warm thanks to Elizabeth and Deborah for all the help they have given me in passing on family memories and notes that Mavis herself had written about her life, which they assured me she would have appreciated being used in her biography.

I extend my thanks to Professor Jane Ridley, at the University of Buckingham, for suggesting Mavis Batey as the character for the biographical dissertation required for an MA in Biography, on which this book is based. My colleagues on this course were generous with information, in particular Jennifer Holmes and Dr David Noy who helped me with some important decision making for which I thank them.

I am indebted to Bryony Norburn for sharing her knowledge of Bletchley Park, and John Chapman, once in charge of the Bletchley Park Postal Services. He kindly suggested various books and gave me a collection of interesting cuttings. Bletchley Park's archivist, Richard Lewis, never failed to provide guidance and, more recently, Mari Haughem, who has cheerfully carried out some rewarding picture research on my behalf. I would like to thank these people and also the veterans who have taken me on tours around Bletchley Park.

Members of the former Garden History Society, now The Gardens Trust, have been constantly available to offer information and give support, and I would particularly like to thank Charles Boot, News Editor and Honorary Librarian, for his kindness in gathering together images of people and places with which Mavis Batey was associated. My thanks go to Christopher Sumner; Mike Thompson; Wendy Osborne, who has offered interesting information about her work on Alverstoke Crescent Garden and Anna Chalcraft, who was happy to talk about discussions with Mavis Batey and their work at Strawberry Hill House and garden.

My research has benefitted from the help of staff and librarians at the Bodleian Library; the London Library; The British Library; and the Oxford Central Library, to whom I would like to extend my thanks. I would also like to thank Kim Wilkie, Landscape Architect and David Lambert, Conservationist, as it gave me so much pleasure to write about their time spent with Mavis Batey, and having fun when working on the Thames Landscape Strategy from Hampton to Kew.

Special thanks to my friends Rose Michel, Patricia Ellis and Dianne Ewing for their interest, and in particular Rosemary Jury for her continuous support, encouragement and help. Once again my thanks to my family for their endless patience. Finally, I remember with gratitude my telephone conversations with the late Jane Fawcett, who will not be forgotten.

If, by oversight, any copyright holder has been overlooked, the author will be pleased to rectify any errors or omissions brought to her notice.

GLOSSARY OF TERMS

Abwehr	The German armed forces intelligence service.
ARP	Air Raid Precautions
Beetle	A term used by Knox and his team to define two clicks on the same rod.
Bomba (pl. bomby)	A machine invented by the Polish to be used when breaking Enigma keys.
Bombe	A fast electro mechanical machine used when breaking Enigma keys – a British device inspired by the Polish bomba.
Buttoning-up	The routine used for recovering the wiring of the rotors in an Enigma cypher machine without a stecker i.e. plugboard.
BSC	British Security Co-ordination
CPRE	Council for the Preservation of Rural England. Now the Campaign to Protect Rural England.
Crib	Probable text used previously and tested against the cypher text and perhaps break the message.

Cryptology	The two-part science of cryptography, encoding and cryptanalysis, the breaking of codes.
DNI	Director of Naval Intelligence
GC&CS	Government Code and Cypher School, 1919–1945.
GCHQ	Formerly GC&CS but post-war became Government Communications Headquarters.
GGG	Abwehr Enigma connecting Berlin with stations in Spain.
ICOMOS	International Council on Monuments and Sites
ISK	Intelligence Services Knox (frequently called Illicit Services Knox)
ISOS	Intelligence Services Oliver Strachey
MEW	Ministry of Economic Warfare
MI5	British Security Service department for running the XX-system and control of double agents.
MI6	British Secret Service: primarily espionage or obtaining accurate information from the enemy by the means of secret agents, and other tasks.
Neptune	The naval portion of Overlord
NID	Naval Intelligence Division
OCS	Oxford Civic Society
Pinch	Thefts of original codebooks or cypher material.
Stecker (g)	Plugboard
PWE	Political Warfare Executive
QWERTZU	The order in which the keys on the Enigma machine were wired to the entry plate.
Ringstellung(s) (g)	Ring setting on an Enigma rota or reel.
RSS	Radio Security Service
Sigint.	Signals Intelligence Agency

SIS	Secret Intelligence Service
SPAB	Society for the Protection of Ancient Buildings
Traffic	Encoded messages.
Twenty	Committee or (XX) Committee, The Double Cross System
ULTRA	Top secret code word for information achieved when breaking high-grade cyphers devised by Wing Commander Winterbotham who had been head of the Air Intelligence Section.
Y-Services	Carried out traffic analysis and broke low-grade codes and cyphers over a wide area.

MAVIS BATEY (1921–2013)
An Introduction

When I heard of the death of Mavis Batey (née Lever), I remembered that she had made an important contribution to society as an outstanding codebreaker at Bletchley Park during World War II. Her achievements as a codebreaker were groundbreaking, making enormous strides towards bringing peace. Mavis worked at Bletchley Park from a teenager at the beginning of the war until it finished in 1945, by which time she had become a twenty-four-year-old married woman.

As there is no biography of this remarkable woman, I thought people might like to hear how Mavis spent her life during World War II as a codebreaker and her later career as garden historian, conservationist and writer. She played a significant role in establishing garden history as an academic subject, and brought the National Register of Parks and Gardens of Special Historic Interest to fruition. Grants were made available and gardens became officially recognised as essential components of European culture.

Wartime destruction inspired Mavis to take an active role in conservation and she became a campaigning force for the protection of landscapes, parks and gardens, fighting threats of encroachment and misuse of land. She led several campaigns saving many important, and often beautiful, landscapes and gardens from destruction by post-war development. Mavis's achievements made a countrywide impact.

I first met Mavis Batey whilst studying the Conservation of Historic Landscape, Parks and Gardens at the Architectural Association School of Architecture in London. I suppose it was because Mavis was writing about St Frideswide's Holy Well at Binsey, near Oxford, and I was writing about the old Charterhouse Monastery, London, that we gravitated towards each other after her lecture, and struck up conversation. These subjects had things in common and we were soon chatting together like old friends. Out of a carrier bag – an accessory for which Mavis became well known – she pulled a draft copy of her work; she thought I might find it of interest and suggested I take it away with me.

As I came to know Mavis better I realised her friendliness was a particular trait. Some in the group were highly educated, but were new to the world of gardens and landscape, and I had the impression that they found it amusing to have this jolly, little, white-haired, rosy-cheeked, middle-aged woman giving a lecture, and at first they undervalued her. Yes, she was a motherly figure, but they underestimated her skills. Mavis was extremely knowledgeable and, driven by enthusiasm, encouraged people into her world of garden history and conservation and was always generously prepared to share her knowledge. Mavis was such a friendly soul that everyone referred to her by her first name, which I will also do throughout this biography.

The biography covers Mavis's life from her childhood years and her work at Bletchley Park, where she was assigned at age nineteen years. She became one of Bletchley Park's top codebreakers, playing an important role decoding German and Italian Enigma cyphers. Mavis met and married fellow codebreaker Keith Batey, and when peace came they travelled with their baby daughter, Elizabeth, to Canada, Keith having joined the British Diplomatic Service.

After a spell in that country, where Mavis enjoyed carrying out the duties of a diplomat's wife, they returned to England where she devoted time to the care of their growing family, and she also started to study social history and landscape. They changed addresses a few times before settling in Oxford where Mavis became a garden historian, conservationist and writer. Eventually they retired to the south coast but Mavis continued to work, sometimes returning to visit Bletchley Park as a veteran.

The British Secret Service Bureau, set up in 1909, was not an organisation where one would find women. Most women wishing to work during World War II were to be found nursing, or working in the Land Army, and were frequently occupied replacing the workforce of conscripted men. Working-class women were enticed by propaganda to work in munitions factories, most returning to domesticity when the war was over. However, barriers were broken down, bringing about a changing Britain where women were becoming recognised as equal to men.

Mavis was one of a very few pioneering women working for the Government Code and Cypher School, and in 1939 she and her colleagues at Bletchley Park were among the first women to enter the field of cryptology. The number of women working there gradually increased, but they filled very few senior posts. Most women seem to have been restricted to mundane, routine jobs, such as cypher clerks who simply typed, and Jean Harris (who later became Baroness Trumpington), who worked at Bletchley Park from 1940, described the work as being extremely repetitive and tedious.

Mavis and her colleague, Margaret Rock, were more fortunate and enjoyed their work as codebreakers. Nevertheless, they did not rise to managerial positions even though they became recognised as exceptional codebreakers. The top posts were filled by men; perhaps this was because they were better educated than the women, or it may have been accepted, without question, that they were better educated. This is the way it was; men were once frequently considered more intelligent than women.

Brenda Colvin and Sylvia Crow were pioneers who became leading names in the field of landscape design, a close cousin of landscape conservation. In 1951 Brenda Colvin was elected President of the Institute of Landscape Architects, the first time a woman had headed an environmental design profession in the United Kingdom. Mavis's career overlapped their final years, and it could be said that this enterprising couple opened doors by putting women on the landscape map, and Mavis most certainly continued in this trend.

Many things changed after World War II, and the recognition of women in the workplace slowly moved forward. When The Garden History Society was formed, the committee of twelve consisted of nine men and three women. Mavis took over from Kay Sanecki as honorary secretary from 1971, but again most of the committee members were men.

Mavis was intensely proud of Bletchley Park's impenetrable secrecy. Many of Bletchley Park's secrets were not for sharing. Employees at Bletchley Park had signed the Official Secrets Act and, when you think of the 9–10,000 people working in all the various sections, it is incredible that the secret of what was happening there never got out. Bletchley's mysteries remained undercover for the next thirty years and only then did information start to be released, slowly trickling out, but many secrets remained, causing difficulties and resentment.

Unlike many people Mavis appears not to have had a problem with remaining silent about confidential information. Mavis and her husband, Keith, had been colleagues, marrying whilst at Bletchley Park, so no doubt it was fonder memories that lingered. It came as a great surprise when, at the age of seventy-seven, her wide circle of friends and colleagues in the world of garden history saw her story on Channel 4 television, in the series *Station X,* telling of the vital work that she and her fellow codebreakers had carried out at Bletchley Park.

It could have caused a problem if Mavis had wanted to seek employment as no reference could be given but it was always Mavis and Keith's choice that she should be with her young children, so none was needed.

They lived at Nuneham Courtenay, Oxfordshire for a couple of years, and the whole family – there were now three children – found it enchanting. They would sail along the River Thames in their boat which Keith named *Sivam Revel* – Mavis's name spelt in reverse – and it was at Nuneham Courtenay where Keith would go fishing, and Mavis would love to ramble around the countryside with the children. It was here at Nuneham Courtenay where her passion for garden history and writing blossomed. Mavis always said she used opportunities as they presented themselves, and so she did, delving deep into the history of the Nuneham Courtenay country estate of the Harcourt family, the creators of the gardens, and the gardeners themselves. She was enthralled and it was not long before Mavis joined The Garden History Society as honorary secretary.

Wartime destruction troubled Mavis as it did many people, and a fondness for the natural landscape, and her interest in local history, caused Mavis to be concerned by the way many of our beautiful landscape parks were threatened by unsatisfactory development. She soon found herself on the executive committee of the Oxford branch of the Council for the Preservation of Rural England, becoming a well-known figure in Oxford. 'You should make your voice known. You never know how things are going to turn out,'[1] she would say when she was campaigning for a particular conservation project to be put in hand.

The choice of their next new home was perfect: the schools were now near home, Mavis was in easier reach of the Bodleian Library and she was able to entertain visitors, friends, the children's school friends, of which there was a continuous stream, and she also welcomed increasing numbers of societies to which she belonged to have their committee meetings in the sitting room. Mavis was most certainly a 'people person'.

Mavis became an important figure in the Garden History Society's story; an inspired leader, along with the chairman, the late Edward Fawcett, who for several years was the director of the conservation course at the Architectural Association. Supported by an enthusiastic committee at The Garden History Society, Mavis and Ted encouraged the research of historic parks and gardens, making it their business to address the conservation problems of those of particular historic interest.

Kay Sanecki, a founder member and previous secretary of the GHS, would have been pleased to learn that Mavis is acknowledged as the driving force behind the society's involvement with conservation, and had met the challenge of the times by taking the society's work on these matters to the highest national level and importance. Mavis had an intense desire to preserve heritage and campaigned tirelessly to save gardens and landscapes such as Painshill Park which, to her delight, was one of the first landscapes to receive grant aid from the newly formed National Heritage Memorial Fund, and her work on the Thames Landscape Strategy from Hampton to Kew was another success.

It was due to her strength of purpose and personality that Mavis rose to become president of The Garden History Society in 1975, continuing until 2000, and remaining an active supporter until the end of her life. Garden history has most certainly achieved status as an academic subject, which was the wish of Peter Hunt and co-founder, Kay Sanecki, and it has a worldwide following.

Keith was treasurer at Christchurch and his rooms overlooked the deanery garden, the same garden as the author Reverend Charles Dodgson, or Lewis Carroll, as he chose to be known, had gazed upon from the library when conceiving the tale of *Alice's Adventures in Wonderland.* The children were delighted at this and Mavis's interest was aroused. She was inspired to delve into the 'unique brand of fun-loving nonsense based on logic'[2] of this imaginative genius. It was many years after our first meeting that I was surprised to come across a copy of her book, *The World of Alice,* in which she again mentioned St Frideswide's Holy Well.

Mavis had always been keen on literature and was studying the German Romantic poets at University College, London; but although interrupted by her wartime career, she always remained a neo-Romantic. Her literary talents came to the fore and she became a prolific writer of garden history. She has many papers, articles and books to her credit, most notably *Alexander Pope, The Poet and the Landscape* (1999), *Arcadian Thames* (1994) and her definitive study *Jane Austen and the English Landscape* (1996).

Mavis's writing reveals her independent nature, always relying on her own thoughts and not trusting the thinking of others; this she said she learned when working at Bletchley Park. Making connections and decrypting codes had influenced her writing. She continued to make connections, as she had when decoding messages, but now it was between original texts and individuals, and this clarified eighteenth-century language, decoding words like 'picturesque', 'taste' and 'wilderness'. These books, like many of Mavis's other writings, are as much social history as garden history.

Mavis explored the economic, geographical, topographical and cultural influences of the times she was writing about, and she also researched the history of anyone she came across who had been connected with a park or garden she was researching, often creating a cast of wonderful characters.

In this biography of Mavis I have included background information as I feel it important that younger people, with an interest in gardens and landscape, should know about the social and political history that influenced the calling for The Garden History Society.

I have been fortunate in finding sources for this biography of Mavis, and one of the last books Mavis wrote was *Dilly: The Man Who Broke Enigmas* (2009), the biography of Dillwyn Knox, her team leader at Bletchley Park, who played an important role as her mentor. This book was a useful tool for me as it contains a chapter entitled *Dilly's Girls*, which includes interesting facts about Mavis's teenage years, what brought her to Bletchley Park and her work and life there. Mavis gave many interviews concerning her Bletchley Park days; some have been published and others have become audio-tape recordings. It is always fun to listen to Mavis chatting away with an interviewer, such as author Michael Smith, who included her in many of his books, recounting her experiences at Bletchley Park.

In 2005 Mavis was interviewed by Louise Brodie for the National Sound Archive. The tapes, *Down to Earth: An Oral History of British Horticulture,* involve a series of informative interviews. Louise Brodie has many years' experience and is an excellent interviewer; she is careful not to hurry her interviewees and allows Mavis time to tell her story, only occasionally prompting by asking a relevant question. Oral history always sets an intimate scene when people become relaxed and enjoy sharing secrets. Mavis sounds calm and collected, sometimes animated, and seldom falters.

The interview is centred upon Mavis's life as garden historian and conservationist. It gives a broad picture of her thoughts on a number of topics, detailing her participation in various garden history projects and conservation campaigns. Garden history was one of Mavis's passions but she was not a horticulturalist. She talks of many of the gardens with which she was involved but also tells a lot more than is expected, going beyond the bounds of horticulture to talk of her childhood, Bletchley Park and her family.

Mavis did not keep diaries, but her daughters, who became interested in this biography, passed to me a selection of notes written at odd times about various, mainly domestic, things which had occurred during her lifetime, and even the smallest notes are interesting.

There are numerous books written about Bletchley Park, many by leading authors, but none has been devoted solely to Mavis, although she is frequently mentioned. One of the most comprehensive books about Bletchley Park, if not the most comprehensive, is *Action This Day* edited by Michael Smith and Ralph Erskine. A series of essays has been contributed by some of Britain's foremost historians, academics and former codebreakers to give the history of the innovative work carried out at Bletchley Park. Mavis contributed to this book, writing *Breaking Italian Naval Enigma*, and her husband, Keith Batey, wrote *How Dilly Knox and his Girls Broke the Abwehr Enigma*.

In old age Mavis planned to write another book; 'I think I will have to do spies,' she would tease. Interestingly, she had on two occasions been accused of espionage.

Another book which is interesting is *Bletchley Park War Diaries, July 1939-August 1945* by Brian Oakley, which gives a succinct chronological account of the various happenings throughout the years of World War II. In 2010 Sinclair McKay wrote a lively book, *The Secret Life of Bletchley Park: World War II Codebreaking Centre and the Men and Women who Worked There*, telling much about the lives of the Bletchley Park workforce.

The Bletchley Park Trust publishes an interesting journal, including many articles on Bletchley Park, sometimes about little known topics which are gradually being released from their growing archives. *The Journal of Garden History* publishes erudite garden history articles written by members, and the newsletter is full of gems about gardens visited, events past and future, and Mavis is not only mentioned but she frequently contributed articles that she had written.

Mavis became renowned for her codebreaking, and upon her death obituaries were to be found in newspapers worldwide revealing a wealth of information, some of which had not become well known, but by the time these details reached the media the Official Secrets Act was almost completely open.

Mavis was proud to have been awarded the Royal Horticultural Society Veitch Memorial Medal in 1985, before becoming, in 1989, a Member of the Order of the British Empire (MBE) awarded for 'services to the preservation and conservation of historic gardens'. Many people unwittingly believe the latter was an award for her work as a codebreaker, which would also have been well deserved.

Mavis's husband died in 2010; they had three children, Elizabeth, Christopher and Deborah, and several grandchildren. They were 'the framework of Mavis's life, but within that frame there is a tapestry of living and learning, the one runs into the other,' recalled Ted Fawcett on the occasion of her seventy-fifth birthday. She was a prestigious character in the garden history world, but had no airs and graces. This silver-haired lady, with rosy cheeks and a friendly smile, was quiet and gentle, although she had proved she could be tough when necessary. Charles Boot, one-time archivist at The Garden History Society, remembers that if Mavis came on the telephone, 'you knew she was smiling, you could almost hear her chuckle trickle down the telephone line'.

Mavis enjoyed writing and had a passion for the history of gardens and their conservation, which she wanted to share with others. The Garden History Society, since 2015 The Gardens' Trust, is full of friendly people always ready to help each other with their special garden history projects and topics, and Mavis was the lady who led the way. She was challenged by the past and left a legacy of lasting achievements which have made a countrywide impact. She never did retire, and it was just months before her death, on 12 November 2013, that she signed off the new Garden Conservation Plan for Bletchley Park, Buckinghamshire, compiled by Dr Sarah Rutherford.

Jean Stone
September, 2019

CHAPTER ONE
The Bliss of Growing Up

Bletchley Park has become a museum, and is now an overly pristine replica of the codebreakers' workplace that occupied this site during World War II. At that time a series of huts had been built streaming away from the grand mansion, which were used as offices, and some of these iconic buildings have now been restored. The Bletchley huts of the wartime years were far from comfortable. The furnishing was spartan with most offices equipped with trestle tables and folding wooden chairs. There was a stuffy atmosphere in the summer months, but the windows were draughty and it was cold in winter – a walk in the open air was necessary to reach the lavatory. Most of these timber huts have now been replaced by more substantial buildings with *all mod cons* and a comfortable restaurant that allows museum visitors to enjoy their visit.

The number of people working at Bletchley Park rose from 100 to around 9,000 towards the end of the war. Many were residents, but the vast majority were billeted out. It is interesting that most of the staff were women, but the female population is by far the least mentioned in exhibitions at the museum. It is easy to imagine all these individuals bustling about the *village*, coming and going in shifts as if by clockwork, sitting at their desks and machines and working like puppets. Each person had his or her own job and was directed to carry out a particular task, unaware of what was evolving, in secrecy, in the next hut. It was no wonder the goings-on at Bletchley Park became known as 'Britain's Best Kept Secret'.

It was here that Mavis Lilian Lever, who had arrived at the beginning of the war years, grew from teenager to married woman when she became Mrs Keith Batey. But what brought her here?

In 1936, Mavis passed the examination for the General School Certificate in German and this coincided with Hitler's troops occupying the Rhineland. There had been a huge advertising campaign which extended around Europe to England. Colourful brochures were distributed offering bargain tickets for tourists to visit this idyllic, peaceful area of Germany where they would be persuaded there was nothing to fear in this progressive country. Mavis Lever was unlikely to have had any particular link with Germany, but she was excited by her German language examination results. She would have been aware that not many girls of her age and from her neighbourhood had the chance to learn a foreign language. So, to put her achievement to good use, she seized upon this opportunity to persuade her parents, who usually chose Bournemouth for their family holidays, to take up the offer. Her elder brother, Stanley, was also keen for a change. It would be a chance for her to practise her German, and young Mavis must have been very excited when her parents accepted the idea. A trip to the Rhineland; Mavis's first trip abroad. This was surely a big step for the family. At that time a week's holiday to Bournemouth, in Hampshire, with its sandy beaches, beautiful walks and places to visit, was a popular choice for middle-class families. Lesser mortals had to be satisfied with a day at Southend-on-Sea or Blackpool, but a holiday cruise along the Rhine was something completely new to the Levers; it would be special.

When considering the family circumstances, one wonders whether it would have been a struggle for the Levers to afford this holiday. Mavis was born on 5 May 1921, in a house in Crebor Street, East Dulwich. It was a friendly community with its own shops, picture palace, and a library which Mavis found particularly useful. The only tension at home was between Mavis and her brother, Stanley, who insisted on playing very loud music on the wireless. This was the era of British dance band music and Stanley's favourite was a band led by the popular Jack Payne. In 1928 Payne became BBC Director of Dance Music and leader of the BBC's first official dance band. For Mavis the situation became worse when Payne did some jazz recording and she could not persuade Stanley to reduce the volume. He had another noisy occupation too – he became the owner of an air gun, and shot pellets at a target; unfortunately, one day he missed completely and shot poor Mavis in the foot. That must have caused a commotion for she was taken to the hospital to have the pellet removed. She hobbled around for a few days but continued her habit of escaping to the local library where she could work in peace. No doubt brother and sister fell out for a couple of hours, but all was forgiven and she was proud of him when he later became a talented cricketer.

Their parents were easy-going and it was a loving home. Their house was in a pleasant street with modest terraced houses of the Edwardian period, but the tidy uniformity of the properties has now been interrupted by refurbishment. It must have looked charming when the small front gardens of each of the little houses were enclosed by iron railings, but these are now gone: compulsorily sacrificed by the owners to help the war effort. There are still sturdy kerb stones dividing the pavement from the road, but the old York stone paving has vanished, and today the street is usually lined with parked cars.

From an early age Mavis could walk to the elementary school without fear of being run down as there was hardly any traffic on the road, and she might occasionally have looked with interest at a horse and cart making a local delivery. Two roads away was the recreation ground supervised by a fierce lady who sat in a hut, knitting. There was no anti-social behaviour in her *rec*, as the recreation ground was always called, but she was kind if someone fell and cut a knee or grazed a hand, and would come to the rescue with a bandage and offer comfort with a sweet.

After a while the family moved to suburban Norbury and from here Mavis enjoyed the tram ride to her grammar school, the St Coloma Convent Girls' School in Croydon, and at the top of her list of scenic tours were the Surrey hills. An all-day ticket costing a shilling would give freedom of the whole bus route, to come and go as you pleased. It was a wonderful, now lost, world, when a twelve-year-old could wander freely in the bluebell woods alone, and make fascinating discoveries of wildlife and nature's secrets.

Mavis's mother went to look at St Coloma School when Mavis was about to take the eleven-plus examination. She was impressed by the girls, whom she thought were nicely behaved, and decided this school must be her first choice for her daughter. Mavis did well and gained entrance to the grammar school and always enjoyed being there. She thought it was particularly good because the nuns belonged to a teaching order and the school motto was 'To work is to pray'. This she thought meant that the girls would benefit from all the extra tuition because, as long as the nuns were teaching, they did not have to pray. 'They would take two hours over your essay, they were absolutely brilliant. It was like having one-to-one tutorials at school'.[1] Mavis looked forward to going to chapel and enjoying the clouds of incense wafting around, releasing spicy perfume. The girls were handed a black veil as they entered through the heavy door, and obviously thought it great fun to cover their heads like grown-ups wearing smart hats, and to hide their young faces beneath the dark net.

Mavis's father, Fred Lever, was a 'letter sorter' working for the post office, and Mavis's marriage certificate shows that he was still a civil servant in 1942, so it may be presumed that he stayed with the General Post Office, or at least had steady employment during the time of the Depression in the 1930s. His forefathers came from Wiltshire and a number of their tombstones are to be found in the churchyard at Fovant. Mavis's mother, Lilian, was of Irish descent, a dressmaker able to contribute to the family income, and her grandaughters remembered that she made all her own beautiful clothes. Mavis recalled:

> Our lives were very self-contained and sustainable; we made few demands on the planet and there was no television to lure us into sex and violence or aggressive advertising to buy what we didn't need.[2]

Mavis and Stanley did not see a lot of their grandparents when they were children as they lived at Bushey which was in the country, quite rural in those days and a distance away, but Mavis would enjoy 'a stay with them for a pick-up after measles or something'. [3]

Her parents must have been good managers with high ideals, since school-leaving age was fourteen years at this time, but Mavis continued at the St Coloma Convent School at Croydon with the intention of going on to university, and even in the final stage of her education, when she later went to University College, London, she could still live at home and go by bus to college.

When it was decided that they should take the holiday in the Rhineland, a travel agent was probably chosen to arrange the family's journey, and there was little reason to think that this would not be a good idea, for at that time travel agents were creating a colourful picture of holidays abroad. The travel agency, Poly, advertised a romantic view of the Rhine emblazoned with a Swastika flag and the slogan, 'The Land of Dreams Come True'; the Thomas Cook travel agency took note that one of their clients returned home singing Hitler's praises. Germany and Italy were 'quite the pleasantest places on the Continent; and quite the most exciting Brave New Worlds in the making, and well worth emulating'.[4] They recommended the Nazi state for 'art, life and music', adding that its hotels were 'exceedingly comfortable'.[5]

The Levers had no grand connections and would not have known that Dr Goebbels was subsidising Thomas Cook's brochures, together with a series of advertisements for German tourism that England's most respected travel agency regularly placed in *The Times*.[6] Even as late as the summer of 1939, when many English families felt trouble stealing its way across Europe, *The Times*, always ready to reassure its readers, carried a bold half-page advertisement placed by the German Tourist Board, 'Germany! Land of Hospitality', it announced, welcoming visitors to the spas of the Sudentenland.[7]

Cheap roving tickets were purchased for a brand new steamer trip along the scenic part of the Rhine, and the Lever family must have become more and more excited until it was time for their departure, apparently oblivious of the political climate prevailing in Germany.

When they arrived they found Germany buzzing with patriotic enthusiasm and the Rhineland was its showcase. Large ships had been built specifically for cruises to be offered free of charge as rewards to the country's workers and their families. Other entertainments and activities were also made available around the country at affordable prices: libraries, concerts, film shows, keep-fit clubs and parks were just a few of the incentives to be given as part of the 'Strength through Joy' or *Kraft durch Freude* (KdF) campaign, similar to the Italian Fascist organisation *Dopolavoro*, which translated as 'After Work'. When extended to *afterwork clubs* in Germany, it became one of the largest organisations of the Nazi regime. Mavis recalled:

> We joined crowds of happy German workers with free tickets; all part of Goebbels' 'Strength through Joy' campaign. They were to be indoctrinated in the myths and legends of German heroes as part of the Nazi philosophy of Aryan superiority, preparing them for the Third Reich, which was going to last a thousand years. Wagner's blonde Rhine maidens were with us constantly, and the band struck up as we passed Die Lorelei.[8]

However, it is doubtful if the family were aware of the many books committed to the bonfire by the Nazis in 1933, and that 'Germans on cruises travelling down the Rhine had to stop singing the Lorelei ballad as Heine, a Jew, had written it'.[9] Heinrich Heine (1797–1856) was a German Jew, journalist, essayist, literary critic and known for his lyrical poetry. As a result of his political views many of his works were banned in Nazi Germany.

Stanley was not shy of joining in the fun and thoroughly enjoyed himself mimicking the German soldiers making the Nazi salute. They thought he was amusing too; he was wearing a school blazer and they could not believe that any boy would wear such a strange garment. It most certainly kept the other tourists laughing when he started to practise the goose-step.

Mavis was overjoyed, happy to have the opportunity to talk with many German-speaking people: 'I lapped it all up, and when I got back I decided to opt for German literature in the sixth form.'[10]

In the years before World War II, the commercial Radio Luxembourg broadcast Chamberlain's speeches, interrupting its usual broadcasting programmes of popular music avidly followed by a wide, but possibly young, audience. However, the British Government purchased air time and expanded this routine to include programmes offering positive information about Britain, its way of life and values, and so promoted a feel-good factor which did perhaps influence some of the public.[11]

Nevertheless, more worrying information was available to, shall we say, those in the know. The year before, and timed to miss the Jubilee of George V on 6 May 1935, Leonard and Virginia Woolf had set off on a journey through Holland and Germany, on their way to Rome, planning to return through France, but not before cautiously seeking advice as to whether it would be safe; this was after all just a year after the Night of the Long Knives. They were warned by their friend, Ralph Wigram in the Foreign Office, that it might not be a good time. The fear of war was awakened in Virginia Woolf, but still they made the journey, and '… what they saw in Germany sank deep into her mind'.[12] In Bonn there were banners stretched across the streets, reading 'The Jew is our Enemy', and writing in her diary she confirmed that some people in England, and no doubt this included the Lever family, did not realise what was happening in Germany.

Mavis had always shone out in the German language class and for this reason her teacher showed a particular interest in her and sometimes gave her extra help. Her visit to Germany also improved her command of the German language, and German literature became Mavis's favourite subject. She always demonstrated the desire to push herself and was given the book *The Romantic Movement in Germany* as a sixth-form prize; this played a part in shaping her future, but not in the way she expected. When leaving St Coloma Convent Girls' School in 1938, Mavis gained a scholarship to University College, London, to study German, and as she had gained matriculation was immediately placed in the second year; she felt she had to catch up, and catch up she did. There was a lot of work to do and many books to cover. She had had six set books to read for A-level at school, and now had to study six books in French grammar, six in Latin and six in English. She thought that was quite a lot to get through all at once, but looking back to her school days she praised the nuns, commenting that they followed a particular lifestyle and did not look upon teaching as a job. She felt pleased when she found the author of her book prize, *The Romantic Movement in Germany,* was Leonard Willoughby, who would now be her professor of German literature at University College. Mavis loved the German *Stimmung und Sehnsucht*, the longing for mountains and depths of forests, and was all set to write a dissertation on the German Romantics.

While at University College it had been arranged for Mavis to spend one term of the second academic year at Tubingen University, South West Germany. She found herself in a remote world as she had no idea what went on outside her own little orbit, and entering university in the second year was extremely difficult. She decided that if she joined the debating society this would help her get into the swing of things, but the first debate was entitled 'Abortion was Another Case for the Legal Profession, For Those Who Wanted It'. Poor Mavis did not know what abortion meant in English, yet alone German.

News came that Hitler had annexed Prague and Mavis was diverted to the German-speaking University of Zurich. Her parents were not worried, they did not think the war would happen, but after a short time it became necessary for her to return home. She then had to report to the British Ambassador in Zurich because, as she was still young, and as she would be travelling alone, it was considered essential that she should have a guardian to make her travel arrangements. She hastily returned to London at the end of the summer when it was said the Siegfried Line was being manned and she found herself plunged into a new world. Europe was in a troubled state and Mavis decided she should get into politics and joined the Socialist Club – mainly because they had better cakes than the other political organisations.

War had not yet touched London but dark clouds were looming. The students of University College had been alerted by the rumblings of Sir Oswald Mosley's Blackshirts, causing chaos as the sound of their hobnailed jackboots penetrated through the cobbled streets of London's East End where they made their violent confrontations on the Jewish community. This disturbed Mavis and, in her disgust at the Germans turning on the Jews, she joined a march on the German Embassy.

The Spanish Civil War was at a peak and causing concern as it had previously been unknown for civilians to be bombed. Many young men and women from Europe and the USA were making their way to Spain to fight against Fascism. Inspired by their dynamic Marxist Professor J. B. S. Haldane, University College had become a revolutionary force, and one Tuesday the students declared a fast, as a way of supporting Republican Spain. Mavis found this confusing, as at her convent school during morning assemblies they had prayed for General Franco. Nevertheless, she found herself sewing red flags for the young men going off to join the International Brigade, and waving them farewell.

Kristallnacht, with its savage attack against Jews throughout Nazi Germany, erupted in November 1938, and Mavis joined the march by UCL on the German Embassy. It may not have helped the plight of the Jews, but the students made their statement.

London had an enormous surge of refugees. The students of University College would have seen whole families sitting around on the front steps of the small hotels of Bloomsbury; neat and tidy families, grouped together, sadly waiting, but not knowing exactly for what they were waiting; they were not happy; they did not smile; they looked forlorn.

The German department of University College encouraged their students to offer their help, and William Beveridge, a former graduate of Balliol, made it his business to set up the Academic Assistance Council, which found work and support for the hundreds of professors who had lost their jobs under the Nazi embargoes. There were other bodies too that gave their assistance. 'Hamburg's leading centre for the study of art, quietly re-emerged as part of the newly formed Courtauld Institute',[13] welcoming immigrants from Germany's art centres; Imperial Chemicals sent Churchill's advisor, Professor Frederick Lindemann, on a recruitment tour offering work and the financial support of ICI to Germany's finest scientists, which was, of course, helpful to both parties.

On a modest scale Mavis became involved in organising jobs in England for German Jewish refugees. She tackled this task by going through the 'situations vacant' columns with a pair she was endeavouring to help. Eventually she found an advertisement for a couple needed in a country house in Kent. She helped them apply for the post and accompanied them on their journey to introduce them to their new placement. 'Unfortunately, Hitler had found the Jewish exodus a perfect opportunity to infiltrate fifth columnists, and it was my bad luck to have been given two of them.'[14] Mavis was quite innocent, but blamed herself. 'Perhaps I should have been suspicious as to why they were so keen on Kent...'[15] 'Her refugees turned out to be spies who were caught photographing military installations.'[16]

Surrounded by unrest, and with Britain on the brink of war with Germany, Mavis now saw the Nazi Propaganda Minister, Joseph Goebbels, as a fraud who had deceived the British public by promoting Germany as a happy and peaceful country; acts of slaughter and devastation lay hidden. Patriotism rose up within her; Goebbels had his doctorate in German Romanticism, the very discipline upon which she had embarked, and she was now halfway through her degree. Mavis was irritated and annoyed, believing it was through his influence that she had become interested in this subject in the first place; a very good reason for her to do something better to help the war effort she thought, not wanting to study anything that might remind her of Goebbels. It was 1939 and war was imminent.

On the morning of Sunday, 3 September 1939, almost every person across the country was listening to the radio. At eleven o'clock they heard the solemn voice of Prime Minister Neville Chamberlain announce '... this country is at war with Germany.'

This grave news had been expected. Many city schools had already evacuated children to the country a few days before this announcement. A week or two earlier each child had been given a small, canvas haversack and their parents had been issued with a short list of items to be packed. Gas masks had already been distributed. To avoid panic or accidents on the day of departure, some children were taken to underground stations by their teachers to practise descending and climbing an escalator; this gave them confidence and helped avoid tears when they finally set off to their unknown destinations.

There was a policy of evacuating 'useless mouths'[17]: a derogatory expression used by the government to describe women and children who could not materially contribute to the war effort. Mavis may not have heard the phrase used, but her mind was made up, she certainly intended to do her bit to help her country.

> I didn't want to go on with academic studies. University College, London, was just evacuating to the campus at Aberystwyth, in west Wales. But I thought I ought to do something better for the war effort than reading German poets in Wales. After all, German poets would soon be above us in bombers. I remarked to someone that I should train to be a nurse. But that person told me: "No you don't, you go and see someone at the Foreign Office. They can use your German." And so I did.[18]

The government was prohibited from advertising for staff, so many people were engaged on secret war work through personal introduction. Debutantes had a strong presence, but Mavis 'was by no means a debutante. Rather she was a fiercely intelligent middle-class girl'[19] and needless to say she was one of the students selected by the Foreign Office. She was interviewed in September 1939 by a lady from the Foreign Office, the 'formidable Miss Moore', to whom she explained her reason for curtailing German studies at university. Miss Moore approved, and was satisfied with Mavis's CV from University College, 'but I don't know if she knew what we were going to do,'[20] commented Mavis, whose adventurous spirit led her to imagine that she might become a *spy*! All sorts of thoughts flashed through the teenager's mind: 'This is going to be an interesting job, Mata Hari seducing Prussian officers. But I don't think either my legs or my German were good enough,'[21] she jovially recalled in later years. There was a delay and Mavis was surprised to learn that the security services were questioning her background. She discovered there had been an interruption to the completion of an investigation, made by MI5 with the local Croydon police, into her blameless past, when she had inadvertently helped the two German spies. They had given her name as their sponsor when posing as refugees.

Mavis must have been relieved when she was cleared of this alleged atrocity, and excited when she was asked to attend an interview. She was sent to the Government Code and Cypher School (GC&CS) which had been responsible since 1919 for dealing with all foreign encrypted messages, particularly those fro m the newly emerging Soviet Union. This small codebreaking department of the Foreign Office had premises in the Broadway Building, opposite St James's Park Underground Station. She later learned that MI6 was on the floor above and was quietly referred to by Mavis and her colleagues as 'the other side'.

In January 1940 Mavis joined GC&CS as a linguist, a student of German literature. Her work involved supplying industrial intelligence for the Ministry of Economic Warfare (MEW) whose mission was 'comparable to the operations of the three armed services in that its object is the defeat of the enemy, and complementary to them in that its function is to deprive the enemy of the material means of resistance'.[22] The task of Mavis's section was to scour the codebooks used by neutral countries to order essential commodities, which they were illegally supplying to Germany, and to blacklist them.

These commercial international telegraphic codes, sent in Morse, were simple and less complicated than secret codes. However, one trying person from an unknown place called St Goch could not be located, so the problem was passed to Mavis, who had a genius for this sort of thing; she had always been interested in puzzles. 'There is much of Wonderland in cryptography and it often pays to be like

Alice and ask disconcertingly innocent questions,'[23] she thought. Her question to MEW was simply: 'How [did] they know when there was a capital letter in Morse code, and they had to confess they didn't as there was no provision for them.'[24] This gave Mavis the clue she needed; she tried changing the capital letter and arrived at StgoCh. She pounced on Santiago, Chile – problem solved, and the culprit was tracked down. Her superiors were impressed and Mavis had earned herself a train ticket to Bletchley Park.

CHAPTER TWO
Life at Bletchley Park

Mavis did not choose to work at Bletchley Park; there were few that knew of its existence and what went on there but she discovered that she had been recruited into intelligence by her professor at University College, Leonard Willoughby, a friend of Dilly Knox, who would become her team leader. Perhaps she felt apprehensive about who and what she would encounter: new people, a new environment and a new job. Would she like living and working there?

It was in early 1940 when Mavis set off for Bletchley Park. She had been given a ticket and told which train to catch and that she would be met at the station. At not quite nineteen years old this was quite an adventure for Mavis, and she must have been relieved when she learned she was going to Bletchley; it was not too far away from home. At Euston she met up with a new recruit, Joy Mitchell, who had also been told to be at Euston at a certain time where somebody would meet her and give her a ticket. Until then she had no idea where they were going, but when they arrived at Bletchley Park they were told they must not give their addresses to their parents. Their parents would be given a special address so that they could write to their daughters, and their own letters would be forwarded to their parents.

Bletchley was a railway town and most of its inhabitants were dependent on the railway for their living. There was little to see in the way of beautiful or interesting architecture and the landscape had nothing exciting to offer.

When Mavis and Joy arrived at Bletchley they took the pleasant walk along the worn path from the railway station and, as they entered the Park by the station gate, Mavis could not help noticing there was a perimeter fence of barbed wire; she later found this went right around the Park. This entrance proved to be very popular as time went on; it was convenient, and a sentry was posted there in daylight hours to admit those with security passes. The path led to the drive and she was surprised when a Victorian mansion came into view. She had been told it had been built in 1883 for the wealthy stockbroker and newspaper proprietor Herbert Leon, a Liberal MP, later to become Sir Herbert, when Gladstone was prime minister.

The mansion was an imposing Victorian Tudor-Gothic pile, a mish-mash of architecture, at that time set in an attractive Arcadian-style landscaped park, with a lake and tree-studded lawns which improved the scene and drew the visitor's attention away from the mansion. The Leon family were great travellers, and they must have been inspired by the styles of architecture seen in the countries they visited, for many of these were incorporated into the building which had gradually extended in size. There were Italianate pillars at the entrance, a copper dome at one end and various Edwardian embellishments, including verandahs overlooking the rose garden, but these assorted additions caused the building to be very oddly proportioned, and Mavis perhaps found the collection of varied styles amusing. However, listening to veterans today, they seem to have developed a fondness for the house; they spent so much time there it almost became their second home.

The Foreign Office had decided to move the Government Code and Cypher School (GC&CS) from St James's, London to Bletchley Park, a rural area, and some staff arrived there about eighteen months before the outbreak of war. Most of the grounds and gardens were swept away before they relocated, but the grounds were still attractive. One reason why Bletchley Park had been chosen was that it was in a prime location, situated and nicely secluded on the A5, the old Roman road, Watling Street, with good communication links to London. Bletchley Railway Station was adjacent to the Park, on the junction of the mainline train service between London, the north of England and Scotland, and also equidistant between Oxford and Cambridge, from where some of the 'professor type' codebreakers were recruited.

Bletchley Park was not the first home of codebreaking; since ancient times cryptographers and spies have abounded. The Chinese and Indians, Ancient Egyptians and Hebrews have all been noted for their secret agents, and in the thirteenth and fourteenth centuries espionage played a key role in the Moguls' conquests in Asia and Europe. Certain gentlemen in Elizabethan England have become well known for their devious pursuits. Sir Francis Walsingham (1532-1590) was secretary to Queen Elizabeth I and is remembered as her spymaster. Thomas Phelippes, who excelled at deciphering letters and forgery, worked under Walsingham, and another Elizabethan spy was Arthur Gregory, who was proficient not only at breaking seals but at repairing them so skilfully that his interference could not be detected. It was Walsingham who arranged the imprisonment of Mary Queen of Scots at Chartley and for her unsealed letters to be read before being given to her. He also deceived her on one occasion by leading her to believe her secret letters were secure, but he had them smuggled in and out of Chartley in a beer keg to be read by his agents. As time has progressed, romantic stories have sprung up around such characters as Mata Hari, helping to pave the way for a mass of spy fiction, and even the young and naive Mavis had thought she might be offered a position such as that of Mata Hari.

The first official British Secret Service Bureau, the predecessor of MI5 and MI6, was set up in 1909 for espionage and counter-espionage, and at the outbreak of World War I, in 1914, the Signals Intelligence Agency (Sigint.), became involved with the task of reading the enemy's wireless messages.

By the turn of the twentieth century underwater telegraph cables had become an easier and important means of communication, and the British companies Eastern Telegraph, Marconi and the General Post Office (GPO) were leaders in the field. However, security became a problem and at the outbreak of World War I underwater cables, linking Germany with Britain and America, were cut.

On '6 August 1914 a British cable ship severed five German overseas underwater cables that passed from Emden through the English Channel to Vigo, Tenerife, the Azores and the USA.'[1]

From that time forward it became necessary for communications to be transmitted through airwaves. Guglielmo Marconi had developed the first long-distance communication by radio, and technological developments allowed messages to travel through the ether; no longer was distance over land or even across oceans a hindrance. Messages were sent by keyboard machines powered by electricity, and secret German encoded messages were intercepted and forwarded to the Admiralty. In 1933 a series of breaks in security had repercussions which alerted the Foreign Office; it became necessary to recruit people capable of breaking codes who were absolutely trustworthy.

A special Naval Intelligence Department (NID) was set up for the interception and decoding of messages. Commander Alistair Denniston, from the Royal Naval College at Osborne, Isle of Wight, who was trilingual, was made head of this new department which was more often referred to as Room 40. Winston Churchill, First Lord of the Admiralty, was also involved with Room 40, which was originally located in the Old Admiralty Buildings in London. As the department grew it was moved first to 54 Broadway, St James's, and finally to Bletchley Park where Commander Denniston became operational head of GC&CS. It was at 54 Broadway where Mavis had first worked and the Secret Intelligence Service (SIS) was located. During World War II GC&CS, when working from Bletchley Park, studied methods of codebreaking and devised ways of enabling the secure military codes and cyphers of Germany, Japan and other Axis nations' communications to be broken, allowing the release of vital intelligence to the armed forces – and this was where Mavis became a highly skilled codebreaker.

Prior to World War II, during the Spanish Civil War, Dillwyn Knox, Mavis's future head of department, had broken both the Spanish and Italian Enigma cyphers. GC&CS made little further progress with codebreaking, but with the threat of war imminent the Poles had started work in the 1930s and had become more proficient. They were able to read Enigma cypher machine messages stating that tanks were about to assemble on their borders, and, when the Nazis marched on Prague in March 1938, Britain gave an undertaking that the British Government would declare war on Germany if Poland were to be invaded. Dillwyn Knox, Alan Turing and John Tiltman were the three leading codebreakers from Bletchley Park, accompanied by Alastair Denniston, who visited the Polish War Station in the Pyry Forest, near Warsaw, in July 1939.

There, in secrecy, they met three Polish codebreakers with whom they had instant rapport and affinity, and it was agreed that the Polish Cypher Bureau should hand over their Enigma secrets to the British. The Poles gave the British a replica of an Enigma machine first purchased by the German Navy in 1926 and explained the various procedures for encoding and decoding. The British team returned to Britain gratified at what had taken place. The British team had acquired a good understanding of how the machine worked, but it took considerable practice to achieve the ability to read its messages. The Poles had played a key role in ensuring the British breaks occurred sooner than they might otherwise have done.

At the beginning of WWII the British codebreakers were below the standard of the Germans in their proficiency at cracking the codes concealing naval and military messages. The German armed forces were encrypting all radio messages for security reasons, and Dillwyn Knox 'and his section were working on the solution to Enigma, the enciphering system of the machine selected by the Nazi Government to distribute as standard issue to the German forces'.[2] The machine itself was well designed and rather like a typewriter, but a little larger. The German military had adapted the commercial Enigma machine for their own use. It had five wheels, of which three were in use at any one time, and each had twenty-six letters, a transmitting and receiving keyboard and an electrical keyboard; settings were changed daily. Variants would later be used by the German armed services, police and diplomats.

Breaking the Enigma codes was vital – it would give access to encoded messages from U-boats, the Gestapo and German High Command, details of bombing raids, the location of shipping and army manoeuvres. The Bletchley Park codebreakers' target was to retrieve and break the codes of every message for this would be a major factor in the safety and survival of the United Kingdom.

Mavis reported to Commander Alastair Denniston who, before transferring to Bletchley Park, had worked in signals intelligence since 1914. At the end of World War I he retained his position and became head of the GC&CS at Broadway Buildings, at that time known as Government Communications Headquarters. When moving to Bletchley Park as operational head of GC&CS he played an important part in maintaining continuity in signals intelligence.

The commander's meeting with Mavis was in his office, formerly Lady Leon's morning room to the left of the mansion entrance. In stature he was quite small and had chosen this room because it looked out over the drive and from here he would be able to keep watch on all those coming and going. Over the years he had already achieved a lot, and went on to make more progress, which sometimes involved undertaking dangerous trips across the Atlantic for diplomatic talks with the Americans. On one flight when returning to Britain, his plane came between two German planes, one in front of his and another just behind, and both were shot down.

At first he had a chat with Mavis and his quiet and warm manner must have put her at ease, but in a more serious and firm voice he reminded her that she had signed the Official Secrets Act and impressed upon her the importance of this. He told her she must never disclose to anyone anything about the work she was doing, or where she was working, and Bletchley Park was to be referred to as Box 101. The level of security at Bletchley Park was extremely high and it was largely Denniston who had set the standards. 'Careless Talk Costs Lives' was a slogan which appeared on posters displayed on trains, buses and other strategic places all around Britain during the war years.

Security was of utmost importance. Admiral Sir Hugh Sinclair, whose idea it had been to purchase Bletchley Park, which he reputedly did with £7,500 of his own money, saved the house from demolition and redevelopment. However, he was aware of the need to upgrade security if it were to be used by the Secret Intelligence Service. In August 1938 there was a rehearsal to test Bletchley Park for the SIS departments. Rumours about what was going on there had been flowing around the local villages, and these became even more intense when groups of middle-aged men and young girls were put up in local hotels and spent their days at Bletchley Park. These strange people were members of GC&CS who were to colonise the mansion and its grounds. They had been told to keep a suitcase packed, a 10s. note in their pocket, and await a telephone message that 'Auntie Flo is not so well', then they were to make their way to Station X. Bletchley Park was tenth in line of a number of buildings acquired by M16, and the Roman figure X thus became a name adopted by them.

Admiral Sinclair had his own chef brought from London to provide gourmet dining for his group, and everything pointed to their having some sort of *Jolly*. The chambermaids imagined all sorts of shenanigans going on; they were, after all, 'Captain Ridley's Shooting Party'. This was the code name given to the group to keep the locals off the scent. And so it did. The true reason for this escapade remained a secret within the Park, as well as outside, until post-war days when official papers started to be released in the 1970s.

Mavis had learned about the importance of security when working at Broadway and quickly became aware that at Bletchley Park work was not discussed outside the group you worked with, and other groups did not discuss their work with you.

In November 1939, the year before Mavis arrived at Bletchley Park, there had been what became known as the 'Venlo incident'. A great deal of information about British intelligence was given to the Germans by two SIS officers when based in Holland, who were kidnapped at Venlo on the Dutch border. They had been expecting to meet with two representatives of the German High Command who they had been led to believe were planning to overthrow Hitler, but the SIS officers had walked into a Nazi trap.

The incident brought the Netherlands into the war and British security became of vital importance. 'Power and experience had hardened Churchill. Some 60,000 Germans living in England had been interned or deported within the first months of his leadership.'[3] Winston Churchill demanded absolute silence to any approach made by Germans claiming to be opposed to Hitler. Colonel Stewart Menzies, the new head of SIS, decided it was not sensible for GC&CS and the SIS wireless communications section to share the same property, and subsequently SIS Radio Station, and Section VIII of SIS, were relocated to Whaddon Hall.

It was not until after the war, in the 1950s, that staff got to know exactly how much information the two men had given away. This was made possible by a Gestapo handbook, written by SS General Walter Schellenberg, recording information and providing Hitler's staff with a detailed analysis of British political and economic structures, including an accurate description of British Intelligence working at 54 Broadway. This was where Mavis had worked at the beginning of 1940 when the Germans had positioned an agent outside the underground station opposite, posing as a match-seller but taking photographs of people coming and going. Mavis said she 'would be intrigued to know whether [she] was in a Nazi file. A floor-by-floor breakdown was given naming their departmental heads. A special wanted list of those to be arrested even gave their home addresses, and in some cases car registration numbers'.[4]

Winston Churchill became proud of the Bletchley staff who later earned the description that Bletchley Park was possibly the best kept secret in modern British history.

After Mavis's meeting with Denniston, his secretary, Barbara Abernethy, took her to Dillwyn 'Dilly' Knox's cottage, known as Cottage 3. It was one of three small buildings in the stableyard that had previously housed a groom. Dilly, as he was known, was to become her team leader. He did not like organisation and was not suited to a production line, so it was here that he set up his own research unit to break untried Enigma variations. However, when he found the cottage unsuitable, he complained, and it was converted and enlarged by joining the two adjacent cottages. There were several early codebreakers who were attached to the British Secret Service Bureau who later worked at Bletchley Park, and Dilly Knox was one of them. He had been a great pioneer of codebreaking since WWI, an ace cryptographer and the chief at GC&CS, specialising in breaking non-plugboard versions of Enigma and responsible for breaking the U-boat code. Unfortunately, from 1941 onwards he became a sick man, suffering from lymphatic cancer. The senior staff endeavoured to make his life as comfortable as possible although he was one of the most eccentric personalities at Bletchley Park. This sometimes caused difficulties as he threatened resignation whenever a call was made for a change in routine.

In January 1940 the first Enigma key was broken, and to maintain secrecy the Cottage immediately became out of bounds to the rest of Bletchley Park. Mavis found it a strange place after the Broadway building at St James's. About eight girls were working there when she arrived, including Joy Mitchell, the girl she had met at Euston Station. Dilly was sitting by the window puffing away on his pipe which he took from his mouth when Mavis entered the room. He looked up through his horn-rimmed spectacles, saying: 'We're breaking machines, have you got a pencil?'[5] It was an odd thing to say, but Mavis must have gathered that he meant gaining entry into the codes, and then breaking them to retrieve the messages.

'That was it. I was never really told what to do. "Here, have a go",[6] he said, handing her a batch of coded messages spoiled by his scribbles. Mavis recalled:

'I think looking back on it that was a great precedent in my life, because he taught me to think that you could do things yourself without always checking up to see what the book said. That was the way the cottage worked. We were looking at new traffic [encoded messages] all the time, or where the wheels, or the wiring had been changed, or at other new techniques. So you had to work it all out yourself from scratch…'[7]

The pages given to Mavis to work on at the GC&CS at Broadway had been filled with neat and tidy code-groups and, although not immediately comprehensible, she was able to read them. In contrast, the messages Dilly handed to her were not easily decipherable as they were obliterated in places by his scribbles in purple ink. Mavis felt desperate. 'I am afraid it's all Greek to me,' she complained, and he replied saying, 'I wish it were.'[8] When Mavis later discovered he was a distinguished Greek scholar who had been a classicist deeply involved with deciphering ancient papyri fragments at the British Museum, she felt embarrassed.

In spite of her strange introduction Mavis became extraordinarily proficient at codebreaking, and later an expert in finding her way into new codes and cyphers that had never before been broken.

Dilly Knox had four brothers and Mavis learned they all had a great ability for words. They were clever children and always able to occupy themselves, and one of their pastimes was to write a family magazine. All five of the Knox boys were devoted to *Punch*, and Eddie Knox, who went on to become a famous editor of that publication, started their family magazine with gossip, news and jokes. This was not unique, it was something many families encouraged at that time. The children of the Strachey family also indulged in this hobby, but their topics must have been very different. As a boy Dilly also became engrossed in Greek lexicon, and at the age of twelve years he contributed an exceptional cypher to their family magazine, but when he went on to write two more instalments Eddie would not allow him to do so, but they all enjoyed problem solving which became another of their interests.

By the time he was codebreaking in adult life Dilly had developed a unique knack of using his imagination to open up codes and cyphers. Like Mavis, Dilly and his brothers were great admirers of Lewis Carroll and they were addicted to 'chopped logic' such as the nonsense based on ambiguity that Carroll frequently used in *Alice in Wonderland*. 'Which way does the clock go round?' Dilly would ask. And if you were stupid enough to answer clockwise, he'd just say: 'Oh no it doesn't, not if you're the clock. It's the opposite way.'

> And that's sometimes how you had to think about the machines. Not just to look at them how you saw them, but what was going on inside. That was the only way in which one was really trained. But trained is a bad word because that was the one thing you mustn't be. You have got to look at each thing afresh and wonder how you could approach it.[9]

All Dilly's brothers were clever, and Dilly had won a scholarship to King's College, Cambridge where he made several friends who possibly accelerated his interest in language. John Maynard Keynes was at King's and later at Bletchley Park, and he became a lifelong friend of Dilly, as were most of his friends from King's. This bonding was a trend amongst members of the intellectual and secretive discussion group, the Cambridge Apostles, sometimes known as the Conversazione Society. Maynard Keynes was a member, and although he had been proposed Dilly never took up the invitation, but he was friendly with many of them. A number of well-known names had been members of the society, including Bertrand Russell, Leonard Woolf, Lytton Strachey, E. M. Forster, Rupert Brook, Eric Hobsbawm and Victor Rothschild. Other members of the society included agents of the Cambridge Spy Ring: Guy Burgess, an M16 officer and secretary to the deputy foreign minister, who worked in close liaison with Bletchley Park, Donald MacLean, Foreign Office secretary, and Kim Philby, M16 officer and journalist.

It was probably from members of the society that Dilly acquired the habit of never accepting a first statement, but to always ask questions. This was part of their philosophy and Mavis tells us there were two questions that Dilly constantly asked, 'Why do you say that?' and 'What do you mean by that?'[10]

Dilly became an outstanding codebreaker, and his research team at Bletchley Park were Tony Kendrick, who was once head boy at Eton, Peter Twinn, a mathematician from Brasenose College, Oxford, previously at GC&CS in the Broadway building, who was the first mathematician recruited by British Intelligence before WWII to attack German cyphers, and Alan Turing, who was particularly admired by Dilly. There were also two career civil servant clerks, Joyce Mail-Fox and Rachel Ronald, and two new recruits, Elizabeth Granger and Claire Harding, the daughters of two members of Denniston's Ashtead Golf Club. Joyce Mitchell, Mavis learned, was a speech therapist; also three actresses were recruited by Dilly as he believed they would be proficient in understanding the rhythms of the messages. Mavis understood: 'The girls he chose had a background connected with linguistics, phonetics or literature. It was all a question of linguistic patterns of syllables for him. Others, recruited by Commander Denniston, had secretarial training and acted as registrars.'[11]

Margaret Rock was a graduate mathematician and statistician from Bedford College, London who at thirty-six years old was older than the other girls and, along with Mavis, one of Dilly's favourites. She had arrived at Bletchley Park in early 1940 and had joined Dilly in Cottage 3. Mavis got to know Margaret well and learned that her father was a doctor and she had attended Portsmouth High School which was part of the Girls' Day School Trust.

Dilly was sympathetic toward his female staff and concerned for their welfare. He would enquire as to whether they were happy with their billets, and if they made good progress he would make sure they were rewarded with an increase in pay.

A sprinkling of debutantes were taken on at Bletchley Park, as young ladies of the upper class were thought to be trustworthy and able to keep secrets, 'background was so important',[12] and on the whole they were well educated. However, all women aged between eighteen and forty, who were not in a reserved occupation such as teaching or nursing, were to become eligible for conscription by the government into the forces, or factories, or perhaps the Land Army, and this was soon to become the rule. Only if they volunteered prior to conscription would ladies be allowed a choice. Bletchley Park may have seemed a good idea for those whose parents knew someone who could recommend them. The government was unable to advertise for staff so many people were engaged on secret war work through personal introduction.

In 1940, approaching her nineteenth birthday, Jean Campbell-Harris, daughter of an officer in the Bengal Lancers, who later became Baroness Trumpington, enjoyed a privileged family background. However, for those subject to this system of directed labour, which was soon to be compulsory, Bletchley Park may have seemed a suitable alternative. Jean Campbell-Harris was not yet eligible for conscription, but it was on the horizon, and having spent so many years in school uniform she did not relish the thought of a year in services attire. Her parents were unsure what to do with her, but a lieutenant commander in the navy, a friend of her father, said he knew someone who worked at Bletchley Park and that this should be considered.

At the time, Jean was unaware of this conversation, but a few days later she found herself in a Lyon's Corner House sharing a table with a jolly man called Frank Birch. He questioned her as to whether she could speak German, French and Italian and gave her something to translate. "'Well," he said, "you'll do. Here's your ticket, take the train tomorrow morning to Bletchley."'[13] Jean followed his advice and spent the next five years working at Bletchley Park. She was not in Dilly's section, but Mavis and Jean did know each other and occasionally enjoyed each other's company.

Frank Birch, who had interviewed Jean, was formerly of King's College, Cambridge, where he was an historian, but became a codebreaker in 1916, first at GC&CS at their Broadway premises, later becoming a lifelong friend of Dilly. In September 1939, he transferred to Bletchley Park where he became head of the German Naval Section working in

Hut 4. Early copies of the *Allgemeines Funkspruchbuch (AFB) (Basic Guidelines to Radio Messages)* were primarily created for warships and merchant ships and later used by Zeppelins, but there was a key to be solved before the information contained could be deciphered. The copy used by Birch was captured from a Zeppelin, and shows his notes and scribbles with details of U-boats that had been sunk during the First World War.

Frank Birch and Frank Adcock, both historians and fellows of King's College, became recruiters of 'professor types', primarily choosing men from Cambridge colleges whom they knew well; consequently twelve King's dons served at Bletchley Park during WWII.

It soon became apparent that it was a particular kind of individual who had more than average ability to break codes: mathematicians who enjoyed playing brain games, chess playing, solving and inventing puzzles, and linguists interested in language – all were seen to be candidates. University students who it was thought would be useful were earmarked prior to the outbreak of World War II; those with languages and mathematics appear to have been at the top of the list, and there were several old Etonians among the recruits.

During World War I mathematicians were said to be introverted personalities, so much wrapped up in their own world that they would be unable to cope with the horrendous reality of wartime situations, and this attitude lingered. Sir Alfred Ewing, former fellow of King's and professor of engineering at Cambridge, was of this opinion so put forward classicists, historians and linguists. However, between the wars Polish military intelligence found it necessary to have professional mathematicians, and Denniston too came to this conclusion and took on some mathematicians along with the professional types he was recruiting from Oxford and Cambridge colleges for codebreaking at Bletchley Park. Although at first meeting with some prejudice, the mathematicians were soon found to be indispensable and worked along with the linguists, classicists and historians who made up the first recruits admitted to Bletchley Park. Chess players were thought to be suitable as they were patient when considering endless permutations, and leading chess players Hugh Alexander and Stuart Milner-Barry were recruited.

On 3 September 1939 Alan Turing from King's and Gordon Welchman from Sidney Sussex College, a brilliant mathematician and also an expert chess player, and John Jeffreys arrived, all professor types from Cambridge colleges who had been on an emergency 'call-up list'. 'They would make significant contributions to the exploitations of the initial breaking of the Enigma machine',[14] but it was Alan Turing who stood out from the crowd.

When attending Sherborne School in Dorset, his headmaster had once written, 'If he is to stay at a public school he must aim at becoming "educated". If he is to be solely a "Scientific Specialist", then he is wasting his time.'[15] Since childhood Turing had been known for his habit of drifting into his own world, and his mother captured an image of him in this state when he was a ten-year-old at preparatory school. She gave the drawing to his matron, calling it *Hockey, or Watching the Daisies Grow*. Her son was completely oblivious to the noise and excitement of the hockey match taking place all around him; there he stood, quietly bending over a clump of daisies. Turing developed into a shy and obsessive young man, but he was a genius.

Turing, or the Prof, as he became known, was around twenty-seven years old when he joined Bletchley Park. He arrived carrying one of his own creations which he had been working on at Princeton University in the United States. He called the contraption an electric multiplier machine, and it was mounted on a breadboard. Already exceptional in that he had carried out research into both computing and cryptography, he was author of a brilliant paper of 150 pages on Enigma, written in 1936, that positioned a mathematical machine controlled by a program in its memory. This was the forerunner of the first electronic digital computer which Turing would formulate in 1945. In spite of his eccentric ideas and mannerisms he was admired by Mavis's boss, Dilly Knox – they had both been 'King's men' at Cambridge – there was a certain camaraderie between them and they worked well together; Mavis too was also soon to admire him.

At Bletchley Park there were a number of eccentrics, some of whom would have been considered too eccentric to be employed by most government bodies, and it is to be commended that in spite of their idiotic mannerisms and habits these men, who were geniuses in their fields, were treated with respect and understanding at Bletchley Park.

Dilly believed he did his best work for Room 40 when lying in a bath at the Admiralty Old Building at Whitehall; he thought the steamy atmosphere to be perfect for the cracking of codes. His friend, Frank Birch, found this amusing and, when writing his satirical history of Room 40, *Alice in ID25*, he explained:

The sailor in Room 53
Has never, it's true, been to sea
But though not in a boat
He has served afloat –
In a bath in the Admiralty.

Mavis was very considerate of Dilly: 'He would stuff his pipe with sandwiches sometimes instead of tobacco he was so woolly-minded, but he was brilliant, absolutely brilliant.'[16] If Dilly mislaid his pipe, work would stop, and everyone in his section would join in a search. Later in life when looking back, Mavis remembered that his eccentricities soon became noticeable when she first arrived. 'He would contrive, absent-mindedly, to try to leave the room via the cupboard door... His enthusiasm for hot baths never waned. He was – an unusual privilege this, in difficult times – allowed real milk for his coffee, which came fresh from a local cow.'[17] If Dilly wanted to visit his punch-card operators when they were working a late shift, 'he would limp across from the cottage, often in his grey dressing gown, indifferent to rain and snow, to tell them his new idea'.[18]

Upon her arrival Mavis found the huts to be cold and dismal. Industrious builders worked outside in the park constructing more low buildings to house what would become ever increasing numbers of staff, but working conditions inside the huts were not to be admired. As winter advanced they became colder; some had a central coke-burning stove with a black iron chimney piercing the roof, but the heat did not circulate. It must have been difficult for the staff huddled in their scarves and overcoats, and wearing mittens whilst patiently striving to concentrate and break the Enigma codes. As staff numbers increased, lack of facilities became intolerable and one section head reported that there was only one lavatory to be shared by two hundred staff; only the administrative staff in the mansion were more fortunate. Work on the mansion had been put into progress immediately it was occupied: direct telephone and teleprinter lines to London had to be installed urgently and other smaller alterations were made to the organisation of rooms.

Mavis remembered having meals in the dining room in the mansion in the days before the canteen was built. She happened to be sitting next to a Frenchman when unexpectedly the news of the fall of Paris was announced on the radio. He suddenly burst into tears; Mavis immediately recognised the importance of the news and was possibly shocked when she realised how serious things were becoming. She did not attempt to talk or comfort the man but went on to finish her lunch, thinking of the next long shift and the threat of invasion which could follow. She often mentioned this occasion in later life, perhaps hoping the man had not thought her heartless. Everything was new to nineteen-year-old Mavis and perhaps a little strange, so it is more probable that she was shy, embarrassed or worried.

In spite of the discomfort and unusual events like this Mavis felt at home with her colleagues at Bletchley Park. Looking fashionable during wartime did present problems but they took care of their outward appearance, and the girls sometimes borrowed each other's clothes for a special occasion. 'We were never scruffy... that was true of everyone during the war,'[19] she said, but Alan Turing, Josh Cooper, Dilly Knox and Angus Wilson were the exceptions and they were tolerated in a kindly way even though there was little known about illnesses such as autism, Asperger's syndrome and dyspraxia. The term bipolar had not come into use, but all were conditions from which they may have suffered. Angus Wilson would wear blue shirts and apricot-coloured bow ties, and his hair was long; Turing was known to turn up looking like a tramp, using a striped necktie to anchor his trousers, with fingernails chewed so badly that his fingers were raw. When the weather was fine he frequently rode around the countryside on his bicycle wearing his gas mask, but this was not so stupid as it might appear; he suffered from hay fever and believed this might avoid his having an attack.

When it was announced that cups had gone missing from the dining room Turing would chain his mug to the radiator, but Josh Cooper, who did not know where to put his mug when he had finished his coffee, would throw it into the lake. Angus Wilson, however, when in a paddy and told, ' "Do stop it, Angus, otherwise; we'll put you in the lake!" he replied, "Don't worry, I'll do it myself!" He threw himself in, and he had to be pulled out.'[20] But in spite of their odd mannerisms and habits they were intelligent and exceptionally clever in their own fields, and Bletchley Park would never have achieved what it did without them.

It was not uncommon for codebreakers to suffer temporary or permanent physical or mental collapse due to the pressure of work; Hugh Trevor Roper had problems for several months during 1941 and Dorothy Hyson became exhausted by her shift work as a cryptographer, but in post-war days she went on to continue her life as an actress. Other staff too suffered in various ways.

Although Bletchley Park was not a military base the men were doing vital work, but some had a feeling of guilt at not being in the front line, so it no doubt helped them feel a little better when they were offered the opportunity to join the Home Guard. It was thought to have been the youngest Home Guard company in the country, but nevertheless it was taken very seriously by most men and they took pride in being more competent in military matters than their Intelligence Corps colleagues. They did drill in the stable yard and had rifle practice in a nearby deep clay-pit which it is said was a passable imitation of the Somme in 1916, however, legend tells of practice with broomsticks before rifles were issued which must have caused considerable mirth among those who preferred to be spectators.

Activities were strictly compartmentalised mainly because of the high level of security involved. There was no time to see the job through; you did your bit, and it was then forwarded on to the next stage. For some the work was extremely boring; the codebreakers would complete their part of the task, it might then be passed on, perhaps to the next hut where the procedure was continued without the codebreakers knowing exactly what their input had contributed to the final result. 'That was the way it was,' remembers Jean Trumpington, 'you did your work with blinkers on.'[21] However, Gwen Davies recalled, 'This left plenty of room for gossip, and that was wonderful; apocryphal stories about everybody flew everywhere, personalities were safe to talk about.'[22]

Concealment must have been difficult at first, but then it must have become a habit; this had to be a good habit because the Official Secrets Act always had a threatening presence. News could be exciting but emotions could not be shown; you kept your secrets, but no doubt each person wondered what other important facts the staff in the other huts were concealing. Traffic could be good news, or even frightening, but it had to remain secret.

Mary Knight, when in her nineties and writing her memoirs in 1999, recalled that '... the secrecy of the place was paramount and we had to swear that we would never speak about our work to anyone outside Bletchley at any time, or even to anyone outside our own Hut.' [23]

When at the age of twenty years Mavis's future husband, Keith Batey, first arrived at Bletchley Park, his landlady firmly requested that before accepting him as a lodger she would like official notice that he was not one of the unpopular 'conchies' – a conscientious objector avoiding military service. When it was confirmed that he was not she was very glad to take him as a guest and treated him very well. Mavis said that men were always treated better than women – they had their washing and ironing done for them.

Mavis soon got to know her colleagues and enjoyed their companionship. Most of the staff were billeted out and it was the luck of the draw as to where they lived. Those doing more vital work were billeted in the village – others were ferried around by bus. Mavis was first placed at a manor house; they ate things like Spam and potatoes but they did have a manservant to wait upon them. Her hostess advised that a maid would run baths for her, but that would cost 10s. each week. Mavis had to decline this offer as it was not possible on her wages as she earned only £1. 10s. a week; and her board and lodging cost £1. 0s. 0d. a week. Poor Mavis had to manage with one bath a week. Her next billet was at a grocer's shop, a good place to be in wartime as sometimes they had extra bits of bacon and that was a real breakfast-time treat. She looked after the children occasionally, did some baby-sitting, helped with the chores and did her own washing. Her grateful landlady insisted on taking a cup of tea to her guests in the morning, and then one day she told Mavis she would be away the following week and that her aunt would be coming to look after them as she was going to have a baby. Mavis was horrified that they had been letting her wait on them, but her landlady just laughed and told her they were not the only ones who could keep secrets.

Mavis said that some people thought they were incarcerated, but she joined a psychology group at the Workers Education Association (WEA), helped with the canteen on the station, and for a while was in the Air Raid Precautions team (ARP). The strange thing was that nobody outside ever asked what they were doing at Bletchley Park, but Mavis said that doing these additional jobs brought them together. Mavis fitted in well, but other people had unfortunate tales to tell.

This was a completely new world to Mavis, but she got along well with the staff and soon settled down to enjoy life in this unusual place.

CHAPTER THREE

Mavis Has Her First Big Break

In June 1940 Italy joined the war and things became intense. German U-boats held a threatening presence in the Atlantic; the loss of British merchant shipping sunk by them was substantial and continued to increase. The delivery of supplies of food, fuel and arms was suffering, and it became necessary to delay merchant shipping still further in order to enable them to assemble in convoys to be escorted across the Atlantic by warships. It was vitally important that the Naval Enigma should be broken, but no progress was being made.

Alan Turing had earned himself the reputation of being exceptionally clever and, in August 1940, his invention of what became the 'bombe' led to the breaking of the Air Force Enigma. It was believed that he and the brilliant Peter Twinn might also go on to break the Naval Enigma, but Frank Birch, head of the naval section, became frustrated at the lack of progress. He was exasperated by the methodology of Turing and Twinn. They may have been brilliant, but in Birch's opinion the two men were not practical and did not have the determination of practical men. Alan Turing appears to have been pessimistic about the breaking of the Naval Enigma, and indeed the eventual outcome of the war. It was in 1940 that he converted an amount of his savings to silver ingots which he wrapped in brown paper and took by perambulator to a place in Bletchley's countryside where he buried them. This was to be his insurance against German interference with his bank account, should the Germans win the war.

Dilly was not happy when losing Turing, who was to work with Twinn, or that Gordon Welchman and John Jeffreys were running Hut 6. However, Alastair Denniston did his best to appease him and Dilly was given charge of the Cottage research unit to break untried Enigma variations, which included the Abwehr machine. One reason for this was that Oliver Strachey, brother of Lytton Strachey and friend of Dilly Knox from university days who had been recruited by Denniston in 1919, was called upon to set up a section known as Illicit (or Intelligence) Services Oliver Strachey, which was to be operated from Elmer's School at Bletchley Park.

Denniston was firm but always considerate of Dilly who was allowed to choose his own team. Although previously Dilly had not favoured mathematicians, he now selected Margaret Rock who proved to be an excellent and worthwhile choice. She joined Mavis and they worked extremely well together and between them tackled several important projects, and the reorganisation proved to be a good move.

Unfortunately, the loss of shipping continued, and still there was no progress with breaking the Naval Enigma Code. The feeling of frustration filtered through to the codebreakers and they too were becoming anxious. Various techniques were explored, including the Wild Cat Scheme which involved Bletchley Park sending out dummy Morse messages that it was hoped would provoke a useful response; but none came.

Admiral Godfrey, Director of Naval Intelligence, was aware of how successful the staff located in Room 40 of the Admiralty Old Building had been when dealing with U-boats during the First World War. Denniston had played an important role in Room 40, and in 1919 he became head of the newly founded GC&CS and retained this position until February 1942. Dilly Knox started in Room 40 in 1915 and he was joined by his friend Frank Birch who was an actor. Godfrey wrote to Frank Birch saying that he was setting up an organisation to arrange the theft of German codebooks and/or cypher material. His solution would involve establishing a combined committee of talent in his own and Birch's department who could think up cunning schemes. Asa Briggs wrote that Godfrey 'loved drama and it was characteristic of him that within the Admiralty he selected as his personal assistant Ian Fleming…'[1] a great showman and the future author of James Bond thrillers, and together they would be able to plan daring operations.

Godfrey arranged that Fleming should also work with Dilly; it was, after all, Dilly who had broken the First World War U-boat code. Dilly, always ready with suggestions, would have told Fleming that the Enigma's key for one day might be obtained by asking for it in a bogus signal. Mavis points out in her biography of Dilly that '… he would have explained to Lt-Cdr Fleming that it was not the actual Enigma machine that was needed, as it was often thought. We already had a working model of it, but that was useless by itself as there were millions of possible settings; it was the key that was needed.'[2]

Fleming was something of a pin-up among the female staff. He was working in London on naval intelligence at that time, and although he dropped in at Bletchley to see Dilly on a regular fortnightly basis he presented no problems with the young staff. Mavis knew that Dilly was very protective of his girls and she was sure that if a man with a reputation such as Fleming's should join him, they would never get to meet him. And they did not.

Fleming did produce a cunning scheme involving a daring line of action to obtain a pinch of the daily key settings from a German naval vessel. He would have liked to have played the leading role with the crew of five, but had the escapade taken place he would have been forbidden to put himself in such a dangerous position, as if he were captured he could be interrogated. Unfortunately, 'Operation Ruthless', as the scheme was called, was never activated as circumstances, including the weather, were unsatisfactory, but nevertheless the path had been laid for future cunning schemes to be put into action. For the present there was the feeling that something of importance was about to take place, and Bletchley Park looked forward with apprehension, but time dragged on and an air of gloom prevailed.

Meanwhile, life became more challenging for the girls in the Cottage after Italy declared war in June. For Mavis, as one of the more recent members of staff, this was particularly important as, instead of doing routine jobs of little consequence, they were now working to break the Italian Naval Enigma. It was tedious work and a hard slog when trying over and over again to break a code, but knowing there were men whose lives depended upon their success they worked unstintingly and held no grudges. Their team was responsible for saving the lives of many men and nothing equalled the relief and exhilaration felt when a code was broken.

Work on the Italian Naval Enigma became even more important, and Dilly's girls were thrilled when presented with new fields to be explored. They were taught Dilly's 'rodding' system, the technique he had invented in 1937 used to break messages that had been enciphered on Enigma machines without a plugboard, or *stecker,* as it was called in German.

The first commercial version of an Enigma machine was of this type and, after equipping it with different sets of rotors, a few countries adopted it for use by their armed services. Dilly devised a way into this machine which had been used by the Italian Navy in the Spanish Civil War and continued to do so in a limited way after their entry into the Second World War in June 1940.

There had been teething problems in the 1930s when the Germans increased the number of code-letter wheels to the machine so strengthening its security. However, the Frenchman, Major Gustave Bertrand, was working with the Polish mathematician Marian Rejewski who had been able to help with this problem. Mavis, always fair, insisted that Bertrand's assistance should be acknowledged, and Keith Batey, too, registered his opinion about this:

When the Germans improved the plugboard of Enigma they sent out a manual.

And the idiots actually gave a plain text telling how one set up the machine and this manual gave you the answer. The Germans realised, and recalled the manual right away – but Major Bertrand got hold of one none the less. That's what gave the Poles the entry they needed.[3]

First, Dilly's team had to find out which of the various models of the Enigma machines were being used, but this did not take too long. The machine the Italian High Command, or *Supermarina*, was using was the one without a plugboard. The commercial machine that Mavis had worked on at GC&CS when at the Broadway building, also had no plugboard so Mavis became intrigued – her experience there had given her confidence. By introducing his rodding method Dilly had made the task of breaking the Italian Naval Enigma – an otherwise tedious routine – into a simple word game that could be played without understanding the mechanism within the machine. The process is succinctly described by Sinclair McKay:

'Knox's "rods" were, in the most basic terms, a painstakingly calculated slide-rule style representation of the wiring and rotor position of the machine upon which cypher-text letters could be moved and rearranged.'[4]

Dilly's fascination for words and Carrollian 'chopped logic' went back to his childhood games, and it is a coincidence that he invented his rodding method for breaking codes and that his Bletchley girls regarded this as a game.

Dilly and his team were cautious as there was a possibility that the 'K' Enigma, for which Dilly had worked out the rodding method, might be inappropriate. Settings changed daily and messages were received infrequently rather than several on the same day, so although rodding was an asset the procedure could be tedious and 'remained a major feat of cryptography.[5] There were only a few girls who could understand the mechanics of the machine; nevertheless, in spite of this, they were all able to use the rodding method and achieve results. Mavis also voiced her opinion about the procedure:

The good thing was the psychological effect of knowing that we were no longer working in the dark and that we were dealing with the 'K' machine, whose wheel wirings Dilly had broken in the Spanish Civil War. Each message had to be broken separately however, as the indicating system was never solved, presumably having been taken from a codebook.[6]

The wartime Naval Enigma messages slowly crept in and were intercepted with great excitement as the girls were able to produce crib charts to speed up the rodding process.

It became apparent that submarines, the Italian *sommergibili,* were a chosen vessel of attack, a prime example of intelligence that Dilly chose not to share with the girls. Mavis did not learn what they had been dealing with until years later when records were released. The Italians had invented, and were using, a midget submarine – a human torpedo – manned by two frogmen who sat astride the vessel wearing divers' suits. They were carried by a full-size submarine and were launched close to the target. The first knowledge of these lethal apparatus were messages at Bletchley Park, received by *Dilly's girls*, when in October 1940 two *sommergibili* made an attack in Gibraltar.

For reasons of security the codebreakers at Bletchley Park were seldom told about the operations they were supporting, and *Dilly's girls* would not have known exactly why and how their codebreaking concerned warfare in the Atlantic and the Mediterranean, although they were aware that it was exceedingly important. As far as Dilly was concerned he always held the belief that there was intelligence he did need to know and that his staff did not. This was his way of shielding his girls from some of the more unpleasant warfare activities, although it was inevitable that they would gather a lot of information when dealing with incoming traffic.

The girls continued to work hard until Bletchley analysts proved something was afoot. The girls knew this would mean a 'Jumbo Rush', their pet name for an emergency or something very important about to happen. That day they had broken new wheels introduced by the

Italians so leaving six possibilities for rodding and charting for the right-hand wheel. There was no leave, no sleep, and little time to eat. The task had to be completed as quickly as possible and girls had stood a stuffed elephant on the table to remind them of the meaning of a *Jumbo Rush*.

Dilly's complete team set to work and nineteen-year-old Mavis Lever broke an Italian Enigma signal. She had no Italian; her small vocabulary consisted mainly of musical and cookery terms and ingredients for the few Italian recipes with which she was acquainted, but it was not long before her limited knowledge had expanded to include words related to shipping. Mavis became very enthusiastic and spent many weeks working patiently on the rodding process, which was a laborious procedure as they were looking at new traffic all the time, or for instances where the wheels or the wiring had been changed. There was no easy way into a code.

> Dilly suggested we should try something as simple as PERX (for) at the beginning of each message, disregarding those that 'crashed' (that is to say, had those letters in the enciphered text where the crib was needed, it not being possible for a letter to encipher as itself). The encoded text was written out on squared paper across the page and the appropriate rods set up under it, the letters on the rod fitting the same size squares.[7]

It demanded a great deal of patience, but Mavis worked on, until in September 1940 she had a second lucky strike. She had stayed behind to work during the evening shift whilst it was quiet; she was working in the Italian language and eventually became adventurous, disobeying instructions. When S, rejecting X, appeared of its own accord from the first coupling, she decided not to discard the position as she thought that PERSONALE might be a good guess, and it was: 'Fortunately, there was a run before the wheel turnover, and a "beetle" (two letters side by side – one of several terms devised by Dilly) 'meant that one of the remaining bigrams in the column would have to be used, suggesting other words to try.'[8] Mavis knew she had a struggle on her hands with the remaining text, but with the help of her mini Italian dictionary she was soon able to follow the method of the machine and decided to persevere with five other couplings. She eventually achieved the results she wanted. She had worked into the early hours of the morning; she was tired but excited and filled with enthusiasm – she knew she had achieved something very important but did not know exactly what the result of the code she had broken would reveal.

At this point Mavis should have handed the message she had retrieved to Dilly but, becoming increasingly ill, he had gone home. It has been recorded that 'Mavis had made the first break into the traffic sent on the wartime machine.' [9]

Dilly was overcome with excitement when Mavis handed the deciphered message to him the next morning. As a result of Mavis's work the Italian Naval Enigma was read each day from September 1940 until the summer of 1941 when procedure changed. Dilly was fully aware of the advantages that would now be available, and that evening he showed his appreciation by taking Mavis out to dinner at the Fountain Inn, at nearby Stony Stratford.

This was Mavis's first experience of being driven in his Baby Austin and it was an 'horrendous drive from Bletchley with Dilly gesticulating and quoting *Herodas* and '*himmliche rosen*' *ad lib,* with total disregard for the oncoming traffic.'[10] She was apprehensive and nervous of the blackout, particularly as it was thought by many that preparations were in place for a possible German invasion, but fortunately Dilly did 'manage to avoid the tank traps along Watling Street.'[11] They arrived safely, even though Dilly had a reputation for being a very fast driver who believed that, if he drove over crossroads at speed, he would have less chance of knocking down a pedestrian.

Dilly preferred to have women rather than men working for him, and it was said that if he saw a tall, pretty girl around the Park he would put in a request for her to join his team. This was strongly denied by Mavis, and she adamantly stated that they were selected solely by notes supplied by the fierce Miss Moore who had interviewed her at Broadway. It is said that the girls became known around Bletchley Park as *Dilly's Fillys*, and it was rumoured that they were even known by this title in the Foreign Office. Dilly took it in good part; he was not a womaniser, but genuinely enjoyed the company of ladies and he felt their nimble fingers gave them a particular advantage when codebreaking.

It is possible that he suppressed homosexual tendencies but, if so, he behaved like a gentleman in the manner expected of him at that time. In her biography of Dilly, his niece, Penelope Fitzgerald, writes: 'In his last two years at Eton, Dilly conducted some "intellectual and sexual" experiments with [John Maynard] Keynes, and at King's for a short time he was the object of Lytton Strachey's desire', but she states that Dilly was 'impervious to the golden glow of homosexuality that suffused Cambridge in those days.'[12] It was perhaps that he was fascinated by Mavis's girlish innocence. Mavis was fond of him but their friendship was platonic. They enjoyed a shared interest in literature and poetry, both being besotted with the works of Lewis Carroll and Jane Austen. Mavis soon accepted his eccentricities and, in a kindly manner, would help him search for his spectacles, frequently found in his tobacco pouch, and forgave his explosive temper. Mavis cared about Dilly, he was her mentor and soulmate, and she thought of him as Lewis Carroll's White Knight in *Alice in Wonderland*, the queerest bird that Alice has ever seen, endearingly eccentric and concerned about her welfare.

Over dinner at the Fountain Inn the conversation turned to how life would be post-war, and Dilly asked Mavis what she would like to do. Thoroughly absorbed with what was going on with codebreaking at Bletchley and the war that was raging beyond its boundaries, Mavis had no plans for her future life, but on the spur of the moment she said she might try journalism.

This seemed to please Dilly and he promised to introduce her to his brother Evoe, who was a poet and held the editor's chair at *Punch*; he would help to get her started. More helpful to Mavis at that time was that he was so pleased with her work that he decided to have her put up a grade which, of course, would mean an increase in pay. She felt proud when she was told that she would be promoted to the more important position of machine cryptographer and delighted with her pay-rise as she had been earning only 35s. a week, from which she had to pay a guinea to her landlady.

At Bletchley Park, Italian Naval Enigma messages continued to slowly arrive, and on the night of 20 November 1940 the girls suffered another serious interruption of their sleep; a single German plane, believed to be returning from bombing Coventry, and carrying some surplus bombs, needed to lighten its load, possibly enabling the crew to increase the speed of their flight home. It released the bombs on the first suitable target, which happened to be Bletchley Park campus, or perhaps the adjacent railway sidings were their aim. However, it was Elmer's School, close by Bletchley Park, where the Bletchley Park Diplomatic Service was based, that suffered a direct hit, causing damage to the typists' room and the telephone exchange. Fortunately there were no casualties, just a bit of disruption that was soon overcome, and work continued on the Japanese codes.

Another bomb damaged the nearby vicarage of St Mary's Church and the third was near Hut 4, by the mansion. There were various reports about the damage caused, and there was a small crater, but it is stated in the Bletchley Park Diaries that the hut was lifted off its foundations and a naval rigger team had to reinstate it the next day – but work on naval air and intelligence undertaken in that hut scarcely ceased. 'The next bomb fell on the stable yard but fails to go off, which is just as well as Dilly Knox and his "harem" of girls are at work there in Cottage 3, breaking the few Italian Naval Enigma messages, and struggling to get to grips with the Abwehr Enigma.'[13] Nevertheless, they were soon busy again and racing to make progress.

There were said to be two more bombs that did not explode, and it would appear that the Germans believed that Bletchley Park campus was no more than an ordinary military base. If this was so, it was a very unusual army camp for it often had high quality musical evening entertainments in the Assembly Hall.

On 14 and 15 November 1940, when there had been a full moon, intelligence revealed the Luftwaffe was planning an imminent major attack. R. V. Jones, MI6's principal scientific advisor, had invented a device to discover how Luftwaffe pilots navigated when they flew over England by night during the Battle of Britain and the Blitz. He unravelled the Lorenz beam navigation systems they were using and was sometimes able to jam, sometimes to divert, their beams,[14] so given the possibility to 'bend' these beams the pilots could be put off target. In this instance Bletchley Park was unaware of the exact whereabouts of the target, but they knew that the Germans were using X-gerat, a device which became known as 'beam-bombing'. The bombers could be guided along a navigation beam, operated by radio, until it was crossed by another beam; the point at which the beams crossed was their target. This could be the centre of a city, and there, they would release their bombs. The beams were kept on course by radio and picked up by a Y-Services outstation which would pass on the information to Bletchley Park on Brown Enigma cyphers. The attack was expected on 20 November and the Midlands were the expected target: Birmingham, Coventry or Wolverhampton were all possibilities for the *Moonlight Sonata*.

The British did build 'jammers' to bend the beams and in many instances they did work, so rather than hit factories, or other important targets, bombs were dropped randomly about the countryside.

Keith Batey's duties in Hut 6 were largely on the Brown Enigma cyphers. These gave information about the radio beams guiding the pilots of the German bombers to their targets and so allowed RAF fighter aircraft to intercept them. He was always saddened by the Hut 6 codebreakers' inability to break the Brown key on the night of the devastating raid on Coventry but the coded names of the towns and cities targeted needed a codebook and none was available. This was a tragedy for which Churchill was erroneously blamed.

CHAPTER FOUR
The Battle of Matapan, March 1941

No doubt still feeling pleased with her promotion, a few months later Mavis was once again on the evening shift and working alone as she often did. There was a short spell when nothing of importance had been happening, and during this time, as frequently occurred in slack periods, dummy messages were being received. The enemy believed that if messages continued to make an appearance without a break, and without gaps, it would not be noticed when important new traffic resumed. Fortunately dummy traffic was usually recognisable, even though on one occasion a young lady wasted several days working on a message only to find it was a passage from Dante's *Inferno*.

In the next stream of traffic Mavis quickly noticed an exceptionally long message, which she immediately picked up and saw there were no Ls in the script – she guessed that the operator had made a mistake and had pressed an incorrect key. On that particular night she was beginning to get tired and then she reached the final stage of what was known as 'buttoning up' on the QWERTZU diagonal. This was the usual method of recovering the wiring, but it was proving very confusing owing to the repetitive nature of the crib. She decided to seek the advice of someone from the Hut 6 watch and, as luck would have it, it was Keith Batey who offered his help. 'We put our heads together and over the calmer light of logic and much ersatz coffee, the problem was solved.'[1] They discovered that for security reasons *Supermarina* had changed the wiring of one of the wheels, and once this was reconstructed there were no more problems.

Keith later let slip that he had noticed Mavis about a year earlier, but because during working hours they were all confined to their own sections he did not have the chance to see her again. If Mavis had pounced upon this opportunity to talk to Keith, it will never be known, but this was the beginning of their romance.

The Italians gave them a big break by 'insisting on their operators spelling out full stops as XALTX and in order to keep the message in five-letter groups, the end one would have Xs added, so that there might be an eight-letter crib XALTXXXX right at the end of a message.'[2] However, the operator made a mistake entering an incorrect full stop. 'Little did Mussolini know that a humble full stop would be responsible for the defeat of his navy in the Mediterranean,'[3] Mavis would chirp when telling her story in later years.

Mavis had gathered that the message had been important, but for security reasons this information was withheld and she had no idea exactly how important it was; the team knew there was still more codebreaking to be done and things became even more exciting.

On 25 March 1941 a three-lined message was received and the first word, SUPERMARINA, the Italian translation of Naval High Command, was recognised by Dilly's girls as a crib. The girls used the rodding procedure and a complete message was deciphered stating, 'Today is X-3, Today's the day minus three.'[4] It was from the Naval High Command in Rome and addressed to an Italian commander on the Greek island of Rhodes. Their previous exercise had proved to be useful and the charts became helpful.

Mavis knew immediately that to receive a message like that indicated that something of great importance was about to happen. Each of the three days had different key settings, making things more tedious as each message had to be broken separately. More and more relevant messages came through and Mavis worked on through shift after shift, day after day, night after night, scarcely eating, and sleeping spasmodically. Eventually, at around eleven o'clock on this dark, wet night, 'I rushed, ran, absolutely tore down to take it to Intelligence, to get it across to Admiral Cunningham.'[5] The girls were excited. They knew it was something important, and were heard chanting the phrase like a mantra – 'Today's the day minus three'. They waited anxiously.

Mavis had made the first break into the traffic sent on the wartime machine and had solved the first signals revealing the Italian Navy's operational plans before the Battle of Matapan had taken place.

It had been a marathon. Now there was just the tidying up to do, making sure that the rods were not left around on the desks but returned to the appropriate jam jars. The weary Mavis made her way by torchlight along the dark gravel pathway to the railway station thinking she would be able to catch a train to her billet in Leighton Buzzard, but all was in vain. When she approached the driver of the Royal Scot which was taking on water, in reply to her request for a lift he answered, "I'd do anything for you, Missie, but I'm afraid the train can't get into Leighton Buzzard". [6] Most of the girls found shift work unpleasant. 'It was awful. You worked nine to six, four to midnight, or midnight to nine, and they changed the shift every week, so you could never get a proper sleep pattern,'[7] Jean Trumpington had complained. But nights like this were even worse, thought the lonely and very tired young lady who fell asleep on Bletchley Station that night and was awoken hours later as the milk train steamed through.

By solving the first signals, the decrypted message proved to be another important achievement. It had been forwarded to Admiral Sir A. R. Cunningham, Commander in Chief of the Mediterranean, and revealed the Italian Navy's operational plans before the Battle of Matapan. The Italians were planning to attack a Royal Navy convoy carrying supplies and soldiers to Greece; the content of the message gave details not only of their plans, but also instruction to the commander in Rhodes, which was occupied by the Italians, alerting him that the airport was to be bombed and the route between Alexandria, Crete and Piraeus should be put under surveillance.

By solving the first signals Mavis had made it possible for Admiral Cunningham to be forewarned and able to set to sea on the evening of 27 March to confront the fleet of Admiral Angelo Iachino.

Intelligence from another source was received and various confusing tactics were carried out. A curious incident, instigated by Admiral Cunningham, happened in Alexandria when, after a meeting with his staff officers, he suggested to Lieutenant Hugh Lee that they should have a round of golf. Lee agreed and was amused to learn it was to be a ploy. He was told that while at the sporting club they would have a conversation about a dinner party to be thrown that evening at the ambassador's residence in Alexandria, and that the British fleet would remain there for the night. He was to ensure that their discussion was heard by any would-be eavesdropper. As luck would have it, when leaving the club Cunningham saw the Japanese Consul, a known spy for the Axis, and also a keen golfer, who was obviously trying to hear what was being said. So Cunningham raised his voice, and on calling "Is everything ready for the dinner tonight?" Lee replied, "Yes, everyone's invited."[8] Cunningham walked over to the car carrying an apparently heavy, but empty, overnight bag. They drove away and made a diversion to the ambassador's residence where Cunningham was temporarily living, and had a cup of tea with Lady Cunningham. However, by seven o'clock that evening they were sailing out of the harbour on HMS *Warspite* on their way to battle.

On the night of 28/29 March 1941, as a result of Bletchley Park's work in breaking enemy codes and the following ULTRA information, Cunningham was able to intercept the enemy off Cape Matapan.

> … the Royal Navy crushed its Italian counterpart with three British battleships sinking an entire Italian cruiser squadron of heavy cruisers and two destroyers, with the loss of three thousand Italian sailors. The Italians had no radar so the British caught them completely by surprise.[9]

The battle fleet of Admiral Angelo Iachino included about twenty ships, amongst them his flagship, the 41,000 ton *Vittorio Venito*. It was an outstanding British victory which resulted in the Italian Navy leaving the British to control the eastern Mediterranean; crucial in the evacuation of Greece and Crete, so avoiding many casualties and saving lives. This was the first unexpected major Royal Naval victory in fleet action of World War II and the battle was claimed by Winston Churchill as the greatest fight since the Battle of Trafalgar. Mavis had reason to be extremely proud of the part she had played in bringing this about.

The Battle of Matapan lifted not just the spirits of the people of Bletchley Park, but also those who rejoiced at the headlines of Britain's newspapers. Newsreels in cinemas all around Britain showed Admiral Sir Andrew Cunningham standing proud on the quarterdeck of his flagship HMS *Warspite*, guns booming and lights flashing as he observed the defeat of the Italian Navy. He became the nation's hero.

On the evening of 29 March, the day the battle had been won, John Godfrey, Director of Naval Intelligence, rang Bletchley Park and asked to speak with Dilly Knox. Unfortunately Dilly was at home so Godfrey left a message: 'Tell Dilly that we have won a great victory in the Mediterranean and it is entirely due to him and his girls.'[10] His girls were delighted by the news, their only disappointment was that they could not share their success with their friends and families. Mavis felt particularly proud, but perhaps her biggest achievement, in terms of the results achieved, was to solve the first signals revealing the Italian Navy's operational plans before Matapan. She knew that not only did they break the Italian Enigma cyphers that led to the Royal Navy's victory at Matapan, but the messages were sent by their team leader, Dilly, using the special procedure known as ULTRA, the top secret codeword for information achieved when breaking high-grade cyphers. Every person in the team was excited, and Dilly was so elated that he wrote a poem as a tribute to his girls naming them each in turn. The rhyming tribute for Mavis was *rara avis*. Their tea lady, an expert at handling the temperamental urn that kept the girls awake with cups of tea or coffee, had signed the Official Secrets Act, so she too was mentioned.

Mavis found it flattering and included the poem *Swollen Heads* in her biography of Dilly.

When Cunningham won at Matapan
By the grace of God and Claire,
For she pilots well the aeroplane
That spotted their fleet from the air.

When Cunningham won at Matapan
By the grace of God and Nancy,
Now she is a girl, the Admiral said,
That might take anyone's fancy.

When Cunningham won at Matapan
By the grace of God and Mavis,
Nigro simillima cygno et, praise Heaven,
A very rara avis.

When Cunningham won at Matapan
By the grace of God and Margaret,
It was thanks to that girl, the Admiral said,
That our aeroplanes straddled their target.

When Cunningham won at Matapan
By the grace of God and Phyllida,
And made that impossibly self-willed girl
If possible self-willeder.

When Cunningham won at Matapan
By the grace of God and Hilda,
And sank the Vittorio Veneto
Or at least they can't rebuild her.

When Cunningham won at Matapan
By the grace of God and Jean,
And if Jean Harvie had been there too,
Hoots man, what might na ha been?

When Cunningham won at Matapan
By the grace of God and Mrs Balance,
Indeed, he said, the Cottage team
Is a team of all the talents.

When Cunningham won at Matapan
By the grace of God and Elisabeth,
The credit was almost entirely ours
But possibly God did his a bit.

Many people believed that Dilly saw cryptography as a theoretical problem unrelated to real events, however this was not so. Aerial reconnaissance was significant in Cunningham drawing up his battle plan, but it was Dilly who immediately informed the Admiralty in order to ensure that its appearance in the press would acknowledge its success as being entirely due to air reconnaissance.

An additional verse was written as a tribute to 'Nobby' Clarke and Admiral Godfrey, the DNI, who had made ULTRA possible:

When Cunningham won at Matapan
By the Grace of Godfrey and Nobby
Though not of our outer or inner rooms
They're allowed sometimes in the lobby.

Dilly was not to be forgotten, and Mavis remembered that Nobby Clarke – an old friend of his in Room 40 days – who was in overall command of the naval section at Bletchley Park at the time of Matapan, summed up the situation with an extra verse for Dilly's Matapan poem.

When Cunningham won at Matapan
By the grace of God and Dilly,
He was the brains behind them all
And should ne'er be forgotten. Will he?

When the excited young ladies heard that their hero Admiral Cunningham was on his way to Bletchley Park to thank the codebreakers, they rushed down to the local Five Bells to buy some bottles of wine. It may not have been of the quality usually served to an Admiral, but it appears to have had a jolly effect on the team who at one point appeared quite inebriated.

The girls, who now doted on the Admiral, crowded around him. He was wearing a spotless naval uniform and looking very confident; but surrounded by admiring young ladies he probably felt hemmed in. When the bemused Admiral cast his sharp, blue eyes over the group, no doubt they twinkled teasingly.

He was particularly keen to see the original coded messages to the enemy, especially those to Admiral Iachino, as his plan of attack had been based on them. He was obviously quite proud of his James Bond style tactics and he told his audience how he fed the Japanese Consul false information, and how dumbfounded the consul must have been when next morning he found the harbour absolutely empty of all shipping.

'When we weren't working hard, we were being extremely naughty,'[11] remembered Jean Trumpington. Possibly in the anticipation of this momentous occasion, the girls had something to do with the Cottage walls being freshly white-washed, and giggles had to be stifled when Admiral Sir Andrew Cunningham smilingly lounged against a sparkling, but damp wall. It was fortunate that he did not discover the white blotches upon his smart, dark suit until after he had left. Considering how narrowly focused their lives were, the young ladies must be forgiven their prank.

On Saturday 6 September 1941 Winston Churchill unexpectedly arrived at Bletchley Park. He had been fascinated by cryptology and secret intelligence since he was First Lord of the Admiralty, and as prime minster during WWII he continued to take an interest in the procedure. The logic employed in breaking the codes, and the subsequent success in the ability to read the internal messages of the German navy and military, were of vital importance. Just two weeks after he was appointed prime minister, Bletchley Park broke into the German Air Force Enigma, and this impressed him so much that he arranged for a box of intercepts to be secretly forwarded to him on a daily basis.

Churchill was taken on a tour of the many Bletchley Park activities and it was a very busy scene that he came upon. First he inspected the Hollerith machine installation in Hut 7, where the machines of the forty-five operators working there were brought to a sharp halt. Instant silence was broken by an introductory explanation followed by demonstrations when the machines were then brought back into action. The head of the room, Freddie Freeborn, could not have led the performance with more precision had it been a regiment of the guards. As the prime minister made his way to the door the machines were once more brought to a standstill, and he bid his farewells before going on to Hut 6 where he met Alan Turing who was unfortunately overcome by shyness, but Gordon Welchman kindly took over.

Before his departure Churchill climbed onto a heap of builders' rubbish outside a hut and addressed a group of codebreakers who had gathered around: 'You all look very innocent; one would not think you would know anything secret!'[12] He then made up for his remark and, continuing to address the young ladies, he called them 'the geese that lay the golden eggs – and never cackle'.[13] It later became known that he referred to his daily messages from Bletchley Park as his 'eggs'. The address was made with deep emotion and received in much the same way; Mavis was stirred to remember this moment for years to come.

Churchill had met an extraordinary range of personalities and was clearly baffled that those who were obviously ill-disciplined and eccentric folk were making such an impression on this key battleground of the intelligence war. He continued to be constantly in touch with Bletchley Park. Their work was of vital importance to the war and he took trouble to see that whenever possible life was made a little easier for the staff. When he heard that only one tennis court remained after others had been destroyed to make way for a new Bletchley building, and rounders was the only possible ball game, he arranged for two tennis courts to be provided. Another surprise awaited the popular Bletchley Park Tennis Club when they were allowed to use the summer house as a changing room.

After his visit a group of the senior personnel wrote, praising the technological assets which had been provided, and made a personal appeal to Churchill for extra staff needed for the continuation of their important work. He was aware that the important work could not make progress if there was a shortage of staff. A written instruction was immediately issued by him to his chief of staff instructing him to make sure they had all that they had requested, and at the top of the notice was one of his famous stickers: 'Action This Day'.

CHAPTER FIVE

The Twenty Committee: Double Cross XX

In December 1939 Hugh Trevor-Roper was recruited from Merton College, Oxford to work with E. W. B. Gill in Radio Security Service (RSS), a branch of MI5 based close to Bletchley Park at Hanslope.

Trevor-Roper was clever and had devoted much time to acquiring a vast knowledge of German intelligence. He was a headstrong young man, no doubt keen to make a name for himself, and indeed he did. Later in life, in the year 2000, after he had risen to become Lord Dacre, when interviewed by Graham Turner for *The Daily Telegraph*, he invented himself as a flamboyant MI6 agent who carried on fox hunting through the early years of the war: 'Occasionally, when I had a staff car, I found it compatible with my conscience to make my visits to the Code and Cypher School at Bletchley Park coincide with my hunting days with the Whaddon.'[1]

Walter Gill was a specialist in electromagnetic phenomena, a lecturer in electricity, and in World War I he had been a leading codebreaker in the British Army Signals intelligence organisation. He served in an army wireless service section in Egypt where he ran an aerial up the Great Pyramid at Giza.

The two men took up positions with MI5 at Wandsworth Prison, but finding there was a minimal amount of traffic to deal with they became bored and frustrated, and at home in their flat one evening these amateur cryptologists started to experiment and cracked some simple Abwehr hand cyphers.

In March 1940 they were charged with intercepting illicit wireless in the UK and breaking some simple hand cyphers from a Hamburg control station. When the matter reached the ears of Bletchley Park leader Alastair Denniston, they were reprimanded and advised not to concern themselves with matters that were not their business. Although at first GC&CS dismissed this operation as being unimportant, it became an embarrassment, and Bletchley Park decided to carry Trevor-Roper and Gill's research forward.

Intelligence Services Oliver Strachey (ISOS), sometimes referred to as Illicit Services Oliver Strachey, was now operating from Elmer's School. By December 1940 Strachey had successfully broken the most important hand cypher and, through ISOS, MI5 was able to keep the messages of double agents under observation and was alerted in advance of the arrival of German spies. It was found that Abwehr were operating a professional espionage network across Europe, their mission being to penetrate Britain prior to a planned invasion by German troops, so forming an advanced guard able to check on morale. However, with the fall of France the invasion did not take place.

This was a stroke of good luck for the British who immediately made a plan for a clearing house known as the Twenty (XX) Committee, or the Double Cross system, to be set up in London where the co-ordination of operational activities was to be arranged. The first meeting was held on 2 January 1941, they met every week and there were in all 226 meetings, the last being on 6 May 1945.

Their leader was John Masterman, who had been a prisoner of war in World War I and had acquired an ability to follow the German thought process. This enabled him to work out what the Germans would do next when faced with a particular problem, in contrast to how the British would confront a problem. Another officer capable of this was MI6 representative Frank Foley, and both were useful to the Twenty Committee which exercised a steady and consistent supervision of double agents' work through the last four and a half years of the war. When discussing various plans for deceiving the enemy, they always accepted proposals put forward by MI5, and on only one occasion was there a disagreement and this was put to a vote.

The German spies, all of whom had been taken prisoner, were dispatched to Latchmere House, Ham Common, Richmond, where they were interrogated. Those found to be suitable to work as double agents were trained to send back false information to their German controllers.

By the end of 1940 Double Cross had a dozen double agents under their control, with MI5 in charge of security in the United Kingdom; MI6 with German spies abroad, was responsible for overseas operations. It was a risky business that had to be conducted with the utmost precision and security; one of their duties being to decide what information should be filtered back to Abwehr.

The double agent used his own hand cypher which had been allotted to him by the Germans before leaving his country, and each agent was directed by his own British case officer to send out false information by wireless transmitter, to be received by his controller stationed in a neutral European city. Messages received would then be analysed and transmitted to Berlin on the Abwehr Enigma machine. At first the British wanted to give the impression of a strong defence and continued with the aim of misleading the Germans, therefore putting the Allied forces at an advantage in the field. Unimportant information would be included with that of supposedly greater importance, so giving the messages an apparently genuine content. MI5 was in control of all German espionage activities in Britain, and German response to the agents' requests for information would keep the British up to date with the extent of Abwehr intelligence.

John Masterman was aware that there could be problems of security, and there was concern about leakage as well as other operational difficulties, 'the Double Cross system was always in danger',[2] but with careful surveillance danger was avoided. 'The agents did justify the trust reposed in them and in the Double Cross system.'[3]

The part played by Bletchley Park codebreakers during the war was important, but there were other units, with people in the naval, air and military sections breaking lower-level codes which were also valuable. Many people were unaware of the large number of outstations that had connections to Bletchley Park; similarly many people, civilian or otherwise, were completely oblivious as to what went on there. Little was known of those stations known as Y-Services; some of their operators had never visited Bletchley Park and its Station X – for them it was just the place where intercepts were sent and from where cryptic instructions were returned giving the frequencies to which the recipients should listen, and until October 1943 traffic analysis was also carried out and low-grade codes and cyphers were broken. The Y-Service had roots going back to World War I, and in the early years the procedure was not appreciated for its true value, but as time went on it came to be realised just how important it was.

The effort to break the Enigma would mean many more staff, and thought was given to the size and layout of the Bletchley Park hut where operations were to take place and decisions had to be made regarding equipment that would be required. Gordon Welchman was largely responsible for this when working as head of the naval section located in Hut 6, which dealt with all listening assets. There were messages in German to be analysed and returned to Y-Stations with information on the appropriate frequencies with which to engage.

There had been a fall in the amount of Italian naval traffic so it was decided that Italian codebreaking should be passed to the Bletchley Park Naval Section. Before the high-grade Enigma traffic was recognised as being of importance, it had been sent early in 1941 to Gordon Welchman to be worked on by the Hut 6 team, but when no progress was being made, it was in the following summer that Dilly along with Margaret and Mavis began to tackle the unsolved traffic, described as unknown variations of Enigma research. When he accepted the challenge Mavis was particularly pleased for him as she was aware that Dilly and his family had always been interested in spies; and as a boy he and his brothers had devised various games revolving around espionage, and Dilly had thus become keen to be involved with current research.

Organisation was not one of Dilly's best attributes so he spent time with Strachey at Elmer's School learning about the organisation and distribution of the spy network, 'covering Spain, Portugal, the Balkans and Turkey, to see how the ISOS hand-cyphered messages related to Dilly's Enigma messages sent on from the neutral capitals to Berlin after December 1939'.[4] They also studied cribs from previous hand-cypher traffic which they hoped would be useful. Things moved along a little more quickly, and it is possible that an element of competition encouraged them to achieve speedy results.

Dilly had a friendly relationship with Strachey and liked being involved with research alongside him. By October 1941 he had made great headway and, keeping Alastair Denniston informed of his progress, suggested they should have a meeting. Although he mentioned he would be absent on 30 October, what he did not say was that he was suffering from a return of stomach cancer, but he was at that time unaware that his terminal illness would perhaps prevent him from returning to Bletchley Park. Denniston did not approve of Dilly's way of going about things and his familiarity with the Elmer team, so a certain amount of bickering took place. Following Masterman's lead that information should be shared with as few people as possible, Denniston, who was obsessed with secrecy, considered it unnecessary for Dilly to know about ISOS activities. However, Dilly objected, believing that if they did not share this information his breaking of the Abwehr code would be hindered, and this view was supported by Mavis. Correspondence was exchanged between the two men, Dilly complaining about the way in which various communications were handled.

Dilly also wrote to Colonel Stewart Menzies, Deputy of SIS, insisting that the material should be passed on in its original format. At this time he was working with Mavis and Margaret, and he wrote saying: 'In my opinion, Bletchley Park should be a cryptographical bureau supplying its results straight and unadorned to intelligence sections at the various ministries. At present we are encumbered with

'Intelligence Officers' who maul and conceal our results yet make no effort to check up on the arbitrary corrections.'[5]

Dilly was secretive about his illness, and in spite of what he referred to as 'a minor ailment' he endeavoured to continue his routine at Bletchley Park where his 'lightning inspirations', fired by black coffee, were excitedly triggered. Although seriously ill he was determined to carry on working. Letters continued to and fro; discussions were frequent, resignation threatened, but if Dilly had one of his inspirational moments he worked on diligently, sometimes all night through, when true serendipity, and even the Carrollian logic of *Alice in Wonderland*, would sometimes lend a hand. Mavis and Margaret understood his eccentric behaviour, and were particularly concerned about his health. They would do their best to ensure that he was never left alone in the office, particularly when he insisted on working late into the night – so there would always be one of the girls there to give him a hand if needed, which, of course, included a continuous supply of black coffee. He was extremely conscientious and it is unfortunate that Denniston was unaware of how ill he was, as he would probably have been more considerate of his behaviour.

In spite of the ill feeling between Denniston and Dilly, Margaret and Mavis started to concentrate on cracking the top German Abwehr cypher used by the German military intelligence service. This Abwehr cypher used an unusual form of Enigma and was much more complex than the Italian Enigmas. However, luck once again played a part in Dilly's quest to solve the breaking of the code.

Dilly's friend Fredric Freeborn was in charge of Hut 7 where Hollerith punch-card equipment was used to make rapid searches of data. There had been difficulties in finding staff to operate these machines. Similar machines were used by John Lewis Partnership, a well-known London chain store, and an official request was made to use some of their trained female operators. At first all was well and ten girls were chosen to work at Bletchley Park. However, problems arose when the Ministry of Labour and National Service withdrew permission for Bletchley to use the 'Lewis Girls' and there were delays, but when Churchill became involved this would appear to have eased matters.

After Dilly had paid a visit to Hut 7 to explore his friend Frederic Freeborn's Hollerith card-sorting and tabulation section, he had a serendipitous moment which fired one of his 'quick as lightning inspirations'. There were distinguishing features which did not surprise Dilly, and for the first phenomenon he coined the name 'crabs', because matters moved sideways, and 'lobsters' was the name he gave to simultaneous turnovers used for finding the keys. Dilly was sure these items would be the way into the code.

When it became clear that Dilly would be working very late, Phyllida Cross stayed in the back room at the Cottage ready to make coffee, cope with his non-existent filing system and, if necessary, hunt for his lost spectacles. When all in a rush he told her excitedly what he was about, she tried to understand, but she had to confess she did not comprehend a word.

Overnight his thoughts must have simmered because next morning he greeted Margaret and Mavis at the Cottage door; now overcome with excitement he said, 'If two cows are crossing the road, there must be a point where there is only one and that's what we must find.'[6] Of course, the two young ladies understood exactly what he meant.

Dilly organised a 'lobster' hunt as he thought lobsters served a more useful purpose than 'crabs', but this involved a great deal of tedious work spread over two days. Margaret and Mavis worked hard to evaluate a number of key-blocks until it became possible for Dilly to discover how many turnovers each of the wheels held.

On 28 October 1941 a joyful Dilly sent a report to Denniston about the breaking of the Abwehr Enigma machine. Denniston's circulation arrangements improved; this must have pleased Dilly. He probably knew that a group of Bletchley's senior cryptographers had written to Churchill complaining they did not have enough resources to do their codebreaking efficiently and that Churchill's approval was immediately given. Dilly wrote to Denniston requesting an increase in staff. He currently had seventeen girls and of whom only two, Margaret and Mavis, plus himself were German linguists and able to take part in his lobster hunts. He needed two more girls, who he said must be given time to learn the tricks of the machine. Denniston arranged for David Rees to be transferred to Dilly's section, and Keith Batey was put on secondment from Hut 6 in November. An air of intrigue was hovering both inside Bletchley Park and beyond the gates of the Park.

In November 1941, just as Dilly's Spy Enigma was being broken, some people at the Park heard a rumour that was a little worrying. It was caused by none other than the author Agatha Christie. Her new counter-espionage detective novel provoked a twitchiness among the senior staff; the name of one of her leading characters was *Major Bletchley*. It was known that Dilly was a friend of Agatha Christie and whispers started to flow, but he knew that he had not revealed any information that would have given her reason to make connections with secret activities. Dilly did not want to be linked with this matter but he was keen to help. The use of the name 'Bletchley' had to be investigated without causing publicity. Any future breaches in security had to be prevented. The big boys put their heads together and it was decided that Dilly should be the first to try and discover how this choice of name had come about.

Dilly and his wife, Olive, invited Miss Christie to tea at their home, Courn's Wood. Olive made sure their rations would stretch to scones with butter, and she had some home-made jam. Tea would not have been a problem as Dilly drank a lot of coffee – frequently the chicory variety that helped eke out their wartime rations. Conversation was carefully steered around to the question of the name of Miss Christie's major and what had prompted her to call him Major Bletchley. Fortunately, it turned out to be an innocent choice. Miss Christie did not know of Bletchley Park and she did not know that Dilly worked there. She had been held up at Bletchley Railway Station when changing trains, and finding it to be a horrible place she chose its name for the horrible character in her book. Dilly was put at ease by this information and, after what had been a tense few days, the little group no doubt made the most of this unexpected tea party.

Back at Bletchley Park they continued to get outstanding results, and Dilly was able to report to Denniston that, 'The hunt was up and scent was good. One very fine lobster among others was caught and after two days, Miss Lever, by very good and careful work, succeeded in an evaluation which contained sufficient non-carry units to ascertain the green wheel.'[7]

There was now cause for much excitement. It became apparent that Dilly's invention of the lobster process meant that a long crib was no longer necessary. Mavis likened the process to dendrochronology – the ring-dating of trees by the overlapping sequences. The first message was broken on 8 December 1941, and Denniston was so impressed with Dilly's work he immediately wrote to Menzies with the result, praising Dilly for his work and his modesty in attributing the success to Margaret Rock and Mavis Lever: 'Knox has again justified his reputation as our most original investigator of Enigma problems... He attributes the success to two young girl members of his staff, Miss Rock and Miss Lever, and gives them all the credit. He is of course the leader, but no doubt has selected and trained his staff in his somewhat unusual methods.'[8]

Dilly's achievement in breaking the Abwehr Enigma used on higher-level communication links allowed the XX Committee to have complete confidence in their double agents, and Dilly and his girls were still remembered many years later when the following statement appeared in *The Daily Telegraph*:

Knox took over the task of breaking it [the code] using Mavis Batey and Margaret Rock as his assistants, to test out every possibility. On 8 December 1941 Mavis broke a message on the link between Belgrade and Berlin, allowing the reconstruction of one of the rotors. Within days, Knox and his team had broken into the Abwehr Enigma, and shortly afterwards Mavis Lever broke a second Abwehr machine, the GGG, adding to the British ability to read the high-level Abwehr messages and confirm that the Germans did believe the phoney Double Cross intelligence they were being fed by the double agents.[9]

Dilly and his girls were excited about the success and although no doubt concerned about Dilly's illness, Mavis must have been particularly happy, but it is unlikely that she had known of Dilly's comments at that time. She modestly believed it was his greatest triumph in cryptography and intelligence, which she considered were for him always inseparable, and they made a vital contribution to the system. She did not even consider the task could not have been completed without her import and the Double Cross could not have advanced.

Denniston had found Carrollian logic a problem, but Dilly's girls were well versed in this style that had once more played a part. Colours and numbers, crabs and lobsters, names coined by Dilly, had entered the scene and 'Lobster' became the name of this particular Enigma machine. A favourite quote of Dilly's from Lewis Carroll's *Sylvie and Bruno* book was:

> In Science… in fact in most things, it is usually best to begin at the beginning. In some things, of course, it's better to begin at the end. For instance, if you wanted to paint a dog green, it might be better to begin with the tail, as it doesn't bite that end.[10]

Dilly and his team continued to work hard using 'somewhat unusual methods' and 'it became a real *Wonderland* situation when lobsters, starfish and beetles could all be coaxed to join in the dance'.[11] The two girls understood immediately, unlike Denniston who had become so confused by Dilly's methods that he had decided, in his admiration, to sit back and let matters take their course. He was not to be disappointed and decided that Dilly's section should be allowed to develop further. After speaking to Dilly he wrote to Valentine Vivian, who was in overall charge of counter-espionage within SIS:

> With regard to Knox's success and the resultant labours I would suggest that the series be issued as ISK [Illicit Services Knox]. Secondly, it will be necessary for the emending party to be reinforced to deal with some 50-100 extra telegrams per day and I suggest this is an opportunity to develop the ISOS hut on lines parallel to Hut 3.[12]

When the first messages were issued on Christmas Day 1941 Dilly was working almost permanently at home; he was, nevertheless, delighted that his section had become known as Illicit Services Knox, and he was probably even more pleased to be given additional staff, and it was no doubt a proud moment when they became known officially as Intelligence Service Knox. Quoting Archimedes, Dilly had always made it clear that if given 'A Rock and a Lever, he could move the universe'. His team continued to keep track of the German operators and Dilly was at ISK for the creation of the new Abwehr machine network to be known as GGG that Mavis had broken in February 1942 using Dilly's methods. Keith and Mavis were both now working for Dilly and both played a critical role in breaking the cyphers of the Abwehr, German military intelligence, which later enabled the Double Cross deception operation to safeguard the success of the D-Day invasion.

Intelligence Services Oliver Strachey (ISOS) also became a crucial weapon against Abwehr and, working alongside Intelligence Service Knox (ISK), together they played a vital role in the decryption of signals and had several successes, including the ambitious disguise of the target area of the Normandy D-Day landing.

MI5 and MI6 had *turned* large numbers of German agents sent to Britain or reporting from other parts of the world and were using them to feed false intelligence to the Germans. The Abwehr Enigma messages deciphered at Bletchley showed that the Germans believed the false intelligence they were being fed and also provided a warning if any of the double agents were under suspicion, in which case steps would be taken to ensure they regained the Abwehr's trust.[13]

Dilly had been determined to break the Abwehr Enigma and, greatly assisted by Margaret Rock and Mavis, it was his last, and possibly his most important, codebreaking challenge. Mavis and Margaret continued to work hard, finally getting to grips with the technology of the machine which enabled them to regularly break the messages. The Abwehr decrypts forwarded to MI6 by them were vital to locating German spies and confirming they had fallen for the Double Cross information they had been fed. The girls were successful, but unfortunately Dilly collapsed after working day and night with little to eat. He was taken home and returned to Bletchley only occasionally.

Dilly remained head of ISK and was content with this position, Margaret working with him at his home, whilst Mavis remained at the Cottage, visiting occasionally. On 13 February 1942 Peter Twinn was put in charge; and after Keith Batey had been transferred from Hut 6 on secondment, he proved his excellence and became a high-powered member of the Enigma codebreaking team. Dilly remained in close contact with Twinn, and there was no problem when Twinn decided to take things into his own hands. Twinn had joined Dilly in the stableyard Cottage, which when war broke out became the Enigma research section. Twinn worked hard and Dilly was quite at ease with the arrangement when Twinn took over the running of ISK.

Dilly was in constant touch with Twinn and was concerned that the ISK section was not getting enough feedback from the St Albans outstation. Twinn decided he should take up the matter with Commander Edward Travis, telling him that certain improvements should be made, particularly with communications. He complained about the lack of comment received from SIS, or anyone outside Bletchley Park, although they had provided decodes of the whole of GGG traffic since 14 February until 4 May, and since then his team had broken five days of a completely new network. In response Travis confirmed that he had dealt with the situation and that he thought things would improve.

When Admiral Godfrey became involved, a 'rush service' was put into operation at Hanslope, where their traffic was intercepted. Improvements were made and the girls removed Jumbo from the cupboard and from then onwards he made constant appearances. The girls seldom got to know the reason for any particular 'Jumbo Rush', but they did learn that 'Action Stations' meant that men's lives were at risk and that involved working around the clock.

With the increase in numbers they moved from the Cottage to Elmer's School and the former Hut 6, and finally to Block G which also housed ISOS. By the end of the war they had become 100-strong, but in the meantime they were receiving 100 or more messages a day. The Abwehr Enigma was thereafter broken most days until a new machine was introduced in December 1944. 'In total they made 140,000 Abwehr Enigma decrypts.'[14]

As time progressed, Dilly deteriorated further, and Mavis would often be seen strolling with him in the woodland around his Chiltern home at Courn's Wood.

CHAPTER SIX

From Mutual Suspicion to Mutual Respect

The birth of the 'Special Relationship' between Britain and the United States of America has been enduring and is still in place today. The United States had been reluctant to go to war in Europe and President Roosevelt struggled to come to terms with this attitude. However, as Hitler's atrocities spread, in 1940 negotiations for the United States to enter the war were started, and during that year a group of four American men, two naval and two military, were sent to check out Bletchley Park. The group set off from Annapolis, Maryland, aboard the British warship HMS *King George V*, and the journey was long, difficult and dangerous; when arriving on the British coastline they were worried by threatening German aircraft. Nevertheless, upon reaching Bletchley Park, although looking dismal when looming in the darkness before them, immediately upon entering the building, they were put at their ease by a friendly welcome.

During their stay of several weeks, they were taken on trips to the Cotswolds and Loch Lomond. The visit had been kept secret and they were also taken around U-boat tracking stations and radar stations, but at Bletchley Park a great deal of discussion took place and an agreement was made for Britain and the United States to share technical information concerning German, Italian and Japanese codes. 'One of the key elements of their visit was their mutual interest [with Britain] in cracking the Japanese codes.'[1] Hugh Foss and Oliver Strachey had been successful with this in 1934 when working with GC&CS – John Tiltman, a former army officer, who had cracked Japanese military codes as early as 1933, had been called back to Britain from India to again work with them. Bletchley Park did its utmost to keep Anglo-American cryptanalytical participation concentrated upon Japan, about which their own knowledge was now weak. The United States on the other hand were behind in their mastery of German military cryptographic systems and the British knew that they would be keen to share the British bombe (which had been inspired by the Poles and developed by Alan Turing). At first the two countries were not in a formal alliance; America had not yet entered the war. Churchill and his leaders were anxious to encourage the United States to become their ally; co-operation between the two nations in these fields would therefore be favourable and the knowledge shared would lead to the saving of thousands of British and American lives.

It was fortunate that Brigadier General George V. Strong, when at Bletchley Park, had reason to urgently cable William Friedman, America's top cryptanalyst, at SIS Washington, reporting Britain as 'a gold mine of technical information'.[2] Friedman's rapid response gave approval to a complete exchange of codebreaking, including US work on Japanese diplomatic cyphers. The British were amazed at this news, and did not hesitate to give their acceptance of the offer. By 1940 the Americans had developed their own 'Purple' decryption machine for Japanese codes and, by coincidence, joined the war on 7 December 1941, the same day that Dilly Knox broke the German armed forces intelligence service Abwehr code. Britain later made great advances with Japanese codebreaking.

The Americans took up their positions at Bletchley Park and the number of US service personnel posted there by 1944 reached 110, and by May 1945 was expected to be around 238.[3]

Space became a premium concern when the top secret machines known as 'bombes' were introduced at Bletchley Park. These were ultra-fast electro-mechanical machines recovering Enigma daily keys by testing a crib and its implications at all possible wheel or rotor orders and initial settings: *bombes* were 'inspired by, but not based on the Polish *bomby*',[4] explained Mavis. These large bronze machines measured 6ft high x 7ft wide x 6ins deep, and an order was placed for seventy machines, requiring 700 men to operate them. It was thought it would be difficult to find enough men to take on the operation, but a solution was soon found and the decision was taken to replace the male workforce on this machine with the Women's Royal Naval Service (Wrens).

The WRNS was created in the First World War (1914–18) to release men from technical and combat jobs that could be done by women. In the mid-1930s when war was looming it was decided to build up a women's reserve of 1,500 to take up certain jobs previously carried out by men in the Naval and Royal Marine services. In 1939 unmarried women aged between eighteen and forty-five years, later lowered to seventeen years, and married women without children were enlisted.

A number of these women were elected to take up positions at Bletchley Park to man the bombe machines. Eight of these new arrivals were chosen to conduct a trial run on the top secret bombe machines, which tested the Enigma settings being used by the Germans. It was impressed upon them that the work they would be doing was highly secretive, and they would have to work fast to get their results through to Hut 6 and Hut 8 as quickly as possible, as they, in turn, were dependent upon them to get urgent intelligence to the British military and Naval commanders. The women proved themselves to be competent of doing the job and an order was placed for seventy more of these large bronze machines, and girls arrived to operate them. Again it was impressed upon them that they would be doing highly secretive work. By the end of the war there were 2,963 Wrens working at Bletchley Park.

The bombe machines were located at various requisitioned country houses around Bletchley, and some were installed in huts at

Bletchley Park and operators were then bussed in from their billets. There were a number of difficulties – the billets became famed for their lack of baths, there were difficulties with laundry, and there was a shortage of dentists and doctors, but nevertheless Superintendent E. Blagrove reported: 'There was a magnificent spirit among these pioneers and wherever they turned they found great co-operation and many helping hands. The stimulation was the knowledge of the essential work on which they were employed.'[5]

The Wrens found working conditions unpleasant. As well as setting up the bombe machines they were responsible for keeping the carbon brushes clean and making any necessary adjustments to the filaments and so avoid short-circuiting. Like the huts, they were warm in summer and cold in winter, but the Wrens suffered most in summer. The machines generated heat when running at full capacity, and some were surrounded by 6ft-high blast walls which intensified poor circulation of air and added to the acutely stuffy environment.

All staff working in the huts suffered from the same problems – hot summers and cold winters – but the Hut 6 girls came up with an ingenious idea to prevent them from having to go outside in the winter in order to pass their paperwork on to Hut 3. They fixed up a tunnel from hatch to hatch between the huts, with a tea tray on a pulley which could be used to transfer the work between the two huts. They then found draughts of wind blew through the hatches, but that was no problem: they fixed up doors at each end which alerted them with a bang upon the arrival of their haul.

For some people it was a shaky start when the Americans joined them. In July 1942 a Bletchley Park liaison officer visiting Washington became irritated by what he considered the regimental gossip of American wives at dinner parties. He was also obliged to attend what he thought was a tedious picnic where Soloman Kullback, one of the US Army's leading cryptanalysts, 'placed obstacles in the way of British requests for information'.[6] By September the British officer had written home, 'Sometimes I think they are just a lot of kids playing at "Office".'[7] He thought they had many childish qualities and criticised their taste in women, cars and drink and even their demonstrative patriotism, but he admired their friendliness and generosity – and excused himself by writing, 'Hell! Anyone would think I didn't like them. But perhaps it is as well I'm fond of children.'[8]

The Wrens had no problems in forming friendships. It is frequently said that the American forces were very popular with British women during the war, many of whom considered them to be prize catches, and they were envied by the less well paid British men. It was a common joke during the war years for the American forces to be described as 'over-sexed, over-paid and over here'; and no doubt they caused a stir at Bletchley Park just as they did across Britain – but many were known to have been sober, shy, lonely young men, straight out of high school. Nevertheless, it must be said that their uniforms were very smart and made them look important, and their film-star accents could also be alluring. Their generosity with sweets, cigarettes, and of course chewing gum, could also have been an added attraction in drab and rationed wartime Britain. They were generous to the local children and a group could often be found hanging around at the gates of Bletchley Park hoping to be given sweets and no doubt chanting 'Got any gum, chum?', which was the question frequently posed around barracks and other places where children gathered to collect the pet names the young Americans painted on their jeeps – a game that replaced the old habit of collecting car numbers.

Entertainment became very lively. In spite of cultural differences, there was a friendly atmosphere both at work and at play and only a few minor difficulties were encountered. The Americans had a very easy-going attitude to life; so relaxed, that at first they were regarded with suspicion as it was thought they had no sense of the importance of security. They brought in alcohol, which they offered around, but more than once were told 'We don't drink here'.

The English were always thrifty, but during the days of wartime rationing and shortages they were even more careful, and one young American was heard to say, 'You English! Why do you keep everything in *god damn* shoe boxes?' These were the days of clothing coupons, and the English felt poor and ragged beside these rich young men with several uniforms each, but the gregarious Americans were happy to share their drink, and even their exotic food and nylon stockings which they must have requested from home.

The staff at Bletchley Park were overworked and found it tiresome to have to teach these people, whose knowledge of Europe was almost non-existent, and in turn the Americans sometimes admitted they found it off-putting to be taught codebreaking by young girls. A group of young Americans visited Bletchley Park just before taking up their positions. 'It just so happened that I was in charge the day one of the Americans came round... He could not believe he was being told how to break codes by a nineteen-year-old – but I had got a corner into the work and knew what I was doing,'[9] Mavis adamantly recalled.

During the period of the arrival of the Americans at Bletchley Park, when Mavis's boss, Dilly, had a serious recurrence of his illness, and she and Margaret Rock visited him, he often enquired about the Americans and Mavis did her best to keep him cheerful and up to date with news and developments. On one occasion he wanted to hear about the American visit when they came to see how the Abwehr machine worked. Mavis had noticed the difference between British and American behaviour, but she made light of it and told an amusing story of two service types that she had come upon: one large and bullying with two ribbons, the other lean and acquiescent with only one. After five minutes of light-hearted discussion the leader said: '"We've sure got your machine [the *Abwehr*] taped now," which, of course, he hadn't.'[10] The other man made what Mavis and Margaret thought was quite an intelligent observation, only to be crushed by his senior officer with, "'Don't be ridiculous," and he replied meekly, "Sorry, it was only an idea."'[11]

Mavis and Margaret had managed to get the ingredients together for a chocolate cake which they baked ready for their visit, and Mavis confessed that the younger man had awakened their maternal instincts and they made sure that he got a much larger piece.

When the men left they commented that they had never had such hospitality nor met such charming people. Mavis sent a note to Dilly telling him about the event and brought it to an end jokingly writing, 'I hope we are not going to have a whole string of Doughboys to drive dizzy.'[12]

During the course of their meeting Mavis decided that 'it was the lack of hierarchy that amazed all the Americans as in Dilly's section anybody, however junior, with a bright idea was listened to and it was often worthwhile'.[13] Important matters, particularly security, were treated in a well-disciplined manner by the British, but the atmosphere within the huts was easy-going and there was little sense of hierarchy. There would be one person in overall control, but the codebreakers tended to work along with each other, if it was felt to be beneficial.

Some difficulties appear to have been caused by a preliminary distrust between the two nations, no doubt due to the cultural gap, but the Wrens did a lot to smooth things over. The outgoing and generous personalities of the Americans went down well with the Wrens. There was little sign of a transatlantic cultural gap; on the contrary, many of these girls were looking for adventure; they were a lively and fun-loving crowd wanting to partake in the American lifestyle they had seen on the silver screen. Could it have been that the English officer writing home had been an old fuddy-duddy?

The British belief that the Americans were extremely lax in security measures, causing many Bletchley Park officials to be reluctant to share intelligence, derived from breaking the German Enigma cyphers. The Americans, however, were thought to hold an historical distrust of the British since the war of 1812, and resented any indication that America was thought to be the junior partner at Bletchley Park. Although the British and American cryptographers worked well together at first, it was not long before those in higher American ranks became disenchanted; they were after a bombe machine but British Intelligence denied them ownership. There were two reasons for this. First, the British were very tight on security but the Americans were not; and secondly, upon their arrival the British had only six bombe machines, all working at full capacity, and could not afford to part with even one. However, MI6 insisted this excuse should not be given to the Americans as they might decide to request a blueprint for the bombe which, it was reasoned, could easily get into German hands.

Diplomatic tensions remained but the relationship between senior cryptographers did not suffer, and it has since been written that, 'The addition of the American contingent was so smooth that we hardly noticed it.'[14] A mutual trust gradually evolved, an agreement was made concerning the pooling of cryptographic knowledge, and Denniston gained favour by sending Alan Turing, England's top cryptographer, to give assistance in the United States. They were then able to develop bombe machines based on his designs. Half a dozen or so Americans, who were expert cryptographers, came to Bletchley, and gradually more followed, slipping effortlessly into positions in the various huts.

'Although I have done many interesting things and known many interesting people, my work at Bletchley was the most satisfying of my career,'[15] reported Bill Bundy, when interviewed by the BBC in 1999. In August 1943 Bundy had led a US Army unit, Signals Security Detachment, to work at Bletchley Park alongside the British staff in Hut 6. It was extremely busy, with constant traffic making it necessary for organisation along production-line methods. Gordon Welchman was the first head of Hut 6, followed by Stuart Milner-Barry who took over at the same time as the arrival of the Americans, and he continued to do an excellent job. When Bundy returned to the United States he and his brother became high-level advisors to successive American presidents, but he continued to remember his Bletchley days when giving a talk in 1982 to the American Cryptogram Association:

> I think the level of performance in Hut 6 was as near perfect as anything I have ever been or ever expect to be associated with... There just weren't mistakes. You didn't send down programs that didn't fit. They might not have been the wisest ones; that was a question of judgement, of course. Things were not mis-sorted. Making mistakes in testing could have meant that you'd missed the fact that the key had been solved.[16]

This is a reflection of how well Bletchley Park was managed. Staff were chosen carefully; they were frequently highly intelligent and usually the most proficient in their own field. Whether the task in hand was of the greatest importance or the most trivial it was tackled with the utmost attention. They were conscientious, each person aware of exactly what was going on in his own section, but committed to working in secrecy as far as other sections and the outside world were concerned.

Mavis recalled that when William Friedman, America's top cryptologist, visited Bletchley Park in 1943, he made similar comments to Bundy, finding himself astounded by what a bunch of amateurs could produce, saying:

> In a technical sense, we are ahead. But in a practical sense, judged by accomplishments, these amateurs have very largely surpassed us in detail, attention to minutiae, digging up every bit of intelligence possible, and applying high-class thinking, originality and brains to the task.[17]

It is doubtful if either Dilly or Mavis would have agreed to being called amateurs. Many Bletchley men had been working with codes since WWI, and some had been university professors. Dilly had utmost confidence in 'his girls', he always sang their praises, and whenever one of them achieved a special goal he always made sure that, if they deserved it, they were rewarded by an increase in salary. Nevertheless, men were always paid a higher wage than women since it was believed that with families to support they needed more money.

Mavis was happy that the other comments made were complimentary so she did not complain, but she would have been quite justified if she resented being called an amateur, as she excelled in her codebreaking activities, and her command of the German language was good. It is unlikely that the remark was meant in a derogatory manner since Denniston had built up a long-lasting personal relationship with Friedman when flying to the United States in 1941. It was on that occasion that he had meetings with leaders of the cryptological organisations, and together they laid the foundation for later co-operation from which Britain benefitted.

All feelings of distrust and suspicion had been swept away, and there was mutual respect between Britain and the United States. A

'Special Relationship' now prevailed at Bletchley Park, at every level, and the social life there was possibly the best that could be found in Britain during those depressing wartime years.

Before the arrival of the Americans there was a shortage of male dancing partners at Bletchley Park. Now the girls were able to enjoy dancing, jitterbugging and Latin American, and the social life became something to be remembered. The Wrens were usually responsible for arranging dances; they did this well and the senior staff frequently joined in. Mavis seldom attended the dances as Keith did not dance, but nevertheless there were plenty of other activities they did enjoy. On one occasion permission was given for a dance to be held in the ballroom of Crawley Grange, owned in Elizabethan times by Thomas Wolsey, but now the home of a group of Wrens and their bombe machines.

Unfortunately they were told that alcohol was not allowed, but the enterprising Americans arrived in a jeep with a well-stocked mobile bar which they parked outside the grounds. Disaster followed and they were forbidden to leave their quarters for a month. However, the dances did continue. Another dance was to be held in a hangar at a nearby American Air Force base, but this became a solemn occasion when the Glenn Miller Band did not arrive as their aeroplane was reported missing. The Wrens, the whole of Bletchley Park and the townsfolk were in shock.

The Recreational Club offered activities for those with a more subdued taste, including a library, and a drama group which put on reviews, frequently raising money for charity. There was choral singing and a Scottish Country Dancing Club, bridge, chess and fencing. Things were in full swing, and there was even a ladies' hairdressers, set up by the Woburn hairdresser, Mr Wesley. This new branch in Bletchley Park became an essential service, and was greatly appreciated. Mavis's hair was always neat and tidy and this became a lasting habit. A 'shampoo and set' or a 'trim, shampoo and set' was available for ladies in uniform at a cost of 3s. 9d, and for civilians at 4s. 6d. The men were not neglected and they could have a haircut or a shampoo for a shilling. However, there was a shortage of towels, and clothing coupons were needed to purchase new ones, if they were available, so it was essential that everyone took their own.

There just remained the question of the rules of the rounders matches to be sorted. The rounders pitch was a concrete patch marked with two circles, one for the batsman and one for the bowler, and this arrangement had to be explained to the Americans who were accustomed to something rather grander. The rules of the two teams differed and at the end of the game they found a difference that could not be agreed upon; each team was convinced that they had won. Barbara Abernethy, Denniston's personal assistant, later reported, 'It ended with drinks all round; actually we agreed we'd won by our rules, and they'd won by their rules. So that was all right. But they never asked us to play again.'[18]

Although it is often thought that people were more or less incarcerated at Bletchley Park, Mavis rejects this comment: 'That isn't true at all, we could do anything in the town.'[19] Bletchley Park folk were probably like any other group of people; there were those who clamoured to enjoy the world around them, and what it had to offer, and those who were lazy and stayed on campus and enjoyed just what was put before them. Mavis also recalled: 'Lord Asa Briggs said to me, as he did to a few other people: "It was our university, Mavis. Those five years are tremendously important at that age... what it did for me, I was very grateful for, we were all thrown in at the deep end." '[20]

Those working in shifts would get two days off every fortnight, according to the change of shift times, and some people who had bicycles used them to get out and about – and there were two young ladies who made good use of their free time by cycling into Oxford or Cambridge.

Mavis made the most of her opportunities. She remembered she was much into Sigmund Freud who had almost a cult following. Having studied German Romantics she felt she had become 'much better acquainted than anyone else with Freud, because I went to Zurich University... And I actually heard Freud's disciple Carl Jung.'[21] Was this really Mavis showing off? Whilst at Bletchley, Pelican published sixpenny editions of *The Psychopathology of Everyday Life*, so Mavis delved into this, as well as enrolling for the Cambridge extra-mural course on psychology that she attended with the townsfolk. That's the way Mavis was, always interested and always keen to try new tasks, and this was the way she continued after the war had come to an end.

Mavis was never attracted by an American, she was very happy with Keith, but naturally enough there was a rash of romances at Bletchley, some became serious and a few girls returned to the homes of their American loved ones after the war – but there had been a few steady romances between Bletchley staff which had been going on earlier. In later years Mavis used to look back to the night when she sought Keith's help, and Keith too would fondly remember that moment when their eyes met late one evening, 'This little girl arrived from Dilly's outfit with this message, or problem – she didn't know how to solve it. I didn't see her again for another year.'[22] That was the way things were; because of the rules concerning secrecy, people tended not to linger in other huts, and each of the units tended to keep to themselves. Mavis remembered that things became easier when Keith was transferred to the Cottage from Hut 6, and then she and Keith were engaged, but when she confided in Dilly – as they had got to know each other very well – perhaps secretly a little jealous – he tried to put her off marriage, repeatedly saying, 'He's just one of those clever mathematicians from Cambridge.'[23]

Keith's work at Bletchley was very important to him and he played a leading part as one of the most outstanding codebreakers. He reconstructed two Enigma cypher machines and played a key role in breaking many others, but he had a modest nature, and in spite of several successful codebreaking triumphs he avoided praise. Mavis was frequently interviewed about her own and her boss Dilly's achievements, but it was Keith's habit to remain in the background and allow Mavis to steal the limelight, although he would occasionally cut in with a pertinent remark. However, many of his contemporaries were serving in the armed forces and, although Keith was doing an exhausting job and helping the war effort, he felt guilty that he had what was considered by some to be a 'cushy number', out of danger's way. Gordon Welchman, when writing his story of Hut 6, writes of one young man who received a scathing letter from his old headmaster accusing him of being a disgrace to his school.

Keith did not relish the idea of active combat, possibly because he had seen what it had done to his father who returned from Passchendaele during WWI suffering badly from shock. Sadly he was never a well man after that experience and died in the late thirties.

Keith applied to be allowed to join the RAF, but permission was refused. After making an appeal it was with reluctance that he was allowed to join the Fleet Air Arm. It was thought this would be more satisfactory as, if he should be shot down over enemy territory and subjected to interrogation, he could possibly reveal the secret that the Enigma cypher had been broken. If flying with the Fleet Air Arm, his life could be lost at sea, or there would be a chance that he could be picked up by the Royal Navy.

Keith was born in Longmoor, Cumberland in 1919. His father had been a soldier but suffered injury on the Somme. He received a war pension, but it fell upon his mother, a part-time teacher, to contribute to the family income. She managed well and their two sons were well brought up and both had a good education. Keith went to Carlisle Grammar School and was successful in obtaining a state scholarship to read mathematics at Trinity College, Cambridge. Along with several of his friends and acquaintances from Cambridge he was recruited by another Trinity scholar, Gordon Welchman, to join him at Bletchley Park where he was head of Hut 6. The young mathematicians knew nothing about the jobs they were taking on, but they found they were to have exciting times.

'There were no rules against "courting". We thought we had been very secretive, but when we announced our engagement we were told that there were bets on when we would.'[24] They were very surprised by this, and marriage followed not too long afterwards on 5 November 1942. Holy Trinity Church in Marylebone, London was their choice rather than a church in south London where Mavis's parents lived, because it was more easily accessible to Bletchley by train.

There was a slight hiccup when making the arrangements as they did not meet the residency rules and live in Marylebone. However, this was overcome by Mavis leaving a suitcase in a friend's flat nearby the church. The wedding was a small affair with few guests. Margaret Rock was Mavis's lady-in-waiting and Keith was accompanied by his best man, Peter Twinn, his codebreaker friend from Bletchley Park. Keith stood proud in his new Fleet Air Arm uniform and Mavis, looking elegant in a light blue suit and carrying a black felt bag, was delighted when Keith's cousin, Veronica, presented her with an ornamental horseshoe decorated with little sprigs of heather.

They snatched three days for their honeymoon and went to the Lake District, where they were joined by Keith's brother, Herbert, who came from Carlisle to visit them. He was two years younger than Keith; he read physics at Oxford and then became a vicar of St Bede's, Cumbria, so it seemed a sensible idea to travel to the Lakes as travelling and meeting up with relatives could be difficult during the war years. Keith was soon to be off to join the Fleet Air Arm in Canada – but Mavis was very disappointed when he and his brother spent the three days playing chess. She was a feisty young lady in those days and, feeling neglected, and then irritated, she did not hesitate to kick the chessboard up in the air, sending kings, queens and knights flying across the room. On 8 November, just three days after Mavis and Keith were married, the twenty-one-year-old Mavis went back to continue her work at Bletchley Park whilst her young husband sailed to Canada to start his training for the Fleet Air Arm.

On returning to Bletchley, knowing Keith would have left Liverpool and was making the crossing to Canada, she was feeling anxious and then, when having lunch in the canteen, one of the section heads noticed that Mavis was looking forlorn. He came over to her and asked if she would like to see how far Keith's convoy had progressed. He took her to have a look, and after a short time a submarine suddenly appeared on the screen, coming alongside Keith's convoy; Mavis was stunned but the kindly officer told her to go and have a cup of coffee and they would deal with it. Mavis went away for a short time. Thankfully, when she returned the submarine had gone.

Once again Mavis felt it was a good thing that they were not allowed to know too much.

While Keith was away in Canada Mavis wrote a constant stream of letters to him, but later found they had not been received. A very large bag of her mail was returned to her after the war and she believes that she must have unwittingly included useful information that would be interesting if it had reached enemy hands. She told Keith a lot about everyday life, even down to what they had had for dinner, thus revealing if there were any food or fuel shortages. Unfortunately, Mavis's daughters do not know what became of the mailbag with its secret hoard. However, early on Mavis did get a few letters from Keith. He wrote, 'I knew all along that I shouldn't enjoy flying... I undertook it as a hard job that had to be done.' He hated dishonesty and hypocrisy and he was irritated and wrote to Mavis saying, 'I have listened to so much humbug and nonsense about "having a good war", "a great life this flying", and such remarks as those who regard war as a pleasant and enjoyable pastime are wont to make.' Keith must have been relieved when he was returned to Bletchley Park, as his specific skills were much in demand and needed as changes in the Enigma had taken place. His feelings of having had an easy war meant that when Bletchley Park Medals were given out at the turn of the century, he refused to receive one as he said medals were for bravery. He and Mavis were always supportive of each other so she also refused, in keeping with him... but Deborah smiles when she says, 'but then when he died she accepted hers'!

Mavis was undoubtedly worried about Keith's safety, so perhaps it was a blessing when it was decided that he would be more usefully employed at Bletchley Park, and he was brought back home just three months later. He was transferred to Hut 6 that had been moved locally to Elmer's School. They then had time to join in the fun with the Americans, dances continued and occasionally they would join in and have a drink with their English and American friends, some of whom they kept in touch with for the rest of their lives.

CHAPTER SEVEN

D-Day and Victory
in Europe

After the defeat of France and the Netherlands in June 1940 many people became anxious, even terrified, believing Britain would be the next to suffer invasion. There was immense speculation but the pessimistic attitude was swept away when Britain made ready for battle. There was mass evacuation along the coasts, beaches were mined and coils of barbed wire were stretched out along the foreshores. First there were intermittent small-scale daylight air raids, but the Germans shifted their targets to focus first on the London docks and warehouses, with the London Blitz starting on the afternoon of 7 September 1940. The last daylight air raid of that period was Sunday 15 September. 'That day more than 200 German bombers set out for London and 158 reached it, but that day they lost thirty bombers with a further twenty more damaged.'[1] The Germans then switched to night bombing, and during October the raids were largely directed against London, 400 bombers attacking on the evening of 15 October. At night the bombing raids were relentless; war-weary Londoners fled their homes only to find them gone when they returned the following morning. The great Blitz lasted until 16 May 1941, when the Luftwaffe started building up for the oncoming invasion of Russia, but resumed in 1942.

The RAF reacted to the Luftwaffe air attacks – Spitfires and Hurricane fighter planes were the prime air defence maintaining Britain's mastery of its skies. 'The RAF alone dropped fifty times as many tons of bombs on Germany during the course of the war losing some 12,000 bombers and 50,000 air crew.'[2]

The end of war in Europe was fast approaching, but bombing did not cease. New technical missiles, pilotless jet-propelled planes, known as V weapons were targeted on London, and from June 1944 the V-I flying bombs and V-2 rocket attacks razed great swathes of property to the ground: '... on average each V-1 damaged 400 houses in the London area, and each V-2 damaged between 600 and 750.'[3] They often crash-landed, missing their targets, but nevertheless caused a substantial amount of damage, and lives were lost. A rocket came down near Stanmore bombe outstation, but fortunately damage was not extensive as a blast wall had been erected as a means of protection.

The common names given to these missiles were 'doodlebugs' or 'buzz-bombs'. It was very disturbing to hear one buzzing along, the noise getting louder and louder as the device got lower and lower, then suddenly the sound would cut out completely. Many people became almost petrified when this happened; often there was silence, followed by horror when the weapon did its worst.

Mavis and her fellow codebreakers at Bletchley Park were working on double agents giving misinformation to confuse their German controllers. When on duty Mavis was frequently able to read the Enigma and would see the response, but there were times when, perhaps for security reasons, this was not so. One incident when the content was not divulged was when the V-1s started to arrive and the target was for the rockets to fall on central London. The Germans wanted to make sure they were hitting their target and asked for a report on where the V-1s were falling. Mavis clearly remembered:

At that point, the bombs *were* falling in central London so intelligence here wanted them to cut out at a different point. So this double agent was instructed to tell his masters that they were falling north of London. The result of this was that the Germans cut the range back a little and as a result the rockets started falling in south London.[4]

Mavis remembered Dilly, when he would say, 'there is a need to know, and a need not to know' and she agreed that on this occasion it was better that security had prevented her from knowing anything about this Double Cross operation or its success. Norbury was the part of London where Mavis's parents were living. 'I had no idea and it is just as well that I didn't. So when I saw the devastation at Norbury, I did not know that it had anything to do with anything I was doing. It would have been a terrible shock to know that.'[5]

' "I remember," said Mavis, "that we knew D-Day was coming [soon] because I can see myself going up to London on a train from Bletchley and thinking, *I suppose I am the only one on this train who knows.*"'[6] The girls had for some time known that things were coming to a climax and hopefully a victorious end. They partly based this idea on the fact that the Home Guard, who had continued their training throughout the war, had disbanded the previous Christmas. Their captain, the late Gerald Taunt of Hut 6, had commented that, 'they gave a welcome quietus to a survival that had outlived its relevance, but which in its time had generated enthusiasm, comradeship, and a great deal of harmless fun,'[7] and Mavis and her colleagues could not agree more.

Various operations were carried out and one successful plan, made in May 1943, was devised by Charles Cholmondesley, the RAF representative on the Twenty Committee. It was called 'Operation Mincemeat' and was perhaps disturbing to some. The decision was taken to drop an unknown dead body disguised as a Royal Marine Officer – victim of a fictitious aeroplane crash – off the coast of Spain, close enough that it would be washed ashore. The body carried personal information and documents including love letters and a photograph of a lady, but most importantly a letter from Lord Mountbatten, the Chief of Joint Operations, in which he made a joke about sardines. There was a known level of collaboration between the Spanish and the German authorities and it was correctly assumed that the documents would be shown to the Germans – who would come to the conclusion, because of the joke made about sardines, that the Allies' landing point would be Sardinia. Hitler himself reported that the British planned attack would be directed mainly against Sardinia and the Peloponnese.

It was important that the Allies should know of the German High Command's reaction, and Churchill, who was at the Trident Conference in Washington, was sent the message 'Mincemeat swallowed whole'.[8] Needless to say, all Bletchley staff who were involved were delighted when news came through that the Germans were moving troops to Sardinia, and Mavis and the Twenty Committee were highly amused to learn that the Abwehr were very pleased with themselves when thinking they had worked out what was meant by 'sardines'. The outcome, planned by the Twenty Committee, achieved a magnificent success for, when the Germans moved their troops from Sicily to Sardinia, Sicily was left open to the British and her allies.

In the build up to D-Day the atmosphere was very tense at Bletchley Park. Everyone there was aware an invasion was imminent but very few actually knew the details. John Masterman explains there were three points to consider, 'first to postpone the date of attack, secondly to indicate that the attack would come from the east rather than the west of the threatened area and thirdly, after the real attack had taken place, to suggest that it was only a first blow and that a second, and even weightier assault, would follow in the Pas de Calais area, i.e. at the eastern end of the target'.[9] This was highly secretive work and remained so until 1972 when Sir John Masterman's book *The Double Cross System* was published revealing how MI5 and MI6 persuaded turned German prisoners of war to feed their masters false information about the D-Day landings.

Bletchley Park had prepared well ahead and Mavis had played a leading role in collaboration with Dilly and Margaret Rock; she was responsible, just two months after Dilly had cracked the Abwehr

Enigma, in solving the new GGG Abwehr code, giving MI5 control over German agents operating in Britain. This allowed ISK and the XX system to give false intelligence to be fed to the Germans and so provide the British with a major opportunity for success in the D-Day landings. All minds, certainly those of the Twenty Committee, were concentrated upon the development of a grand strategic deception for the invasion and they spent the preceding months devising a suitable and totally reliable Double Cross deception plan.

Double Cross agents were only part of the machinery of deception; the cover plan was fixed in the Germans' minds by wireless deception for which the Y-Service was largely responsible. Visual deception played a major part, and an ingenious ploy was for a fictitious plan to be drawn up for a sham invasion. In the past the Germans had been aware that an attack could come from a number of vulnerable areas scattered around Europe. By spring 1944 it was obvious that the attack would be sited between the Cherbourg peninsula and Dunkirk. The Double Cross deception plan led Hitler to believe the Allies would land at Calais; consequently huge numbers of German troops were kept there and the beaches of Normandy remained unprotected by them.

When the time came Mavis ensured that Jumbo Rush, their stuffed elephant named after Commander Edward Travis, Deputy Director of Bletchley Park, whose nickname was Jumbo, was once again taken out of the cupboard. During this period leading up to D-Day she knew there would be a constant rush, the traffic would be outstandingly heavy and Jumbo would remind them to keep up to speed.

There were acts of deception carried out, of which most of the Bletchley staff would have been unaware, and Mavis and the other girls, who frequently listened to the BBC News the following day, discovered the results of some of their messages, of which they may never otherwise have learned.

Normandy had been chosen as providing the best beaches for the landing of the invasion force, but it was realised that if the Germans had sufficient forces, when encountered, the British would be brought to a halt and even thrown back into the sea. The Germans were therefore persuaded that there would be no plans for a major assault on Normandy. The enemy was misled by dummy tanks and invasion landing craft left around Kent and in full view in Kentish ports. Mobile wireless vehicles toured the area sending out hundreds of messages to simulate communications of an army based in the south-east, whilst silence was imposed on genuine troops.

Thanks to the Americans the British were now able to use the Purple machine and could receive reports sent back to Tokyo by the Japanese Ambassador and his military and naval attachés, giving detailed information concerning the sites of German fortifications along the French coast including even smaller units such as machine guns. The naval attaché gave Rommel's plan as to how he would counter the invasion.

If Dilly and his girls had not broken the Secret Service Enigma Cypher, the Double Cross deception plan could not have proceeded, and Mavis breaking the GGG code was extremely important, but it must be remembered that there were also those breaking lower-level codes, cracked by Bletchley Park's Military, Air and Naval sections, which were also vital to the smooth running of the invasion.

By 1944 Y-Stations were installed in various locations, including places overseas. These bases, operated by the armed services and the Foreign Office, had the ability to listen not only to the full range of German wireless communications, but simultaneously to locate the positions of enemy submitters on land or at sea. The operators at these stations wrote down the messages received on appropriately printed forms and these were then rushed, often by teleprinter, sometimes by motorcycle courier, to Bletchley Park. The intention was that messages should be forwarded to Bletchley Park by teleprinter, but sometimes, due to the heavy load, the messages would be carried to Bletchley Park by dispatch riders. They were then analysed and decrypted by Naval Section Y before being returned to the field.

There were two kinds of Y-Station: the coastal stations, listening to high frequency, and others, very high frequency, used mainly for listening to voice communications between enemy ships in UK coastal waters; and there were several other listening assets.

Throughout 1944 thousands of messages were intercepted by naval Y-Stations on a daily basis and as D-Day approached the volume increased. It was found to be a slow process, and to improve matters it was decided that a Y-Station should be located in Hut 18 (formally Hut 8) at Bletchley Park which would enable all these various networks to be dealt with there and the turnaround cut to a minimum. 'Party X, of eighteen naval ratings under Petty Officer (Tel.) Appleby arrived by train'[10] and in May they were ready for the D-Day landings. Everybody at Bletchley Park was on high alert.

For the twenty-four hours of D-Day Harry Hinsley sat glued to the chair behind his desk. He was aware that there could be important telephone calls and was not surprised when he answered a call and it was Prime Minister Winston Churchill asking if the Germans knew we were coming. Hinsley assured him that the first Bletchley decrypts were coming in by teleprinter.

A few hours later Churchill telephoned again and this time Hinsley told him that all was going well. Feeling satisfied with the situation he then decided that he should go off to get some sleep.

D-Day commenced at dawn on 6 June 1944. The mass landing on the Normandy beaches of France is remembered as the largest sea-borne armada the world has ever seen. There was a delay of one day said to be due to bad weather, but a short break was forecast and the decision was taken to sail. Three thousand vessels set out from the coasts of Britain: troop and tank transporters were made ready, and many men who had not been called upon for military service prepared a further 3,500 of their own small landing craft, fishing boats, and leisure boats too, to carry men to the five beaches of Normandy. It was such a secret operation that any civilians on air force bases the evening before, were not allowed to leave. The duties of the Wrens had greatly expanded and, 'The greatest number of Wrens to be concentrated on a single project would be employed on Operation Overlord, the allied invasion of the Normandy beaches.'[11] 'Fortitude', the D-Day deception operation, had been put into use and the enemy had been fed a number of radio messages from different locations to fool the German radio interception units. The Germans had been misled, believing the war vehicles in Kent to be on manoeuvre, and were fooled into thinking the plan for the Normandy landings was a sham. Messages went backwards and forwards and finally the true invasion took place. In the days leading up to 'Operation Overlord', the invasion of Normandy, intercepts decoded at Bletchley Park gave the Allies the locations of most of the German Panzer divisions. Hitler ordered two Panzer divisions to the Pas de Calais believing, until the end, that British troops planned to move on to that area.

The girls went on nightshift on 4 June but when there was a delay due to bad weather conditions, they slept and worked where and when they could. When D-Day came on 6 June 1944 they were sitting in Hut 4, once the submarine-tracking room; a narrow room with a long stretch of table in the middle with a map stretched across, complete with miniature boats and submarines. Then, at their machines and ready, every message was decoded as fast as possible. Without the ability to decipher the German code, the Double Cross deception plan, which ensured the success of the D-Day landings, could not have proceeded. This day marked the beginning of the end of the war in Europe.

As the days passed by the girls were brought face to face with the suffering and exhaustion being experienced by the troops. A call for help would be made from the canteen on Bletchley Railway Station, and as soon as the girls' shifts were at an end they would rush over to see how they could be useful. At first they were alarmed at the sight of the dishevelled troops returning from the front; some looked forlorn and weary and the girls would do their best to comfort them. Others of the returning troops were more cheerful, perhaps relieved to be home, and they would enjoy cracking a joke with the young ladies, but Mavis remembered the irascible woman in charge who ordained that the young girls should be confined to the kitchen out of sight, and only the superior matrons should be permitted to take out the tea and chips to the troops on the train. The girls thought the soldiers would have preferred it the other way round. 'We certainly would have done,'[12] confessed Mavis. Nevertheless, when the day of alternating shifts in the Cottage and serving the soldiers came to an end, there was time to relax, and Mavis's thoughts returned to the soldiers and she became acutely aware of how important her contribution through breaking the GGG Abwehr code was in saving soldiers' lives.

Party X worked very efficiently and, during these vital last days of the war, the speed of the process of their messages was a magnificent achievement and they received messages of congratulations from their superiors. Like their many allies the 'team had formed one of the many tiny cogs in the vast machine that was Operations NEPTUNE and OVERLORD leading to the successful invasion of continental Europe in June 1944, and subsequently, allied victory in World War Two'.[13] They continued for a further six weeks and the station was closed down in mid-July 1944.

Paris was liberated on 25 August, battles continued and bombs fell on cities both sides of the Channel, but at last VE Day arrived, on 8 May 1945, and was received at Bletchley Park with a sense of relief. It was reported on German radio that on 30 April 1945 Adolf Hitler had taken his own life, and Admiral Donitz was named as his successor. This disaster had happened in a bunker under the centre of Berlin as the Russians fought their way into the ruined city. Just a few hours before Hitler's death, Eva Braun, his mistress for several years, also committed suicide. Benito Mussolini and Claretta Petacci, his lover of over a decade, tried to flee the country but were captured and executed by Communist partisans above Lake Como: '... their bodies were exhibited in Milan, strung upside down in a petrol station forecourt.'[14] Victory in Europe finally arrived with the 'signing of the unconditional surrender of all the German forces in north-west Europe to Field Marshal Montgomery in a marquee at his HQ on Luneberg Heath at 18.30hrs on Friday 4 May with a ceasefire timed for 0800hrs the next morning.'[15]

It was not until 23 May that the British finally arrested the remaining German leaders, Admiral Donitz, General Jodl and Reichminister Albert Speer, at their headquarters at Flensburg on the Baltic, close to the Danish border.

Bletchley started celebrating on 8 May and the bells rang out from the tower of St Mary's Church. There had been little time to practise, but the bellringers gathered together. They were local people, many of them retired and too old for national service, and younger staff from Bletchley Park. People poured out from their huts and gathered in front of the mansion – announcements were made, followed by cheers. Most were exuberant; the girls in the services had been given the day off and were travelling home to celebrate VE Day with their families. Some off-duty girls went out on to the A3 to hitch a ride to London to join in the celebrations there; others enjoyed the festivities at Bletchley Park. Just two of the bombe machines stayed in operation and unfortunately it was necessary for a few unlucky staff to remain on duty for the rest of the day. Girls put on their best dresses, seldom taken from their wardrobes when working; there were drinks all round and the fun was recorded by group photographs.

'The British codebreakers "contributed heavily" to what was a joint US-British success, "the US history records" '[16] and in the evening the jollity was followed by a dance in the mansion, and Americans and British celebrated – but they did not forget their friends, and money was donated to a war charity.

In spite of the exuberance there were some who felt relieved but saddened by the thoughts of friends and relatives who had lost their lives: many who were reported missing and servicemen who may have been killed – others who had been held prisoner and their whereabouts unknown.

To mark VE Day the director, Sir Edward Travis, sent every member of staff a note thanking them for their efforts made during the war, but reminding them that work would still continue and warning of the danger to security that could arise from careless talk.

Things slowly started to wind down and German messages became fewer and fewer as fighting in Europe ceased. The last German Enigma message that needed to be decrypted was received on 9 May. Tomorrow was another day; it had been Victory for Europe but World War II had not yet been won. Britain was still at war with

Japan – Japanese interceptions became urgent and Bletchley Park cryptographers continued to deal with Japanese traffic as a priority.

Britain had a history of being wary of Russia, and there was now suspicion that Russia could be a prime mover towards another war; their possible aim being to expand their borders to engulf European territory. Polish codebreakers who had sought refuge in Britain again came to Bletchley Park's aid as they had the ability to intercept and read Russian traffic being released from the Ukraine. They came together with a number of Bletchley staff transferred to Bletchley's outstations at Eastcote and Stanmore to work on Russian traffic. Russian language courses became popular and Mavis took up this opportunity.

Finally, on 6 August 1945, there was news that the US had dropped the atom bomb on the Japanese city of Hiroshima, and destruction of much of Nagasaki followed on 9 August 1945. The armistice document was eventually signed on the USS *Missouri* on 2 September 1945.

Members of Bletchley Park staff received an official letter:

Owing to the cessation of hostilities, there is no further work for you to do in this organisation. In these circumstances, there is no object in continuing to report here for duty, and with effect from [space for date], you are free to absent yourself. You must, however, present yourself, with this letter to the Staff Officer, Hut 9, before your departure, to give certain particulars for his records... In accordance with Treasury regulations, your name has been forwarded to the Treasury for consideration for employment in other Government Departments.[17]

With a sense of relief, victory was now accepted gravely and quietly.

The demobilisation of service personnel was strictly controlled; it was mainly based on a points system, as was the rule both at Bletchley Park and throughout the services, however there were some exceptions. Academic personnel were allowed to leave sooner if they needed to complete their interrupted education.

Those people left at Bletchley Park were usefully employed in cataloging all valuable information, books and notebooks, and all premises were scoured for every scrap of discarded paper that needed to be destroyed – huge bonfires burned and not a trace remained.

In April 1946 about 2,000 GC&CS staff were moved to Eastcote, and, in 1950/1954, most went on to Cheltenham. Margaret Rock transferred to Cheltenham, but Mavis did not join this group and stayed on at Eastcote for a year whilst living at Edgware with her husband, Keith.

CHAPTER EIGHT
Post-War Life

Many people who passed through Bletchley Park had previously been on a path to success and were hoping to take up that route once more, but it is noticeable that before, during and after their stay at Bletchley Park more men than women achieved high positions. Roy Jenkins did not shine out at Bletchley Park as he was not known for his expertise in codebreaking, but when leaving, assisted by Prime Minister Harold Wilson, he became Home Secretary and also served as Chancellor of the Exchequer, becoming one of the most influential politicians of his day.

Apart from the official letter recorded previously offering recommendation to another government department, there was little provision for help with the future careers of past Bletchley Park staff, and this may have been important for younger people who, like Mavis, had often enrolled directly from college without finishing their chosen course of study. Some had lost interest in returning to academia, but now found themselves in a world very much changed from that which they had known before being immersed in life at Bletchley Park. There was help available for older, more experienced, important people, but juniors were sometimes cast aside with a payment of £10 0s. 0d. and others were left hoping they would be found a position in a government department.

In pre-war days many young graduates had opted for a place in the Foreign Office, and at the end of World War II some took advantage of the offer made by Bletchley Park to recommend them via the Treasury to various government departments. They were fortunate, as for them there were no difficulties in obtaining references.

Gordon Welchman, a very senior person at Bletchley Park, had no problem in finding employment. After a couple of jobs in the UK he came to the conclusion there was a lack of funding for the future development of the computer industry in Britain, and he found work in America.

In 1974 Gordon Welchman started to write his book, *The Hut Six Story*, which was a complete technical account of activities in Hut 6. The British and American governments did not want these details discussed openly and he met with pressure to remain silent. This he did for many years and it was not until other authors started to publish similar information that his book finally appeared in 1982.

One important reason for Welchman to feel anxious to publish was because he felt that due to the act of silence 'too many people who had worked for him in Hut 6 had never been recognised'.[1] Some died without receiving any public honours for their vital war work. Welchman's own silence had caused his in-laws to shun him, believing that by working at Bletchley Park he had found a way to avoid military service, and others too found themselves in similar situations. Mavis and Keith understood Welchman's attitude, as when Keith decided to join the Fleet Air Arm one of his reasons for doing so was because he knew some people had referred to him as having found a cushy number at Bletchley Park. Some files have still not been released, and it was as late as 2006 that the Ministry of Defence gave official recognition to some Bletchley Park veterans.

During his time at Bletchley Park Keith Batey had shared his billet with Howard Smith, who went on to become ambassador to Moscow and head of MI5. David Rees became a well-respected professor of mathematics at Exeter University, but post-graduate Oliver Lawn, after a term lecturing in mathematics at Reading University, like many others followed the advice given in the official letter of departure sent out at Bletchley Park, and chose administrative civil service. James Hogarth – a naval Ultra veteran – made this choice and he achieved an important position in the Foreign Office. These posts had none of the excitement and romantic aura of Bletchley Park, but it was the people in these official positions who played an enormous part in rebuilding Britain.

James Hogarth's colleagues, J. H. Plumb, who became an historian, and Asa Briggs, later Lord Briggs, another historian, soared to great heights. A number of Bletchley people became writers, others went on to follow careers in the arts. Douglas Craig pursued a career as an operatic baritone and ultimately became a creative executive at Glyndebourne, and Colin Thompson became curator of the Scottish National Gallery.

There were some high achievers among the female staff, notably the film and stage actress, the glamorous Dorothy Hyson, who exhausted by her shift work as a cryptographer, went on to continue her life as an actress and in 1945 joined the highly successful John Gielgud Haymarket Company. Jane Hughes, later Fawcett, first dabbled in becoming an opera singer, but eventually made a great leap forward into the world of conservation and saving historic buildings, and she and Mavis would sometimes cross paths.

Lieutenant Joe Eachus, US Navy, who became a liaison officer, was one of a group of high-ranking Americans who were the first to arrive at Bletchley Park. There was an important meeting which marked the beginning of the 'Special Relationship' between the United Kingdom and the United States of America when a group of high-ranking Americans made their first visit to Bletchley Park. It was also the beginning of another 'Special Relationship' when Joe and Barbara Abernethy became friends. Joe was awaiting divorce, so their friendship continued.

When Bletchley Park closed, Barbara Abernethy first went to GC&CS, renamed Government Communications Headquarters (GCHQ), at Eastcote, in the suburban area of the Borough of Hillingdon, Greater London, and because she had worked for GC&CS since pre-war days she was not asked to leave as many others had, but instead she was allowed to keep her job. It also became her duty to close the Park for the last time and return the gates' keys to Eastcote.

In 1947 Barbara transferred to the United States where she and Joe Eachus married. Barbara then worked for the British Consulate in Boston, Massachusetts, becoming vice-consul in charge of media liaison, and was awarded an MBE for her services in the Consular Service, retiring in 1986; Joe died in 2003 and Barbara in 2012.

Little is recorded of persons of lower rank seeking employment after their service at Bletchley Park, but Mimi Gallagher (née Balance) later had problems which must have caused difficulties for both sexes of lower grades who had been very young when starting there. At fourteen years of age Mimi began as a messenger at Bletchley Park, moving on to become a typist. After the war she transferred to the civil service but found wages low and the cost of living extraordinarily high. Having been at Bletchley Park since she was young she found it difficult to settle in new surroundings, unlike anything she had known before. In spite of the hard work, life at Bletchley Park was exciting, and staff often lived on a knife edge wondering what the next day's news would bring, in spite of the fact that they seldom heard the consequences of their own work.

Now, Mimi found herself living on her own and having to provide for herself, arrange accommodation and food, travel by underground and cope with the high cost of living. Keeping the secrets of her past life was not easy and, when making new friends, it was difficult not to talk about life at Bletchley Park: she was constantly watching what she said. She joined the British Overseas Airways Corporation and stayed until 1953, by which time she was married.

Mimi went to America for a spell and when she returned she applied for a job in the news research department at the BBC; she stated that she had worked at Bletchley Park, adding, "'Foreign Office Evacuated." "What were you doing there?" asked the interviewer. "I'm very sorry, I can't discuss that," she replied.[2] The interviewer was Hugh Lunghi, a distinguished figure who knew Bletchley Park well, and had been Churchill's interpreter at the Yalta conference of 1945 where he had met both Roosevelt and Stalin.

Hugh Lunghi was obviously impressed by her honesty and Mimi eventually found herself working for the BBC World Service, where she would continue to be bound by the Official Secrets Act. Reminiscent of Bletchley Park days it was another exciting world. 'We were keeping watch on world communism. We weren't spies but we had a lot to do with dissidents,'[3] said Mimi, and she proudly went on to say that the Russian writer Aleksandr Solzhenitzyn had visited and her boss was the first to interview him and to befriend him in the UK. Mimi's thoughts of Bletchley Park still lingered and she paid a return visit with a friend but on that occasion it was deserted.

Mavis's husband, Keith, was undoubtedly one of the most brilliant codebreakers to have worked at Bletchley Park. He reconstructed two key Enigma cypher machines and contributed to the breaking of many other codes.

When Keith Batey left Bletchley Park in August 1945 he chose not to go on with mathematics and instead applied to the administrative civil service. He took up a post at the Foreign Office where he spent six months in the South American Department whilst waiting to sit the civil service entrance exam. Another member of the department was Victor Perone, a rotund, Edwardian-styled gentleman who, when the occasion arose, would wear a heavy gold chain across his breast; he had previously held the important position as Her Majesty's Representative in the Vatican. Keith liked working in this office even though he was only a junior, and whilst working there he met Samuel Hoare, chairman of the Bank of London and South America. Keith remembered, '… a more polite, considerate and charming chap I have never met.'[4]

In pre-war days grand, titled families could usually boast substantial private incomes. Now, with the vanishing of large family fortunes, it became important for some men from privileged backgrounds to earn a living; nevertheless, difficulties were often fewer for these people since family background, education and connections could help. 'Sir Samuel Hoare was puzzled. He couldn't understand how there could be anyone in the Foreign Office whose name he did not recognise.'[5]

It was men like Keith who had their sights set on promoting a new society, when the 'old school tie brigade' would possibly become an institution of the past.

Mavis found life easier than some of the young staff. She was now married to Keith and they were enjoying a normal married life. They lived in Edgware for a while and no doubt they were able to support each other in all sorts of ways.

Post-war life continued to be exciting for Keith and Mavis, and after the restricted life at Bletchley Park a new world opened up before them. In April 1947 there was an addition to the family; a baby daughter, Elizabeth, was born whilst they were living in Edgware.

In 1952 GCHQ relocated to purpose-built buildings in Cheltenham, where Margaret Rock continued to work until her retirement in 1963 when she was awarded the MBE. She never married, but became godmother to Mavis's daughter Elizabeth and was a family friend until her death in 1983 at the age of eighty.

Through his position at the Foreign Office an opportunity arose for Keith to join the British Embassy in Canada. Having spent a short spell there with the Fleet Air Arm he thought it would be a fine experience for him to apply for the position in Ottawa, and for him and his family to settle there for a while. After living a hard-working, but exciting, and even an adventurous life at Bletchley Park – never knowing what would happen next – he was keen to take up the situation which he thought would also be something of a challenge. Mavis, always ready for something new, was happy with the suggestion, and even though they had a young baby they were not put off.

It was the intention of Anthony Eden to upgrade the Intelligence of the Diplomatic Service, and Keith found a transfer to Canada to be an interesting goal. Not a born linguist, when he learned that Sir Anthony was changing the rules of entry, and it would no longer be compulsory for applicants to have a foreign language, but a first-class degree – and only have a *wish* to learn a language – he felt a sense of relief. He applied and became a civil servant working for the Commonwealth Relations Office and was posted to Ottawa, Canada, serving in the High Commissioner's Office from 1947 to 1951. Mavis and their baby, Elizabeth, of five months, sailed with him on the outward journey in September 1947, on the liner the *Empress of Canada*.

Mavis must have been apprehensive about her new life. She had a young baby, and probably wondered about the entertaining that she would be expected to do. When growing up, her parents would have friends around and perhaps enjoy a meal together, but more formal dinner parties, as arranged in higher circles at that time, did not happen in the homes of ordinary folk. However, Mavis was upwardly mobile and, although interrupted by the war, she had had a good education and had mixed well with all classes of people at Bletchley Park, but had probably never planned a formal dinner party. Rationing did not help. At Bletchley Park she had become accustomed to eating good, plain food in a canteen rather than enjoying special meals in special places; she was now confronted with arranging and attending dinner parties night after night.

Mavis enjoyed meeting all these new people and learned about another way of living. She was undaunted and soon started learning to cook special dishes and immediately and effortlessly slipped into the role of diplomat's wife. She found herself coping with a gruelling entertainment schedule which involved the composing and typing of menus, managing the lavish entertaining; cooking too was sometimes necessary, with sumptuous dishes rivalling those they had enjoyed on the *Empress of Canada*. She was very impressed with the banquets they enjoyed on board ship and had made a point of keeping the menus. No longer did she have to decide how to disguise the corned beef and Spam they so frequently had to manage with in England. Decisions had to be made as she enjoyed shopping for a whole range of ingredients she had never had the pleasure of using before. They entertained, or would be entertained by, a continuous stream of embassy people just doing the rounds. Life was fun.

Another round Mavis also remembered was pushing baby Elizabeth in her high English bassinet perambulator around the circuit, delivering visiting cards to every person of their own rank at every embassy; these cards, she was told, must be left in the hall. Time passed by quickly and Elizabeth soon enjoyed being dragged around the shops on a sledge, which she found very exciting, particularly on one occasion when on the way home she took delight in throwing the shopping off the sledge – one packet at a time, leaving a trail in the snow along the path behind them. Fortunately Mavis looked around to see what the giggling was about only to find a long line of various coloured bags and packets decorating the snow-covered pavement.

The arrival of their baby son, Christopher, in May 1949 brought more duties to attend to and the pranks of a well-meaning big sister to deal with. There was the question of clothes and what Mavis should wear for these special occasions. One evening, when preparing to go out to dinner, she had run a bath. Elizabeth seemed to be quietly amusing herself, but Mavis turned to find her young daughter had decided she too could help by washing her mother's evening dress, and there it was – floating in the bathtub.

Another problem was when they discovered the babysitter had put a little gin in the baby's bottle to help get her to sleep. That caused a lot of anxiety and for a while Mavis must have been concerned about leaving the children, but fortunately they found the next nurse could not have been more suitable. Even little Elizabeth must have thought she was wonderful. Mavis put the money behind the clock ready to pay the lady when she and Keith returned home, only to be told that Elizabeth had already tried to do so. That certainly gave them all something to laugh about.

There was one custom that Mavis found very amusing and this became her 'Story of the Long White Kid Gloves'. The Russians were very severe about etiquette and absolutely insisted that long, white kid gloves must be worn at all receptions. 'It was ridiculous,' said Mavis, 'they were communists and should not have demanded such a thing.'[6] This was a post-war period when the United Kingdom was feeling the pinch financially; Britain could not afford long, white kid gloves and, perhaps accidentally, Mavis was provided with one long, white kid glove and one short one. At a loss and not knowing how to cope she decided that if she rolled the long one down, just a little bit, it might look as if she had two; she had decided she did not need them both up to her elbows. 'Nobody noticed,' she would joke, 'and we had a lovely time.'[7]

The family spent three years in Ottawa, where Keith worked in the High Commissioner's Office, and became private secretary to Philip Noel-Baker, Secretary of State for Commonwealth Relations. During this time they were able to have some family holidays and they took the opportunity to travel; that, even with two little ones, they did not find difficult. Mavis was delighted when they decided to visit Washington. There would be no problems with their travel arrangements; they did not need to make any – they just set off. There were so many motels, a facility not yet available in Britain, but here they could just take their pick and pull in without having made an advance booking. With two young children it was not easy to judge just how long each stretch of their journeys would take, so this was a good reason for using the motels which they found such a blessing.

Keith became tired of the life in diplomatic circles, which included too much report writing for his liking, he had little interest in politics, and he found it difficult to be diplomatic with people with whom he could not agree. Mavis enjoyed her stay but, always considerate of their children, said they did not like the idea of more overseas postings as when the children got older she most certainly did not want them to go to boarding school. So, in 1950, they decided to return to England, sailing on the Cunard liner *Franconia* from Montreal to Liverpool. The ship had an interesting history. It had been designed by Leslie Paskett, head designer for Cunard, and had been built by John Brown & Company of Clydebank, Scotland. Lady Royden, wife of Sir Thomas Royden, Chairman of Cunard, had launched the ship into the River Clyde ready for its maiden voyage from Liverpool to New York.

This was a ship built to be enjoyed by cruising celebrities such as Noel Coward, Cole Porter, Oscar Hammerstein and Richard Rodgers. Its interiors were luxurious, with garden lounges, a grand smoking room, a health centre and a racquet court; nothing had been neglected as every whim of the clientele had to be satisfied. It became a very popular ship, providing a regular route between Liverpool and New York in the summer, and serving as a cruise ship in the winter months. This routine was followed until 1939 and the outbreak of World War II when sadly the *Franconia* was stripped of its fantastic interior, painted grey and became a troop carrier capable of carrying 3,000 soldiers. What is remarkable is that she was immediately deployed in the Mediterranean, the very area Mavis had been covering with her codebreaking at Bletchley Park. This sturdy ship spent the war years in various parts of the world, but during 1944 she was back again in the Mediterranean carrying American troops, no doubt on their way to join forces with the British ready for D-Day on 6 June 1944. This was an occasion when once again Mavis and her colleagues were ready at Bletchley Park decoding every message as fast as possible.

The *Franconia* had yet another important job to undertake and some of her luxurious fittings were removed from storage to be refitted on board. She was then off to the Black Sea to serve as a floating headquarters for Prime Minister Winston Churchill and his staff who were attending the famous Yalta conference. Accommodation, a little less comfortable for some people, was made ready for various staff, which included secretaries, telegraphers, typists and security guards. Cunard was accustomed to making important people comfortable and, as they were aware that Churchill liked to spend a lot of time in the bath, they installed a shelf just next to the tub, making it possible and enjoyable for him to lay soaking whilst working at the same time.

When the war finally came to an end the *Franconia* had just a few more voyages to and fro across the Atlantic, transporting refugees and emigrants before her government service was complete. She was returned to Cunard to be restored to her former glory before being put on Canadian service from Liverpool to Quebec, via Greenock. Mavis and Keith must have been on one of her last voyages, and it was not without adventure.

As the *Franconia* sailed along the St Lawrence Seaway, Mavis became concerned about the ship's progress, but Keith firmly assured her that her concerns were unfounded. However, shortly after passing

Quebec there was an almighty bang as the *Franconia* ran aground on an island in the St Lawrence Seaway. Keith was very calm about the mishap but Mavis's first thoughts were for her children and she quickly gathered them in her arms, but then she became very agitated when she saw Keith was not in the least concerned and was busy dashing around the deck getting into the best spots to take photographs of the happening. However, all was well and it could be recalled as an exciting adventure. A newspaper in England made the most of the event, reporting, '*Franconia* Shipwrecked – 999 Survivors'. Keith and Mavis no doubt chuckled at this, as they knew there were only 999 passengers and crew aboard at the time, and it was no great catastrophe.

The family were transferred by train to New York and then given a state room on the replacement liner *Caronia,* when they met with another mishap which must have given them many laughs in the years to come. To compensate for any inconvenience they had suffered, Cunard had upgraded them to a more luxurious state room and they were now looking forward to a relaxing voyage back to England, but disaster struck again – Mavis flooded the state room whilst trying to flush away the baby's disposable nappies! Nevertheless, it had been a wonderful journey and they were again presented with excellent menus and, for the next few weeks, they were to enjoy the best food they would have for some time to come, since they expected – upon their arrival back in England – to be met by rationing and food shortages. However, although still recovering from the war, things were getting better; rationing was coming to an end and Mavis would now be able to continue cooking some of the new dishes she had experimented with in Canada. Britain was catching up on household appliances too; shops now frequently sold refrigerators, washing machines and spin dryers – household drudgery was beginning to disappear.

Elizabeth was excited to be returning to what she had been told was their 'real home', and Mavis and Keith were glad to be back, full of enthusiasm for a new and settled future. The cultural scene had made great steps forward whilst they were away: there was now an

Arts Council, new festivals and exhibitions, and, after the disruption of war, education was being reorganised and there would be fresh opportunities for their young family. There was now a National Health Service – only housing could be a problem, but they were optimistic and felt all would be well.

CHAPTER NINE
Return to England

On their return to England in 1951 Keith and Mavis rented a house in Hayes, Kent. Keith remained in the civil service and for a while moved around from one office to another, including a department which was involved with guided weapons. Mavis stayed at home with the children and bravely coped with a difficulty which many women, and even some men, would find difficult to deal with; but this problem remains a family joke and brings peals of laughter when their now adult children excitedly recall the event: 'The place was overrun with mice.' But with her usual confidence, Mavis would reach for the carpet-sweeper and casually sweep them up. Christopher, still very young, was mystified, but little Elizabeth jumped around screeching with glee.

There was another move, this time to Bourne, near Farnham, Surrey, and in 1954 Deborah was born. In 1955 Keith was appointed elsewhere with the civil service and became secretary of the Royal Aircraft Establishment, Farnborough. The family lived at Bourne for around twelve years and even with three young children Mavis found time for historical and countryside pursuits. She joined the Women's Institute and her mornings were spent, along with other members, creating village scrapbooks illustrating local crafts and traditions through oral and written history. It was a useful local history project inspired by the Festival of Britain in 1951, remembering local characters, including the squire who was celebrated in the church and the rude fathers in the church yard.

In the afternoons Mavis would explore the countryside, enjoying her perambulations with her children around the leafy lanes, villages, downs, vernacular architecture and gardens of Surrey, and she would make a point of chatting to them about the things they saw. Mavis loved children and was devoted to all her grandchildren, and occasionally cousins, Jonathan and Julia, would come to stay.

Mavis sometimes had thoughts about life at Bletchley Park, and when in 1960 she heard the film *Sink the Bismarck,* was to be shown locally she decided her young son Christopher might like to see it, but she was not prepared for the effect it would have on her. She remembered she had been in the dining room in the mansion at Bletchley Park when the news came through that the *Bismarck* had been sunk. It was unusual for news to be released in that way, but it was only the work in Hut 6 that was top secret at that stage and the announcement on the BBC Home Service had been received with magnificent cheers. Mavis recalled that when at the cinema, 'I saw it go down and suddenly I really did feel quite sick. I put my head down and my son said to me after a while, "It's alright Mummy, it's gone down..." He didn't know that I was thinking how awful it was that one's breaking of a message could send so many people to the bottom. But that was war and that was the way we had to play it. If we thought about it too much we should never have been able to cope.'[1]

As well as becoming a capable mother and housewife Mavis joined the well-structured local history group at the Workers' Educational Association, and started to write. It was near Lower Bourne, in part of what was then known as the 'stockbroker belt', but formerly had been heath wasteland, the home of vagrants and the 'broomsquire' who would take his brooms, made from heather gathered from the sandy common, to sell to market-day crowds in town.

Mavis enrolled for a social history course, a study of the poor law, pauper history and pest-houses, and her first book grew from this. It is a small, serious book, *Life Let Us Cherish: A Survey of Poverty and Philanthropy in Farnham (1832-1868)*, an in-depth study of the local Pharo family's struggle out of wretchedness into poverty and beyond. The people and places were all real and the chapters deal with *The Pauper Cart*; *The Poorhouse in Church Lane*; *Life on the Common*; *The Pharos Leave the Common* and *A Prize for a Pharo*. There are a series of appendices giving records of the workhouse; a letter written by a pauper begging relief to avoid removal, and another concerning the fate of a bastard child. A further chapter is gleaned from papers of the Parish of Wokingham, 1832, which was found 'willing to give proper and every attention as thought proper' when dealing with a young lad suffering smallpox. It paints a sad picture and reveals Mavis as a sensitive soul with great feeling for the poor and wishing to see wealth more evenly distributed.

During the time they lived in Farnham, Mavis's parents had a bungalow built nearby so as to be closer to their family. They especially enjoyed the company of their grandchildren, who also liked living near their grandparents. Their grandmother was an expert dressmaker, and her granddaughters were impressed that she made her own clothes. She was always very smartly dressed and much admired by the two girls. It was sad that she died of throat cancer very soon after they had moved into the bungalow.

The opportunity arose for Keith to take a different job when in 1964 he was selected as secretary of the University Chest, and in 1965 they moved to Oxford where they lived for a couple of years, and in 1972 Keith became treasurer of Christ Church College, Oxford. The Chest had traditionally been an iron storage box with a lock, and the present chest, made in the seventeenth century, is now known as The Painted Chest, and the term 'the Chest' is currently used at the university to describe the finance department. It was the duty of Mavis and Keith to attend a few parties and Mavis could not help being amused when she was once introduced as 'Wife of the Chest'. Thinking back to a verse in a poem written for her by the High Commissioner when leaving Canada, she most certainly would have had a secret chuckle to herself about an unexpected pun: 'Will they know me there in London – with my now expanded chest? An extra stone and an extra baby – give to life an added zest.'

Although the family were the most important part of their lives, Mavis arranged her time so that she could continue to have other interests about which she became passionate. She could not begin to think how people could part with their little ones. She hated the idea of having a nanny and missing all the wonderful things that were being said when they were four or five years old, and Keith too loved children; they were happy living in Oxford and started to look out for a house of their own.

Mavis was enjoying life. The war was now in the past, the cultural scene was beginning to flourish and the air was thick with enthusiasm, of hopes and ideas. Mavis became interested in what were then relatively new areas of study – garden history, conservation and landscape – and she carefully arranged her life around her children in order that she could enjoy these new interests. It was whilst living at Bourne that Mavis first heard about William Hoskins and became interested in his type of landscape history, which was not just a quest of geology and economics; she also learned how to read the landscape.

Mavis appears to have been astute in making the most of opportunities as they presented themselves. When drawn to the study of landscape she also took an interest in conservation, and soon after arriving in Oxford she joined the Council for the Preservation of Rural England (CPRE). For centuries there has been a cry for the preservation of England's 'green and pleasant land': in the Regency period the gardener and horticulturalist John Loudon (1783-1843) had dreams of parks and gardens as 'breathing spaces for the Metropolis'; he was followed by Octavia Hill (1878-1912) who, keen to protect open spaces, campaigned against the development of suburban woodland and helped to retain Hampstead Heath; the National Trust was born in 1884; and Patrick Abercrombie (1838-1912) played an important role in setting up the Campaign for the Protection of Rural England, founded in 1926.

In 1949, Lewis Silkin, Minister of Town and Country Planning, introduced a bill to Parliament to preserve and enhance the beauty of our countryside, and this triggered new interests and pursuits to the British public who in the aftermath of the war had become even more aware and appreciative of the countryside. Campaigners now endeavour to make sure countryside and towns are great places to live, work and enjoy. National Parks were designated, and the National Trust flourished when embarking on a new role encouraging more and more people to enjoy outdoor activities and more recently work together with the CPRE.

Mavis, perhaps finding herself able to enjoy the outdoors rather than being confined to a hut at Bletchley Park with her head constantly bent over a machine, was swept along by the *zeitgeist* and free to expand on those small snatches of exposure to the countryside she had enjoyed in earlier life.

Remembering Professor William Hoskins from Farnham days, Mavis went to hear him lecture at the Bodleian and had the good fortune to attend his lectures just before he was to retire from Oxford. Her horizons were broadened and she became even more enthusiastic about the conservation of landscape. Mavis was captivated by Hoskins' book *The Making of the English Landscape* (1955) which she said was not just a quest for geology and economics but presented the impact of human activity on the evolution of land patterns of the English countryside – it became the bible of landscape for both academic and general readers.

When at Leicester University College, Hoskins became a friend of the principal, Frederick Attenborough (1887-1973), father of Richard and David Attenborough. Attenborough Senior was a fine photographer and he took to walking with Hoskins on his exploratory journeys through the countryside of the Midlands. Attenborough was inspired by Hoskins' studies, and Hoskins became the force behind the development of the first university department of English local history which opened at Leicester University in 1948. This allowed him more freedom for his research, which in turn led to local history becoming an important subject worthy of serious academic study.

Professor Hoskins was an inspiring speaker both at college and on radio, and his television programmes were also popular. His writing became lively, colourful and poetic, enjoyed a wide readership and was without doubt particularly appealing to Mavis. However, she recalled in later years, 'It seemed to me that the moment I'd got interested in these lovely landscape parks, they came under threat.'[2] Nevertheless, it must have awakened in her a desire to go on to give time to the conservation of historic parks and landscapes.

Mavis attended Hoskins' lectures whenever she could, and remembered, 'He had a favourite list of tools which he advised his followers to use: ecology, geography, archeology, local history and field walking, backed by maps and aerial photography.'[3] These should be used when 'reading the landscape' which he liked to call discovering the 'observables' of England: a buried wall, perhaps part of a Saxon church; a Roman coin; blocks of square masonry; twisted tree roots; and pieces of twelfth and thirteenth-century pottery. Mavis soaked up all the information that Hoskins had to offer and learnt from him that you could read about man's imprint on the landscape by looking at it. Hoskins lived in the old vicarage in Steeple Barton, in Oxfordshire, which lay in the most satisfying of valley sceneries, where the River Cherwell flows, and where he said, 'The cultural humus of sixty generations or more lies upon it.'[4]

Mavis always enjoyed Hoskins' lectures and eagerly followed his advice and instruction. It could be said that as far as the Oxfordshire landscape was concerned he was her guru, but Mavis, being Mavis, was never afraid to put her own ideas into practice.

Hoskins would amuse Mavis, and probably most of his audience, with the way he frequently brought his lectures to a close: 'Enough of me, ladies and gentlemen, let us take to our boots.'[5]

Mavis believed that by 'cultural' he was implying 'agricultural', but as he lived close to Rousham landscaped garden, one of her favourite haunts, she suggested to him that this was also a cultural landscape in another sense, which also needed to be read. Hoskins took an interest when Mavis became involved with researching Oxfordshire historical gardens and researching into designed landscapes, and he encouraged her to take them further and perhaps contribute to *The Making of the Oxfordshire Landscape* in his county series, then being produced, and she may have contributed to this in a small way but she most certainly had other plans.

The Council for the Preservation of Rural England (CPRE) which became the Campaign for the Protection of Rural England, had been pioneering to save the Oxfordshire landscape since the late 1920s. Hoskins' approach strengthened their aim, and Mavis became involved and served on the committees of both the Oxfordshire CPRE and the Oxford Civic Society.

Always a romantic, Mavis was soon taken by the symbolism of a portrait of Queen Elizabeth I at Ditchley, showing her with her feet on Oxfordshire as the centre of her realm. The unfortunate consequence of being in the middle of England, Mavis pointed out, was the proliferation of roads going through the county, and it would not be long before the new M40 motorway would be slicing its way through the countryside. Chiltern villages would become commutable from London and the Cotswolds' villages from Birmingham, producing a housing boom that would need planning control.

Oxfordshire got off to a slow start, but when the CPRE took it upon themselves to give talks in village halls, as a way to urge the parish council to allow them to help make a detailed study of the character of their village and, where necessary, to press for Conservation Area designation to enhance them and control development, Mavis quickly volunteered her help. At first, some villagers weren't sure what was going on, or who they should support, and on one occasion Mavis suffered a second indignity when this time being introduced as 'The Lady from the Council for the *prevention* of Rural England.'[6]

Over the centuries Oxford had developed compactly within its town walls, and in the heart of the city is the well-known flood meadow, Christ Church Meadow, enclosed by the rivers Cherwell and Isis, the Oxford section of the Thames. It is a pocket of green countryside providing tranquil, rural walkways, with secluded routes along the riverbanks. College boathouses stand along the Isis and it is here that rowing teams gather to train and compete. The meadow, still grazed by Longhorn cattle, provides a beautiful setting for outdoor performances and is a popular place for people to gather, to walk and to picnic. Between the meadow and the college is the broadwalk which dates back to the seventeenth century and was threatened in the 1960s when proposed as the site for a new bypass.

When first arriving in Oxford, Mavis found there what became remembered as the 'bloodiest battle' that ever took place over an environmental issue: Oxford University was fighting to prevent the bypass being built through Christ Church Meadow. College and citizens were united in opposing threats to their *rus in urbe* which it was feared would become swamped by industry.

After earlier proposals by other landscape architects had been refused, Sir Geoffrey Jellicoe, the twentieth-century landscape architect, proposed a sunken relief road across Christ Church Meadow. A summary of the events was reported on 20 October 2013 in *The Oxford Times*: 'It was to be 17.5-foot deep into Christ Church Meadow with raised banks to prevent flooding', but also to prevent cattle, "and indeed human beings", from falling in. 'It would involve demolition of 153 houses, and diverting the River Cherwell and Trill Mill Stream across the meadow at a cost of £1.7 million. A heavily planted artificial hill would mask the line of a road as it descended from a new bridge.'[7] National newspapers joined in the furore and public enquiries followed. The scheme was rejected and it changed the way the city heritage was to be protected by leading directly to the formation of the Oxford Civic Society founded in 1969. Although Mavis was not an activist, she followed the developments of the scheme carefully and allowed the society to hold their meetings in her sitting room. The whole procedure must have impressed Mavis and she most certainly stored up information about the process that would stand her in good stead in years to come when she herself would lead campaigns of a similar nature.

The car was said to have its place, but not in the middle of a city. There was a pioneering alternative to the road; the first park-and-ride complex was created. Oxford reaped the benefit and many more towns and cities around the country followed suit and built their own park-and-ride complexes.

From the 1960s onwards committee work took up a lot of Mavis's time. First it was the Farnham Society and other local organisations, and then the CPRE and the Oxford Civic Society.

Since the twenties the CPRE had been involved with the protection of the countryside and she admired what she considered their good thoughts about it as she too had strong opinions on the matter. The sixties was a time of comprehensive developments and they dealt with other issues too when Mavis sat on the executive committee in Oxford. The committee's duties included looking at planning applications, especially when conservation areas were introduced in 1967, seeking out things that were interesting and giving help and advice on particular projects. This was a task that appealed to Mavis; she enjoyed meeting local people and discovering the characters of the various villages. Where the planning authority was promoting something that was not a problem, they endeavoured to help by pointing out whatever was particularly interesting and good.

Mavis found the village of nearby Ewelme attractive and researched its history which particularly appealed to her. For centuries the pretty, historic village has been well known for its fifteenth-century cloistered almshouses, and the school which is said to be the oldest in England is still in use today and now under the care of the local authority. Both almshouses and school were built by Alice Pole, Duchess of Suffolk, who devoted her life to transforming Ewelme into a perfect village. She was the granddaughter of the English poet Geoffrey Chaucer, and it was perhaps this literary connection that first caught Mavis's attention and inspired her to look further into the village history.

Mavis discovered there had been a local industry producing a good supply of fine watercress which was grown in brick-built beds fed by Ewelme Brook. In the 1880s a man named George Smith, of Lewknor, had bought a plot of land, the site of the corn mill which had burnt down. In 1890 he started to dig out and widen Ewelme Brook, which was fed by a spring rising just north of the village and ran rapidly down the main street before turning away to pass by the rear gardens of some houses, and then on to the bridge which crosses Benson Road, before joining the River Thames. The site is set in the lower part of Ewelme village extending beyond the built-up area off to the north-west. George Smith built brick beds which were fed by the brook, and dams which slowed down the flow of the chalk stream to provide large beds of shallow, clear water, giving excellent conditions for the production of watercress over an area of six and a half acres.

A thriving local industry was created and flourished well into the twentieth century. The winter crop would be carried by cart in 56lb hampers to Watlington Railway Station from where it was transported to Birmingham, Manchester and Covent Garden, London. It remained a family business until 1965 when bought by two businessmen, and production continued for another twenty-three years, ceasing in 1988. After closure the beds were quickly invaded by weeds, in particular the great rosebay willowherb, which grew tall and collapsed in winter, choking the beds, which deteriorated and dried up.

Mavis was impressed by the history and the watercress beds which seemed very much part of the village, but they had become a sad scene and she would have liked to have been involved with their restoration. So when speaking with a group of Ewelme village folk in 1967, Mavis drew their attention to the Local Heritage Initiative which was able to provide funding for local projects. However, she was disappointed that nobody seemed interested, and with plenty more to keep her busy she forgot about it.

One man, Des Dix, did become interested and gave up his business to work full time on the restoration and obtained permission to clear and restore the beds. He gathered together a band of people who were all keen to help and who he inspired to become volunteers. In spite of the hard work that would be necessary, they became very enthusiastic about the restoration.

In around 2002 Mavis attended a Heritage Local Initiative Funding Awards meeting for which small groups could apply. To her astonishment one of the awards was to Friends of the Ewelme Watercress Beds. Although disappointed not to have taken part in the restoration project, Mavis was delighted. 'What a long time it took for the penny to drop. Nothing to do with me, of course, but they liked their watercress beds… but there were all sorts of things, nice things like that, that one found out about. That is what the character of the landscape now is to the familiar scene.'[8]

The group had applied, and help was given to get them on their way; they held fundraising events, and the Chiltern Society Conservation Volunteers also helped. With management plans put into place work began on a well-organised programme of restoration and conservation. The beds were restored using historic techniques. The waterfalls, too, received attention, but the wildlife haven was carefully left undisturbed. As well as mallards and moorhens, there are kingfishers and snipe, and a substantial number of fish in the waters.

Mavis did not see the reconstruction when in the final stages of development, but she would have been glad to know that her initial suggestion may have kindled the spirit of the villagers to embark upon the restoration project. Through their own work and initiative, and that of English Heritage, the restored watercress beds are thriving, and the site also became a nature reserve, an Oxfordshire Wildlife site, listed as a place of scenic beauty. Ewelme Brook now has main river status, willowherb, crowsfoot and reed mace are kept under control, historic structures are maintained and water levels monitored. The disturbance of the endangered water voles is avoided and traps are put down to deal with American mink. This site of historical beauty now has public access, with an educational centre offering a programme ranging from informal guided walks to curriculum-based events for both school and university visitors.

This was one of the first among many projects which were to take Mavis's interest. It had no doubt fired her enthusiasm and she went on to enjoy involvement with many other conservation issues and 'all kinds of nice things would crop up; things that were important to villagers themselves and not just tourist attractions.'[9] She knew that local people knew their own villages well, and it was the familiar village scene that was often what the villagers cared about and cherished. She was so pleased to hear the outcome of her original suggestion; she was, after all, with her experience at Bletchley, used to not always hearing about the consequence of her original work.

Literature was never far from Mavis's thoughts and when doing her rounds one day she came across an unsightly double garage lodged on the end of an old cottage and she knew that her team would be able to give advice on how this could be better integrated. William Gilpin had used the term 'not in keeping' when complaining about country cottages which had been painted white. Always interested in language, this fascinated Mavis, who doubted if anyone would have known that this was Gilpin terminology, but she knew it was a direct crib.

There were forty villages in Oxfordshire with properties listing or designating the conservation area status; Mavis enjoyed the opportunity this gave her to work with local people, and picking up from where she had left off when leaving Farnham she continued to enjoy local history even more.

CHAPTER TEN
Nuneham Courtenay

While Keith was working at the University of Oxford, he heard that the Old Town House at Nuneham Courtenay, which had once been a land agent's cottage, had become vacant and was available to rent. This property and its large estate and grand country house were once the stately home of the Harcourt family, but now owned by the University of Oxford who offered Keith a five-year lease. Mavis had enjoyed a happy suburban childhood but now, in her adult life, she became excited by the idea of living in a country house of character, so they took up the offer and moved in on the day the lease began – 1 September 1965.[1]

Their new home was large, and stood in the middle of an eighteenth-century park designed by the eminent landscape garden designer Lancelot 'Capability' Brown. The gardens were big and, although overgrown, it was here that the flower garden designed by the poet William Mason (1725-1797) had once bloomed. Mavis was enchanted and fell under its spell:

> It was derelict. Garden ornaments were buried in the grass. I had to cut my way through, almost losing my small daughter in the process. It kept telling me that someone was trying to say something in that place.[2]

Deborah, the youngest of the three children, felt herself to be in fairyland, and Mavis said she would have to keep watch over her as she was prone to playing hide-and-seek, and if she turned her back, just for a moment, she would quickly disappear. Deborah always objected to this, saying that she was taller than Mavis and never once did she get lost. Oh dear, girls will be girls, and they both probably enjoyed having their own way. Elizabeth and Christopher looked forward to school holidays as then they enjoyed rambling but in term time they were always preoccupied with homework.

It was not a practical move, with three children attending three different schools each located in a different direction; there were no neighbours and the nearest shops were seven miles away, but how could she resist creating a family home in such an intriguing setting? Mavis had been keen to make the move and was determined practicalities would not be a hindrance and that she would cope. Her father had been living on his own since Grandma Lever died but it was decided Grandfather Lever should leave the bungalow as there was room for him to live with his family, and Mavis prepared a lovely bedroom for him at the top of the house.

The children were excited for this was the first time they had lived in the country; the whole family loved the house and estate where they could ramble freely, and the garden was magical. They lived at Nuneham Courtenay for nearly two years and they had fun. Keith bought a boat that he named *Sivam Revel* for Mavis – which was her maiden name spelt backwards – and they would all go sailing on the Thames which followed its course through the valley below.

One might ask how Mavis had been drawn to country matters? Growing up in Camberwell in the suburbs of London she was not far removed from the Shirley Hills beyond Croydon, where as a child she had enjoyed playing. Or perhaps it was her visit to the Rhineland that first awakened her love of the countryside; and then there was the beautiful, but partly demolished, garden at Bletchley Park. All these things may have had an influence upon her.

The Knox family played a significant role in Mavis's love of the countryside. When Mavis was at Bletchley Park she became a friend of her team leader, Dilly Knox, and his immediate family, and his niece, the writer Penelope Fitzgerald. Dilly's Chiltern home, Courn's Wood, where he lived with his family at High Wycombe, Buckinghamshire, had extensive land and he had acquired still more to allow for his passion for tree planting. Dilly had a love of gardening, and one of his eccentric habits was to garden whilst walking in the countryside. He might be seen carrying an axe and would stop to prune branches from trees along the wayside. Eventually, when Dilly had to retire from Bletchley Park and he retreated to Courn's Wood, Mavis would visit him and sometimes work in the garden, or perhaps they would sit chatting, enjoying these short interludes until the time of his death.

On one occasion Mavis was taken by surprise when she was greeted by Dilly's wife, Olive, with an apology that the laundry hadn't come and would she mind sleeping in Dilly's brother Ronnie's sheets as he had just left. Dilly added it was all right to do so because Ronnie was very clean. Mavis may have felt uneasy, but this was wartime and people were used to all sorts of inconveniences. Dilly had invited her over in springtime to see the 'loveliest of trees, the cherry is now in full bloom under the guest bedroom',[3] he wrote. While Olive was preparing supper Dilly entertained Mavis by showing her photographs of the *Mimiambie* fragments from the Greek papyri and explained how to put them together. 'At least we had a table to spread them out on and one can only wonder how he managed to do it on his knees on the train from High Wycombe to London', when working at the British Museum, 'and the reaction of his fellow commuters reading their newspapers'[4] must have been off-putting. Mavis said she learned a lot about the Chiltern woodlands that weekend. Dilly could no longer participate in the planting, sawing and splitting which he so enjoyed, but Mavis helped him shake seeds from pine cones into tobacco tins ready for scattering.

On returning from Canada, one of Mavis's most enjoyable pastimes was to amble around the country lanes and meadows with her children, and they too inherited a fondness for country matters. When the family arrived at Nuneham Courtenay, the only truly country home the children later remembered, they were enchanted, and as adults they still think of it as being a magical time in their lives.

Mavis loved working in the garden at Nuneham Courtenay and was delighted when one sunny afternoon she came across a group from the Magdalen College School sixth form. They were accompanied by their English teacher who began to bully them into helping her untangle the garden designed by William Mason. They got on with the good deed and Mavis was amused when halfway through the task one student threw down his rake and said, 'I don't know why I am doing this – it is an elitist concept.' Always quick with an answer Mavis suggested to him that 'what was elite in the eighteenth century could now be enjoyed by everybody – "So aren't we lucky?" '[5] Perhaps the student then picked up his rake with a clear conscience.

Mavis continued campaigning with the CPRE and her involvement with garden history flourished. Nuneham estate, its garden and its landscape park, became a passionate interest and she decided to embark upon a programme of research. Besotted with the estate's history, she continued over a five-year period to search the archives. She found herself in unexplored territory: the manuscripts at the Bodleian Library had scarcely been searched and there were twelve volumes of the Harcourt papers which Lord Harcourt owned. They struck up an acquaintanceship, and Mavis would go along to the big house and they read through the volumes together. Mavis was surprised when Lord Harcourt told her he believed she was the only person to have read them, and this made her even more keen.

In earlier times Alicia Amherst had mapped horticultural history alongside social, political and technical developments, but Mavis went a stage further and explored the economic, geographical, topographical and cultural influences. Always a 'people person' she also researched anyone she came across who had been connected with a park or garden she was researching, often creating a cast of wonderful characters.

Oliver Goldsmith was admired by Mavis and she was intrigued by his poem *The Deserted Village* which she set out to prove was Nuneham

Courtenay. She learned that the first earl had unfortunately lost his life when rescuing his little dog from the garden's well, and was delighted when she found the poet, William Mason, had redesigned the flower garden and laid it out as a sanctuary. Jean-Jacques Rousseau had lived at Nuneham Courtenay as a guest of the second earl whose wish was that the village 'should be run on the lines of the model estate in *La Nouvelle Heloise*, a work by Rousseau, whose statue was prominent in the flower garden'.[6] Mavis was also delighted when she discovered that the second Lord Harcourt had become a patron of Rousseau and saw his influence in the restyling of the garden by William Mason.

Mavis lived on the estate, enjoyed the grounds and gardens and did so much research on the Harcourt family it would seem as though she had almost adopted them as her ancestors. As each generation of the Harcourts took over, changes were made to the park, gardens and the villa built by Lord Harcourt in 1759 for entertaining and enjoying the prospect. Mavis always maintained that lessons she had learned from day to day cryptology at Bletchley Park stood her in good stead for her somewhat different post-war projects. She knew that you could only get the right answers if you did not build on false premises and, when she married Keith, she considered this was something mathematicians were aware of from birth.

Nuneham Courtenay tugged at Mavis's romantic spirit and it was at Nuneham Courtenay that she became interested in gardens as well as landscape. Led by her interest in social and garden history, landscape and conservation, Mavis became gripped by a desire to record her various projects and writing became her passion.

In her usual manner, when researching she left not a stone unturned. She revealed that the first Lord Harcourt of Nuneham Courtenay was a gentleman of his time; he stood tall and upright, a figure of taste and fashion reflecting his enormous wealth. He was governor to the young Prince of Wales and escorted Princess Charlotte of Mecklenberg from Germany to be married to King George III.

As the call for royal duties eased, the first earl returned to Nuneham Courtenay, his Palladian villa which he knew reflected his refined taste and status. There was a fashion for the grandiose buildings of the ancients seen on the Grand Tour to be emulated in the garden buildings of English landscape parks, these becoming magnificent arenas of classical grandeur. Inspired by his recollections of the Italian countryside enjoyed when he was in Italy, and his familiarity with the paintings of Claude Lorrain and Nicolas Poussin, Harcourt decided to embark upon the challenge of creating a new, idealised landscape park and garden. This would create a spectacular setting for the new house which he had recently built to replace the old family seat, and present a still grander image to display his connoisseurship of the antique. Classical architecture was essential – it would house sculpture collected when on a grand tour, and provide shelter for strollers – a classical garden temple would serve as a parish church. His garden extravagances would engineer a mood, provide places to ponder and enjoy a vista, or perhaps to feast and revel.

In order to extend his garden and park Lord Harcourt took a bold step. Unfortunately it was deemed necessary to sweep away the old village of Newnham completely. It was said to be charming with its sixty little cottages, parsonage and inn, nestling close by the old manor house, and there was a corn mill and farms that straddled the countryside. The village was clustered around a green upon a wooded bluff above the river, looking towards the spires and towers of Oxford, but it was thought to interrupt the classical, sylvan scene. The new village of Nuneham Courtenay was relocated to a position where it stands to this day, with the eighteenth-century cottages built in pairs each side of the Oxford-Henley road. The alehouse, parsonage and school were also relocated here, a mile and a half away from old Newnham, hidden away, so that the view to or from the park and pleasure garden should not be interrupted.

Mavis could never resist having a joke and another of her tales was that on one occasion, when she was ferreting around the site of the old village to see what she might come upon, she was told by an airman, who had been stationed nearby during World War II, that he had heard a story that when the village was moved there had been a massacre and the villagers had all been slaughtered; and years later, 'They dug up human bones' he assured her. Mavis chuckled, 'Yes, they could very well have dug up bones: sheep knuckle bones that were used for decorative flooring in the grotto. Hopefully they had not been digging up the cemetery on the site of the old churchyard.'[7]

William Hoskins had talked of deserted villages during his lectures which Mavis had attended. Most were of the Tudor period, but he touched on those thrown out of landscaped parks, quoting Milton Abbas as the classic example. Mavis approached him after the lecture, 'I told him I thought he might like to know that Oxford University actually owned the true deserted village, so called by Oliver Goldsmith.'[8] Mavis was delighted when Hoskins accepted her invitation to visit Nuneham Courtenay. It was an ideal place for Mavis to live, and from that time onward, alongside her interest in conservation, William Hoskins would visit and discuss the local landscape with which she was so engrossed and it was through him that she became a member of the CPRE, the Council for the Protection of Rural England.

These acts of destruction of villages caught Mavis's attention. In early years, when at Leicester University, William Hoskins had written extensively on deserted villages of Leicestershire, a topic widely researched by many academics, of which Mavis too would have been aware, when Hoskins visited her at Nuneham Courtenay to discuss the deserted village there. Many estate villages had been destroyed and relocated during the Georgian period to make way for the improvement of landscapes and pleasure gardens, and Mavis located eighty of them, including Stowe, Castle Howard, Wimpole Hall, Chatsworth and Chippenham.

Mavis got to know of Oliver Goldsmith (1728-1774) and his poem *The Deserted Village,* in which he laments the destruction of a village whose community was broken up. She was captivated; the story and the poem appealed to her romantic nature. In spite of the opinion of many other academics, who believed the poem referred to deserted villages generally, Mavis was convinced that of all the deserted villages around the country Goldsmith had chosen to write about Nuneham Courtenay in particular, and she set out to prove it.

There was a vogue for wandering in the eighteenth century and Goldsmith had been something of a wanderlust in his younger days; his travels took him on a pauper's grand tour of Europe, but he was an unsettled character, and while living in London he continued to make excursions around the country. Wandering writers seemed to be particularly attracted to what became a Romantic activity – offering freedom and means of self-discovery. It was a popular pursuit and Goldsmith was among the first of many writer wanderers of his era, including Wordsworth and Coleridge, Byron and Shelley. He was a prolific writer, versatile essayist and playwright, and his poetry too was popular. His broad span of interests provided him with numerous topics and his appealing writing style made him a favourite.

He was befriended by Dr Samuel Johnson (1709–1784), another nomadic spirit, and it was he who first helped Goldsmith by finding him a publisher. Goldsmith travelled all over England, sometimes accompanied by Dr Johnson. Mavis points out that he was known to have visited Yorkshire in the 1760s, to have stayed at Bath and Tunbridge Wells, to have visited Dr Percy in Northamptonshire, the Nugents in Norfolk and other friends in Essex and the Home Counties. He had been to Leasowes, near Birmingham and wrote approvingly of Shenstone's 'harmless' garden there. In the spring of 1768 before starting to write *The Deserted Village*, Goldsmith visited Derbyshire, and in 1769 visited Oxford, perhaps not for the first time; in February, accompanied by Dr Johnson, he received an *ad eundem* degree.[9]

Mavis believed that of all the deserted villages in England the village of Goldsmith's poem was Nuneham Courtenay and she made an almost obsessive search to prove it. She recorded her thoughts in an essay, *Nuneham Courtenay: an Oxfordshire Eighteenth-century Deserted Village*. In Goldsmith's essay, *The Revolution in Low Life*, written several years before the publication of his poem *The Deserted Village*, he said, 'it was the summer of 1761 that I had witnessed the eviction of villagers', an eviction which he was later to describe in *The Deserted Village*.[10] The village, fifty miles from London, was to make a new *seat of pleasure* for a wealthy landowner:

It lay entirely out of the road of commerce, and was inhabited by a race of men who followed the prime-evil profession of agriculture for several generations.[11]

Nuneham Courtenay was the only village Mavis had been able to locate fifty miles from London that had been removed in 1761 to make way for a pleasure ground, and she believed there was a striking resemblance between Goldsmith's essay and his poem and that his essay could be regarded as a prose version of the poem. The poem condemns the 'luxury' of 'degenerate times', and explains that the use of good, productive land as pleasure grounds would bring about rural depopulation.

> The man of wealth and pride
> Takes up a space that many poor supplied
> Space for his lake, his park's extended bounds,
> Space for horses, equipage and hounds;
> The robe that wraps his limbs in silken sloth
> Has robbed the neighbouring fields of half their growth;
> His seat, where solitary sports are seen,
> Indignant spurns the cottage from the green.

He writes resentfully of the wealth of the rich accumulated by inheritance and profits from investment in foreign commerce. Mavis finds a link here and agrees that, as well as inherited lands and fortune, Harcourt had considerable investment in the East India Company. Money became evermore important to him and, like Goldsmith's man of 'wealth and pride', he indulged in 'cumbrous pomp'. As a noted horseman, the removal of the village also provided 'space for horses, equipage and hounds'. In her essay Mavis continued exploring the links between Nuneham Courtenay and the poem and puts up a convincing argument.

Goldsmith's poem was published in 1770[12] and received immediate success; several new editions quickly followed. It was a topographical poem, a sociological document describing the depopulation of the countryside when peasants suffered from enclosure of common lands with the clearing of villages and small farms to make way for pleasure parks and the buildings of estate owners. The themes of Goldsmith's poem are the evils of luxury and the contrast of artificial pleasure with genuine joy. Told in Goldsmith's melodic and harmonious verse, not far from nature and the real world, it is certain to have aroused Mavis's passionate feelings for the poor.

Mavis was no doubt fascinated by the charm of his words, his 'painted images' which she admired for their simplicity. He turned to nature for the truth and the pastoral content of his poems was popular: 'Whether he wished to or not, Goldsmith virtually anticipated the Romantic Revival in all but his adherence to neo-classical diction.'[13]

Goldsmith had exquisite taste and sensibility, other literary interests of Mavis. All poetry, Goldsmith believed, should be governed by certain principles of artistic form and expression. These principles controlled his own poetry and it would seem that he indulged in the use of all his senses. Mavis wrote a paper on Goldsmith's *The Deserted Village*. Her research was thorough and could not be faulted. In 1968 her well-received, influential work was published in *Oxoniensia: The Journal of the Oxfordshire Architectural and Historical Society*.[14]

After Mavis and her family had left Nuneham Courtenay she continued her search into its history and was happy when the University of Oxford decided to restore Nuneham House and lease it to Culham Teacher Training College based at Abingdon, and, by strange coincidence, Keith's brother, Herbert, was also a staff member there teaching mathematics, physics and science and the Batey family were now living nearby.

Mavis remembered that years earlier she had seen water pouring through the ceilings of Nuneham House and birds nesting in the gold medallions. She thought there would now be a great improvement, but sadly that took time. '... as we have often seen, the penny-pinching Department of Education and Science is not an enhancer of stately homes and gardens; tarmac on the forecourt, function lights and furniture and minimal garden, maintenance',[15] she reported, after the Garden History Conference, April 1985, had been held in the red drawing room overlooking Capability Brown's landscape park. However, she felt happier when a new, longer lease was entered into with Carreras Rothmans, who she said '... has given Nuneham House back its elegance with chandeliers and suitable furniture and first-class maintenance of the staterooms'.[16] Once again it was used for concerts and sometimes conferences.

Mavis always felt that her time spent at Nuneham Courtenay was the most inspirational time of her life; it was here that the foundation for her lifelong interests was formed and she decided to expand her involvement with the conservation of landscape and historic gardens. While living at Nuneham Courtenay she joined the Garden History Society and, becoming gripped by a desire to write about her various projects, writing became her passion, and the embryo of her first book came into being whilst she was living there.

CHAPTER ELEVEN

Mavis Joins the Garden History Society

Mavis's yearning for the outdoors brought her to become a member of The Garden History Society and she was keen to know why and how it was founded. When at Bletchley Park she had little time to indulge in gardening but she did enjoy what was left of the old estate garden. With the outbreak of war in 1939 vegetable gardening was encouraged and continued to gather momentum in post-war years. Mavis was aware that World War II had created a massive interest in gardening and subsequently garden history and conservation. Nuneham Courtenay had most certainly inspired her love of gardens, and the immense destruction of the war years certainly drew Mavis towards the protection of historic gardens, landscape and architecture.

In the autumn of 1939 the *Evening Standard* published a leader on the war effort and pointed out there was a need to 'Dig for Victory'; those left at home, not in the armed forces, could make a contribution and enjoy a useful activity by turning their gardens over to the growing of vegetables. This was the phrase taken up by the Ministry of Agriculture's press and publicity departments as being a suitable slogan to start the campaign on its way without causing unnecessary alarm. The 'Foot on the Spade' poster appeared in clubs, pubs and on hoardings all over the country and the campaign got off to a good start when launched by the Minister of Agriculture, Robert Hudson, on 10 September 1940:

Just one word to smallholders, allotment holders and those who have a reasonable sized garden to those who may be termed 'back-yarders'. You can help to feed yourselves and others... I ask for the fullest co-operation between all... The results of your work are of vital national importance.[1]

From early 1941, Roy Hay, a knowledgeable gardener and journalist and formerly assistant editor of *The Gardeners' Chronicle,* had the task of persuading the diggers to dig and promotional schemes became extensive. The Ministry of Agriculture published its *Growmore* bulletins, *Food from the Garden, Vegetable Production in Private Gardens and Allotments* and so on, which were issued to police, fire, and Air Raid Precaution (ARP) stations, and a variety of other organisations and societies. Tens of thousands of copies of notes on the campaign were sent to clergy all over the country, and the ministry's plan for each home to cultivate a 10-rod garden was distributed to every rural household.

Competitions were held both locally and nationally, and the *Daily Express* held a 'Grow More Food' competition, offering £5,200 in prizes. Many books were published for the wartime gardeners, and food manufacturer Van den Bergh and Jurgens Limited, the producers of Stork Margarine, in conjunction with the Ministry of Food, published free cookery literature offering advice on cooking with limited rations, preserving vegetables and fruit bottling, etc., to deal with garden produce.

The British Broadcasting Corporation (BBC) played an important part in the campaign. The Commissioners of Crown Lands, and the Estate Paving Commissioners, gave permission for use of 10 rods of ground in a residential square near Broadcasting House – this to be cultivated – and regular plot-side broadcasts were made. There was a complete break with tradition when the celebrities Raymond

Glendenning, Gilbert Harding, Stewart MacPherson, Wynford Vaughan Thomas and others, all new gardeners, turned up to dig wearing their weekend garb.

Britain became a focal point of world horticulture and the most surprising locations were given over to vegetable growing. The ministry's own plot in Hyde Park started a trend that soon spread to the lawns of civic buildings. A concrete school playground was dug up in Bethnal Green and gardeners' classes now grew cabbages, carrots and runner beans; food for the family, and food for their chickens and rabbits, rather than flowers. When the roof garden of Selfridges was damaged by an incendiary bomb, part of the garden was reorganised to grow vegetables:

> Enough lettuce was grown to supply the restaurant for six weeks –
> as well as 40lbs of radishes, 1cwt of tomatoes, cabbages and French
> beans...[2]

At Bletchley Park the walled garden was put to full use as a kitchen garden and the kitchens were glad to have a good supply of fresh vegetables. The 'Dig for Victory' campaign was so intense one can be positive that Mavis would have known about it. Some Bletchley Park staff did lend a hand during their leisure time, but Mavis was still very young and she found the exciting life of codebreaking far more to her liking.

During the war, gardens were not dismissed from the thoughts of the gardening fraternity, and on Wednesday, 18 November 1942, at a lecture at the Royal Society of Arts, the garden designer Percy Cane looked forward with optimism:

> I think there is not the slightest doubt that people will turn from the
> strain and anxieties of war to the peaceful relaxation of their gardens
> with a keener interest than ever before. Cost, both of making and
> upkeep, will be a serious consideration, but existing gardens can be
> altered and new ones designed to meet this need. There is also no
> doubt that cities, towns, recreation parks and roads could be made
> very much more beautiful by suitable schemes of planting.[3]

Percy Cane's approach to gardening was correct. Interest in allotments continued after the war when food was still in short supply, but many back gardens reverted to the traditional lawn. However, by the late fifties gardening went into a resurgence. After the loss of staff during World War II great estates had started to re-establish their gardens. 'Dig for Victory' had aroused such an interest in gardening, many were keen to try their hand at growing flowers which would bring colour and a touch of luxury to the humdrum of still drab, everyday life. As time went by interest in gardens developed further and people became curious not only about horticulture, but also garden history. They looked to the past for ways in which they could arrange their gardens – garden design became important to those with new homes and who perhaps had never had a garden before. Gardening was no longer confined to the upper classes; it had become a national hobby which went from strength to strength.

Peter Hunt and Kay Sanecki were employed by Collingridge Garden Books, Tavistock Street, Covent Garden, and when they moved on to work freelance they continued to work together on some projects and, as Peter had become interested in garden history, they decided to delve further into its mysteries. Peter had worked as editor on *The Shell Gardens Book* (1964) and started to be looked upon as someone of authority who was knowledgeable in the garden history field, and through his research, and questions he was asked, he realised that source material was scattered and fragmented and he saw the need for an informed organisation.

The time was ripe for Peter and his friend Kay to found The Garden History Society (hereafter referred to as GHS). Peter had compiled information on garden history over the years, and was inspired to bring interested parties together for the exchange of ideas. Together he and Kay put garden history into the public domain, a pioneering feat, and interest was quickly aroused. Garden history was not an entirely new subject; Alicia Amherst had published her *History of Gardening in England* in 1895. 'It was the first systematic coverage of English garden history'[4] and went into three editions. It was a huge success and became the cornerstone supporting the future development of the discipline. The first biography of garden historian Alicia Amherst was published in 2010, and its author, Sue Minter, praises Amherst's book for mapping 'horticultural history alongside social, political and technical developments without pleading for any particular point of view'.[5] However, at the time of Amherst's book, topics such as garden history were most definitely the province of the upper classes and it had taken the Second World War to bring it to the people.

Peter and Kay enthusiastically gathered a group of eminent garden historians who met in September 1965 at the Charing Cross Hotel for afternoon tea, and Peter took the opportunity to float his idea of an informed organisation. They had invited Miles Hadfield, Arthur Hellyer, Ken Lemmon and Frank Clark who had all contributed to *The Shell Gardens Book* and all were enthusiastic about the proposal. By 24 November 1965 Kay had organised a second meeting which took place at the Royal Horticultural Society headquarters at Greycoat Street, Victoria, and much to her relief, thanks to Peter's efforts at publicity, about fifty people attended. A draft constitution had been prepared and Frank Clark was elected as president: in 1947 Frank Clark had published the first book on the history of *The English Landscape Garden*. Post-war years brought a vogue for eighteenth-century landscape gardens and he later helped to create the setting for the University of York which followed this trend. Peter Hunt became chairman and Kay Sanecki became secretary, a modest title encompassing the organising of conferences and events, membership, and public relations. The GHS came into being. It was a delighted Kay that '... went home with thirty-seven, three-guinea subscriptions and opened a bank account the following day'.[6]

The early committees included the cream of garden history society who immediately began the hard work of getting the project under way. By 1966 members were able to enjoy a free quarterly newsletter, one shilling and three pence (1/3d) to the general public. Its twenty-one pages were typewritten on A4 paper.

Some worthwhile books, written by committee members, were published, including F. R. Cowell's *Gardens as a Fine Art*, Christopher

Young Mavis dressed for a ballet performance.

Bletchley Park Mansion The National Code Centre.

Station X, the giant redwood tree used early in World War II as a mast to receive signals for M16.

Abwehr Enigma Machine G312.

Margaret Rock colleague and friend of Mavis Batey who became god-mother to her daughter Elizabeth.

Dilly: The Man Who Broke Enigmas, 2010, by Mavis Batey.

The Polish War Memorial commemorating Henryk Zygalski, Marian Rejewski, Jerzy Rozyck, who played a key role in ensuring the British code breaks occured earlier than they might otherwise have done.

Mavis and her husband Keith Batey upon their engagement before their marriage in 1942.

The lake at Bletchley Park where they liked to wander.

Mavis and daughter, baby Elizabeth, in Toronto, Canada.

On return to England Mavis Batey joined the Garden History Society, and succeeded Kay Senecki in her role first as Secretary and later president.

Kay Sanecki, co-founder of the Garden History Society.

Painshill Park saved by Mavis from becoming a plantation of Christmas trees.

Wendy Osborne marking out the design for Alverstoke Crecsent garden with a can of red spray paint.

Wendy Osborne and Gillian Drummond before the Edwardian fountain at Alverstoke Crscent garden.

Mavis Batey and Marco Battaggio, colleague of Kim Wilkie, sitting in the garden at Petworth Park.

Mavis and Keith's new home by the sea, West House.

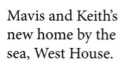

Mavis, Keith and their family.

Mavis and the family.

Mavis and Keith at home.

Mavis and her friend and colleague Edward
'Ted' Fawcett on her ninetieth birthday party
celebrated at Petworth Park.

Mavis Batey after receiving her award of the MBE.

Thacker's *History of Gardens,* and Roy Strong's *Renaissance Garden in England.* The Victoria and Albert Museum had two exhibitions on the conservation of architecture, and when followed by 'The Garden', an exhibition concerned with British garden history and the loss of important gardens in the past, the status of the society was raised. Public interest was stimulated, and today the GHS (now The Gardens Trust) is recognised for the care and conservation of gardens both past and present.

Conservation was an important objective, and a one-day conference 'Reconstruction and Renovation' was held at Stowe in 1968. It was here that Kay Sanecki and Mavis were introduced to each other as they queued for lunch. They got along well, and following their meeting Kay took a group from the society to visit Nuneham Courtenay. Kay, a devoted garden historian, was impressed by the tour given by Mavis, and later Frank Clark too carried out an inspection with Mavis as his guide.

The GHS made progress organising conferences, workshops and garden visits at home and abroad. Edward 'Ted' Fawcett, who had been among the first members of the GHS soon after its formation, arranged, in 1971, a tour of French gardens – the first foreign tour. Ted was tall and wore an air of authority. He had a distinguished war record serving in the Royal Navy and, with his organising abilities, enormous charm and robust sense of humour, could not fail to make a success of the event. Fifty GHS members visited fifty gardens over four days. Needless to say, many more excursions were arranged in the future. When Ted and Mavis met, he told her that his wife, Jane, formerly Hughes, had worked at Bletchley Park, and Mavis recalled that she had worked alongside Keith at one point, in Hut 6, but there had been little opportunity to become friends. Mavis became secretary of the society in 1972, the same year the society's first journal, *Garden History*, appeared.

Kay was now heading towards retirement, and Mavis was waiting in the wings. Nevertheless, by 1970 she had joined the Oxford Department of External Studies as a part-time tutor in the history of gardens and landscape. In 1972 Kay Sanecki was happy to hand over her job as honorary secretary to Mavis knowing that 'a new style of leadership was in place to build upon the firm policies that had been established',[7] but she took up a position at Ashridge House in Buckinghamshire and later went on to organise many successful summer schools there attracting both British and mature students from other countries including America.

Mavis was working with Dr Kate Tiller, who represented the Oxford University Department for Continuing Education and ran their garden history summer schools; this entailed leading tours around gardens and countryside. At first Dr Tiller was apprehensive about garden history as an academic subject, but she went on to confirm that the conferences had shown the answer to be a clear 'Yes'. In the *Garden History Journal* of summer 1996, which contained essays to celebrate Mavis's seventy-fifth birthday, Dr Tiller wrote:

> Garden history has proved an accessible, but when properly undertaken, never superficial pursuit. It brings together the methods and insights of documentary and landscape studies, of historians of society and politics, of art and architecture, culture and literature, and the expertise of botanists, conservationists and planners. In doing so it breaks down barriers between disciplines and, as our conference audiences show, fruitfully brings together informed 'amateurs' and professionals.[8]

The conferences organised covered many periods of garden history and prominent personalities such as Sir Edward Lutyens and Gertrude Jekyll, Lancelot 'Capability' Brown and William Kent; various movements including Arts and Crafts and the Picturesque, and the Georgian, Regency and other periods in history, were explored, with Oxfordshire's local gardens, Blenheim, Rousham and Stowe; the Thames landscapes including Cliveden were also included and, of course, Mavis's favourite garden and landscape at Nuneham Courtenay. Historical sources, both documentary and archaeological, were given attention.

Mavis diligently followed garden history developments doing intensive and continuous research, including the characters of the people who had created the gardens. It was her belief that when researching a garden, as she explained at a conference held by the GHS, the various sources to be addressed were:

Physical evidence through survey, aerial photography and excavation was of first importance. Archive sources included household regulations, estate accounts and inventories; deeds, leases, sale particulars; maps and plans including estate enclosure and tithe; family topographical painting and drawings; architectural drawings and plans; building contracts; oral reminiscences, letters and diaries. It is essential to find out everything possible about the owner of the house... Where did the owner get his money from? Why did he move or enlarge his house or park? What sort of man was he and who were his friends and associates and what clubs did he belong to? What books did he subscribe to and were any dedicated to him? If married what were his wife's family's interests and ownership?[9]

When giving a talk for the GHS in London on 14 October 1985, Anthony du Gard Pasley summarised his philosophy when restoring an historic garden as being: 'restore what you can, where you can, and interpret where you cannot restore'.[10] He thought that to do so successfully, it is necessary to draw upon the poetry, pictures, plays, memoirs and letters of the day, and he cited the research work done by Mavis Batey, particularly at Nuneham Courtenay, as an outstanding example of this approach.

Lord Franks, who had spent time in the United States as an ambassador, returned to Oxford with the idea for summer schools in garden history which would be open to mature people coming over from North America for three to six weeks' study, rather like the English who did external studies. Mavis's children were finishing at Oxford High School and Magdalen School so she was pleased to be available to accept his offer and became a part-time tutor in the external studies department and worked with Kate Tiller to bring the plan to fruition.

Graduates and Smithsonians, a group from museums and research centres administered by the Government of the United States of America, joined the Oxford Summer School and it was popular.

Mavis's students had no set curriculum, 'so they were given access to read in the Bodleian... as it was all new and exciting for the Americans the questions they asked really made one get down to basics'.[11] They could choose any particular gardens they wished to visit and many chosen were Mavis's old favourites.

Landscape history became greatly enhanced for Mavis when she became a tutor. There were small groups of mature students, often distinguished in their own fields, who decided to spend a six-week vacation in an Oxford college to learn more about England, its art, architecture, historic gardens, landscape and related archives. Mavis thought she was lucky as many of her group of landscape students came on sentimental journeys to find their roots. They were all keen to read the English landscape from the coach windows when they were on field trips; it was not just walled gardens, Brownian clumps and landscaped lakes that they looked for, it was barrows, Roman roads, Saxon boundary hedges, ridge and furrow, dovecotes, deer parks, Gothic spires, ruined abbeys and deserted villages. Mavis must have felt rewarded for all the time she had spent with William Hoskins soaking up all the information he had so generously offered. She could enjoy the landscape as he had talked about it, and now she gained a new appreciation of the countryside as seen through the eyes of her students. She also found it very worthwhile to be a member of the CPRE.

When back at home in the United States, her American friends would speed down freeways for hundreds of miles and see sublime landscapes of mountains and canyons; their rural landscapes were nothing but factory-farmed, but in England they enjoyed what Mavis called the everyday countryside, with villages growing out of it, so beautiful, yet something the average English person takes for granted.

New Englanders, Mavis remembered, were always thrilled to find villages with familiar names. Some particularly enjoyed exploring the countryside and there was one student who had ancestors from Farmington and wished to make connections that would link with her family records. The days were too short, so a group of ladies took two cars and, arriving early evening, they searched the churchyard and found the family name on several tombstones, and one student was delighted when she found her name over a butcher's shop.

They could not thank Mavis enough for, as they said, 'opening doors' for them, and Mavis was quite overcome when she received fifty Christmas cards – which she cherished for many years.

Americans came regularly to summer schools and were delighted with the English gardens they visited. In 1979, a visit by the Oxford/Berkeley group, that included a Lutyens house and Jekyll garden, were told that the owner was meeting with difficulties when replenishing the planting scheme without access to Gertrude Jekyll's plans and plant lists. Mavis explained that some of the Jekyll papers, auctioned after World War II, had been bought by American landscape architect Beatrix Farrand of Dumbarton Oaks, and were now at Berkeley. 'The trouble is,' Mavis light-heartedly told them, 'we've got the landscapes and you've got the plans.'[12] A group of her visitors from the University of California, Berkeley said they would see if they could have them copied and sent back to Mavis.

The Jekyll collection of books and papers had had an interesting history, eventually arriving back in England by a tortuous route. They had been donated to the Royal Horticultural Red Cross Sale held in September 1940 in London where Gertrude Jekyll's nephew Francis Jekyll's transaction was assisted by Dr William Stearn of the GHS. The catalogue entry described a quantity of letters and other papers relating to gardens which the late Miss Jekyll (1843-1932) designed or gave advice upon. The collection was acquired by Beatrix Farrand who, until the outbreak of World War II, had been working on the design of the gardens at Dartington Hall in Devon, home of her friend and client Dorothy Whitney, born in Washington and later of Manhattan and Old Westbury, Long Island. Miss Farrand housed the books in her second home at Reef Point, Bar Harbor on Mount Desert Island and the plans are catalogued as the Reef Point Gardens Collection. After the death of Beatrix Farrand in 1959 the collection was transferred to the School of Environmental Design of the University of California at Berkeley, where the originals remained for a considerable time.

Through Mavis's group of ladies the president of the University of California was contacted and he arranged that all the garden plans were put on microfilm and donated to the GHS. Mavis recalled that 'everything was copied and sent back, so suddenly I was confronted with this huge Jekyll record!'[13] She had received seventeen tins of microfilm of the surviving plans; all the garden plans put on microfilm were donated to the GHS. Quite a number of Lutyen's plans came back too, some of them unknown to the GHS. This was because when Lutyens designed the plans, Jekyll could not always get to the site, so he would send a plan to her and she would add an appropriate setting and planting scheme. The archive was formally presented by Dean Milton Stern of Berkeley to Lord Franks, a founder of the Oxford/Berkeley Summer Schools, and to Dr William Stearn as president of the GHS, 'who expressed his delight at the gift and recalled his misgivings when the papers were given to the Red Cross Sale in 1940'.[14] The plans were eventually deposited with the National Monuments' Records.

Mavis always looked forward to tutoring the summer schools along with other courses run by the Oxford Department of External Studies which continued for fifteen years. She found the company of the Americans that visited exhilarating, and membership of the GHS was increased by participants becoming members. One of the society's aims was to become international and from that time forward Mavis made it her habit to look out for further opportunities to introduce members from around the world.

Dr Tiller and Mavis continued to organise conferences and events and, although this was a considerable task, they tackled them with cheerful enthusiasm. Speakers had to be found, and their own lectures prepared, but along with this there were the mundane practicalities to be arranged. Timings, teas and lavatories could not be left off the agenda and many laughs and fond memories still linger with Kate, particularly the commotion at the Women's Institute tea provided at Adlestrop Village Hall when they had to be certain that not one of their 100 participants had been left behind in the Ladies.

And then there was the time when the grand public rooms at Nuneham Courtenay had been rented for a day school on sources for country house and garden history: they had not been warned that the basement rooms below had been let to Boosey and Hawkes Limited who were running a day course on brass instruments. The sound of the oom-pa-pahs echoed around the high ceilings of the Thames-side Palladian villa, no doubt entertaining picnickers along the riverbanks, and most certainly creating a happy atmosphere among the garden historians and mature students – who were not put off attending future courses. 'Only the organisers' nerves were slightly stretched,' remembers Dr Kate Tiller.[15]

Membership of the GHS continued to increase in number by participants joining from the summer schools who were also attracted by the society's aim to become international. The symposium, 'The English Garden Overseas: Eastern Europe', attracted speakers from Poland, Russia and the Czech Republic, and this is a connection which has continued and there have been more visits between those interested in the gardens of these countries.

Mavis's enthusiasm was contagious, so it is no surprise that membership of the GHS soared and remained steady. Mavis always wanted the society to become known internationally, and today it can boast a worldwide following.

When Mavis became secretary of the GHS in mid-1972, she agreed to her appointment on condition she was allowed to bring her CPRE ways to the conservation of historic gardens and, as the GHS desperately wanted Mavis as their new secretary, it was agreed. Until that time the society had been concerned mainly with research and garden visits. In her early days Mavis wrote the minutes and did other routine jobs. Soon she was leading tours around historic gardens, as well as accompanying tours arranged by other guides. In a private paper written c.1989 Mavis explains that the ideal guide 'should not only describe the various garden features, but should relate them to the long history of gardening and garden design as a whole, and place them in their context in the social history of this country'.[16]

Mavis retained her interest in the countryside which she had always loved and she was, of course, still a member of the CPRE which she admired for much of their work, in particular their resolve to preserve access to parks and some private land via footpaths. As a member of CPRE she had been in conversation with a planning consultant friend and had raised the issue of there being absolutely no protection for historic parks and gardens, but she was not believed. We rang the Department of the Environment from my friend's office one afternoon, and he put on his best legal voice and said that he had a client in his office with a very large lake in a park just north of Oxford, and would like to know what section of the act covered the need for planning permission to drain it. 'It was marvellous: the Department of the Environment official went away and came back sounding very agitated, obviously thinking, as we had hoped, that we meant Blenheim. "No," he said, "there didn't seem to be any need, but he hoped there would be local opposition." And my friend said, "Oh yes, there would be. I have her here with me now."'[17] This conversation evidently triggered something inside Mavis and she got off to a good start and an additional focus was added to the GHS agenda.

In 1974 Mavis was asked by the Country Landowners' Association if the GHS would join it in commenting upon the Wealth Tax: she declined, but suggested to the committee that instead they should go along with CPRE, and this they did, supporting the Oxfordshire branch in its approach to access of parkland and so on. A map of Oxfordshire was drawn up showing all the footpaths that went through parks. They found there were eight in Blenheim, allowing access to the whole of the park; there was absolutely no payment necessary. And there was Stonor Park with its wonderful Chiltern beech woods, and the best view of Nuneham Courtenay was from a towpath on the other side of the Thames. Mavis thought that the

GHS should not be too closely tied to the elitist line, and connections should be kept up with the Green lobby. Sustainability, she thought, was important: 'Gardens are really about man's relationship with the environment after all.'[18]

The GHS also gave a great deal of help in recreating lost gardens, and one of the smaller gardens with which Mavis and the GHS first became involved was the villa, first known as Wentworth Place; it was later divided and one part became Wentworth House. The poet-writer of the Romantic period John Keats (1795-1821) went to live there in 1818 for a short period, staying until 1820, so it later became known as Keats' House. It is now a museum celebrating John Keats and is part of the Keats House Trust under the administration of the City of London.

When restoration of the house was carried out in the 1970s the garden was being treated as a 'waiting area' and nothing was being done to recreate it in its former style. The garden was cared for at that time by The London Borough of Camden Parks Department, and they had started to arrange a beautiful garden bedding scheme, but this was inappropriate. Fortunately, the architect, Brandon Jones, chose to consult the GHS about the garden.

When Mavis first approached the council requesting they should do something more in keeping with the architecture and the people who had lived there in the past, her idea was not well received. She recalled that she had once been talking to a post-graduate working on Thomas Hardy who had never been to Hardy's home – he had no sense of place – and this was something Mavis felt very strongly about so she objected to the council's opinion, saying, 'We need a sympathetic area. Don't you know that John Keats was a poet? There were nightingales in the garden.'[19] Mavis knew that 'a sense of place' is arrived at by the merging of lives into land. 'The way a town or house or corner of land is remembered; the ideas and emotions it stimulates; the identities and emotions it carries – these are what make a place',[20] and this is what Mavis wanted to carry forward in the garden of Keats House. The garden could not be restored; the term 'restoration' implies putting back in the original form, i.e. a replica of the original;

however, 're-creation', the making of something entirely new, based upon historical precedent, is what Mavis had in mind and fortunately the council were eventually persuaded and agreed to consider the GHS's suggestions for sympathetic, contemporary planting.

The house is attractive, but of little architectural merit, although it does have pretty windows with iron balconies. Mavis must have been delighted at Keats and the garden, and his poems, with their literary connections; they would present a wonderful challenge to recreate a Romantic garden – Keats was, after all, one of the greatest of English poets of the Romantic school, and the flowers and plants of the Regency period would be a delight to research.

Little was known about the garden, there were no contemporary engravings, paintings or drawings of the layout, nor were there plant lists, but Mavis and her team were undaunted and set about their research in an organised fashion. First, it was decided the design should be that of the Regency period. As well as looking to Keats' writings to see what had inspired him, Mavis looked to the neighbouring houses just outside the old village of Hampstead. The garden adjoined the heathland and the small town houses had gardens planted in the country-garden style, and there were local gardens of the more leisured classes. A stroll around the village gave the GHS an abundance of choice: they learned there were gravel walks winding through shrubberies, perhaps an occasional flower bed or tree set in the lawn, and garden seats and a stone basket or two may have been given a place, and there was frequently trelliswork covered with roses in the background. Sometimes they would chat to local residents and occasionally gather a useful snippet of information.

When discovering the names of the flowers grown around the village, Mavis found there was a large variety. A contemporary survey of the gardens was carried out showing that existing planting echoed that of the Regency period. Next, Mavis turned to early Loudon designs, and, of course, Sandby's painting of the flower garden at Newnham *c.*1770 soon came into her thoughts. The beds were edged with box, and flowers arranged to be taller at the centre or the back of a bed. And she remembered Jane Austen's description of her own garden at Chawton, telling the reader of the casual underplanting of their shrubbery, the mingling of shrubs and trees, which grew freely, displaying their individual shapes and characteristics. Austen wrote of a young peony, a fir tree and a shrubbery border, gay with pinks and sweet williams, of columbines and Orleans plums.

Mavis observed that:

The mingling of cottage gardens and heathlands inspired much of Keats' poetic imagery – sweet peas peeping over cottage walls, laburnums and lilacs, trellised roses and mossy-trunked fruit trees with the heath and its gorse and pine and wild flowers in the background.[21]

It is said that in the spring of 1818, Keats' first year at Wentworth Place, a nightingale built its nest near the house, and Keats would spend hours sitting under the plum tree enraptured by its song. He was inspired and composed 'Ode to a Nightingale', where he mentions the plum tree, and the old mulberry tree where the nightingale had built its nest. The mulberry still stands, but conditions are not quite right for the plum and this has been replaced several times over the years.

Keats' landlord had made paintings of garden and heath flowers, and members of the GHS referred to the Plant Register, which they were compiling, to discover if the plant varieties were obtainable. The Hampstead Horticultural Society asked if they could help with local seed catalogues and they also hoped to identify the nurseryman that Keats mentions in a letter to his sister.

Mavis goes on to tell that Keats spent time nursing his brother during the final stages of tuberculosis until his death; this brought him to the depths of despair. It was in spring 1819 that Fanny Brawne arrived to live in the adjoining house; there was a shared garden which they enjoyed together. They fell in love and were secretly engaged; within a few weeks he had composed some of his finest poems. His feelings for the garden were probably heightened by Fanny Brawne's arrival, and Mavis explains that this was probably the most creative period of his tragically short life, and it was here that he wrote some of his most memorable poetry. Sadly, Keats too contracted tuberculosis and upon medical advice in 1820 he went off to Italy.

In her report Mavis became engrossed with the story of Keats' life at Wentworth Place and what the GHS achieved there, but she writes a fine appreciation of Keats' poems which were richly embroidered with scenes and flowers of the garden. She does not say exactly what became of the garden at that time, but final lines convey her thoughts:

> The sensations of beauty he experienced at Hampstead transcended their origin but because the garden of Wentworth Place was their starting point it should be assured of a place in history.[22]

Mavis's wish was granted. The garden was tended, and the property has become a museum and literary centre dedicated to the memory of John Keats. The house and garden were again refurbished, and on 24 July 2009 it was once more opened to the public; early nineteenth-century species were introduced around the mulberry and visitors sang their praises. Mavis threw herself wholeheartedly into the job she had taken on, and in 1985 she was appointed president of the GHS and remained in that position until the millennium.

CHAPTER TWELVE
Life in the Oxford Dons' Suburb

Mavis had thoroughly enjoyed living at Nuneham Courtenay, but nevertheless she was excited by the family's next move which was earlier than planned. In 1967 Mavis and Keith purchased a large house on the Norham Manor Estate, North Oxford, a suburb popularly called 'the Dons' suburb'; a stimulating and intellectual environment that they would come to enjoy. Mavis was delighted that she would be in closer contact with the GHS, the Council for the Preservation of Rural England (CPRE), and the Oxford Civic Society. She was even more happy to know what a great asset it would be to be able to live so near the Bodleian Library.

The estate was not planned as a total community like Norman Shaw's Bedford Park with its own reading rooms, shops, pubs and clubs, but it was a satellite suburb of Oxford with exclusive clubs in college common rooms and libraries which must be rated amongst the best – if not the best – in the world. The university had moved on since its origins in the eleventh century and there was no longer an obligation of celibacy for dons, but it did require that those who indulged in matrimony should live within a mile and a half of Carfax Tower, which is considered the centre of the city, and governing the height of all other buildings in Oxford. However, Norham Manor Estate was ideal for 'the mile and a half from Carfax' requirement extending right up to Park Town, built in the early 1850s for distinguished Oxford citizens and, it was rumoured, for the kept mistresses of dons.

The children went to school locally and settled in well. Mavis was happy to go along to the Parent/Teacher Association meetings, but Keith had a loathing of such gatherings and chose to stay at home. Mavis enjoyed meeting other parents, but she did wonder how the teachers coped in the catchment area of North Oxford where all the children's fathers were dons. She pitied the poor chemistry mistress trying to give her report to one of the children's fathers who was a professor of chemistry. It must be said that Mavis's children were now teenagers and could be a little headstrong at times, but Deborah now credits Elizabeth, being the eldest, as having blazed the trail and made the going a little easier for Christopher and herself. Mavis, nevertheless, came out of the shadows when after thirty years of absolute secrecy she virtually felt herself blossom – '… it was a relief when the veil was lifted and I could tell them what *silly old square Mum* had done during the war.' That, she no doubt thought, would give them something to think about.

When the Batey family arrived many estate rules had long been forgotten, however an air of academia still prevailed and Mavis found their neighbours both interesting and amusing. They included a philosopher, a Hebrew scholar, a keeper of manuscripts, an editor of the *Victoria County History,* an Ashmolean curator and a more contemporary black hole expert, and there was a scattering of people with literary connections. Not to be forgotten were the indomitable elderly ladies and surviving spinster daughters of the first generation of married dons. One of the Miss Spooners, a daughter of Dr W. Spooner, Warden of New College and famous for spoonerisms, was disconcertingly prone to riding her bicycle with her white stick over the handlebars. More commendable, and particularly amusing to Mavis, was Miss Butler, the daughter of a distinguished Oriel fellow, one of the last of Lewis Carroll's child friends. At the age of 100, she rose from her sick bed and, just before she died, she recited *You are Old Father William*, faultlessly, from beginning to end. Carroll's poem is a parody of a didactic poem by Robert Southey particularly well known at that time by children of Oxford and most certainly known by Mavis.

The author, Penelope Lively, had two pioneering maiden aunts with whom she stayed after the war. They suggested that it would not be long before 'crusaders' had to campaign to save North Oxford houses like theirs, whose privet hedges, their niece said, had survived two world wars. Although protection for historic buildings was given after the last war through statutory listing, few Victorian houses were included. Many years were to pass before Mrs Catherine Cole began her dedicated task of conserving North Oxford.

Catherine Dodgson, another daughter of the Spooner family, whose husband, Campbell Dodgson, was keeper of prints and drawings in the British Museum, was a distant cousin of Lewis Carroll, a frequent visitor to North Oxford when perambulators were becoming an increasingly common sight. He was one of those who preferred the college common room to the permanent matrimonial delights of North Oxford, but as the Maudes, Beatrices and Enids grew into children he was constantly called into their homes to entertain them with Mad Hatter Tea Parties or to read *The Hunting of the Snark*.

Catherine Dodgson was a portrait painter who began to take an interest in the history of her own Gothic North Oxford Victorian suburb. She was dismayed to learn of the lack of knowledge of the area, still referred to as 'an architectural nightmare' as it was when Thomas Sharpe drew up his report for the city council in 1947, and published *Oxford Replanned*.

Catherine Dodgson became secretary of the Oxfordshire Architectural and Historical Society and, in 1962, wrote a series of magazine articles on *Some Vanishing Houses in North Oxford* for her own college, St Anne's, which was busy demolishing Victorian houses in the Banbury Road. She then set up the voluntary Victorian group of the Oxford Architectural Historical Society to study the buildings of North Oxford and to keep the local authority up to its new conservation responsibilities. The Victorian houses were painstakingly recorded and led to the first steps in conservation, and in 1968 it became a conservation area, so halting the demolition and alteration of houses. Although only a newcomer, Mavis was asked to join and went on to enjoy Catherine Dodgson's leadership and friendship.

Mavis must have felt proud to be following after a long line of women of North Oxford who had taken the lead in the emancipation of women by higher education. In 1866 certain wives and sisters of Oxford professors had obtained permission to attend some of the university lectures and even had special classes for women, and in the early 1870s they started a campaign for higher education for women, and by 1878 they were allowed to enter for university examinations and receive diploma awards – but they would have to wait until 1920 for degrees. However, some exciting events did take place.

At the far end of Norham Gardens a house of the typically proportioned style of the houses there was rented, and became Lady Margaret Hall, named after the mother of Henry VII. There was a garden adjoining the University Parks through which the ladies could walk to permitted lectures, but they were, of course, required to be suitably chaperoned.

Knowing that when there was increased pressure for building, gardens always suffered, Mavis agreed with Catherine Dodgson to supplement her work with a study of the gardens of the Dons' suburb to meet the new problems of the 1970s, now that the ninety-nine-year leases were expiring. Mavis and Keith had looked at theirs when they took over their house and found that, amongst other things, they were forbidden to keep pigeons or hang out washing. They had no intention of keeping pigeons, but were relieved to find that the wartime bursar had waived the washing-line restriction and it seemed nobody had remembered to reinstate it.

Many of the houses were being converted for use by institutions and others were divided into flats and maisonettes. Norham Manor Estate was losing the qualities of a leafy garden suburb; front gardens had become car parks and the Victorian houses with their steep-pitched roofs, turrets and gables were standing forlornly in a sea of tarmac. The miniature country house setting designed by William Wilkinson, St John's own Gothic architect, on land released by the college for housing development on their Norham Manor Estate, was fast disappearing.

The Victorian Group and the GHS, which Mavis had joined, came together, and with the help of the council issued a leaflet to encourage re-planting, especially the evergreen hedges, which were not only traditional, but proved useful in screening cars and dustbins all year round. A plant list of suitable trees and shrubs was included and interest was aroused. There were still many Victorian favourites to be seen from the roads: laurustinus, mahonias, hollies, berberis, arbutus, pampas grass, yuccas, and wisterias reached along the verandahs. Here and there a glimpse could be caught of a fern-patterned cast-iron garden railing; there was a pre-Raphaelite statuette in a shrubbery and a length of rope-shaped brick edging along a border. There were also finds from donnish holidays, some fossils, strange archeological ornaments which were perhaps treasure salvaged from college restorations.

Mavis enjoyed calling on the owners of the various houses to talk about their gardens. One day when she had taken up her camera and set off to photograph some of the garden paraphernalia, she met a lady in one of the front gardens of a small house in the North Parade area. It had a superb creeper-covered door with a branched Gothic hinge taken straight out of a mediaeval illustration with Madonna lilies reminiscent of Pre-Raphaelite *Convent Thoughts*, by Pre-Raphaelite painter Charles Allston Collins – it had been created between 1850 and 1851 when it was exhibited in the Royal Academy of Arts. Mavis asked if she might take a photograph and congratulated the lady of the house on the perfect planting up to her Gothic door. She looked bewildered and asked, 'My what door, dear?'. Mavis was glad to understand that some people were instinctively on the right track, even without the leaflet. She wondered whether the lady knew of the painting and that the minutely detailed flowers were painted in the garden of Oxford resident Thomas Combe.

The first lady principal of Lady Margaret Hall was Elizabeth Wordsworth, the great-niece of poet William Wordsworth. She encouraged her students to help with the garden, and a gardening club was formed to take care of the new borders designed by Sir Reginald Theodore Blomfield RA (1856-1942), British architect and garden designer; architect of the main college buildings of Lady Margaret Hall.

Annie Rogers was a devoted admirer of Gertrude Jekyll – and like Miss Jekyll, was a law unto herself. She was a determined campaigner for women's admittance to full membership at the university and also on the council of Lady Margaret Hall. She took over the task of organising the gardening and the librarian provided her with minutes of the meetings. These she stored in her garden trug along with the lists of all the plants she had acquired from friends for her Arts and Crafts gardening. The rock garden at St John's College was a special delight, but the college porters were warned that, although a blind eye might be turned here and there, if Miss Rogers was seen to appear with an umbrella, a favourite receptacle for cuttings, she must on no account be left on her own.

The Bateys' house in Charlbury Road was built in 1902 and there were some interesting features installed by the stonemasons, who had been employed for college restoration purposes during vacation, and filled their time by providing the new brick houses with stone mullions and keystones. A circular hall gave the opportunity for a reduced processional route for taking the ladies into dinner, and for them to withdraw in a becoming fashion whilst the gentlemen took their port. The kitchen area was screened with a scullery and what seemed to have originally been called a 'knife' room. The servants' bells were still there; one was connected to the bathroom but as the family normally ate in the part of the kitchen that had belonged to the housekeeper, the bells were redundant, but were kept in the handsome bell case hung on the wall as an ornament.

Mavis was told by her neighbour that when they went to look at their house, the mistress was out and it was the servant's afternoon off, so Professor Driver kindly showed them round all the rooms including his study and dressing room. However, when her neighbour asked if she could see the kitchen, he had to admit that he did not know where it was, but it was probably beyond the green baize door. Mavis was amused, 'My husband most certainly knew where our kitchen and scullery were!' she announced.

The Batey household was a busy one, constantly full of people coming and going; neighbours would call in, and Mavis was generous and warm, sympathetic and caring, and friends – frequently of her children – would stay overnight, or even for a whole year if the need arose; as it did when one young girl's parents were going through a divorce. Both Mavis's brother, Stanley, and Keith's brother, Herbert, stayed for a while and Grandfather Lever moved with them to Charlbury Road where he had a comfortable apartment in their house. With so many people visiting Mavis, her Canadian experience stood her in good stead and she became a very good cook. When friends of her children dropped in for a home-made fruit cake, a cup of tea and a chat on their way home from school, Mavis always had ready a stack of fruit cakes, and Deborah would often lend a hand with making them. 'We called them rock cakes in those days,' Deborah remembered.

John Herival came with his family. He had worked with Keith at Bletchley Park. Although an outstanding mathematician he made an unrelated inspired discovery which proved to be the key factor in cracking the Enigma. It was an outstanding breakthrough and became known as Herival's tip.

Peter Twinn and his wife were also visitors; he had been a codebreaker alongside Keith at Bletchley Park. When he joined Dilly's team in the stable-yard Cottage at the outbreak of war, like Mavis he was given five minutes' instruction from Dilly, then left to get on with it. He became very successful and was the first British codebreaker to read a German service Enigma. He was modest and would accept none of the credit, but he was Dilly's choice to take over the day to day running of Intelligence Service Knox (ISK) during his sick leave. Keith and Peter Twinn became firm friends and it was Peter who accompanied Keith on his wedding day as his best man.

Bletchley Park was never discussed when they were visiting – thoughts of Bletchley Park usually remained dormant. Instead the men would enjoy themselves playing chess, which was perhaps one of the main reasons for getting together, and the women and children had no difficulty in finding things to do.

Mavis's children grew up while they were living at Charlbury Road and Mavis no longer had to be there when they came home. Elizabeth, the eldest daughter, did her A-level examinations at what was then known as the Oxford Polytechnic and then an external London degree in sociology before going on to do a year's post-graduate teaching course at London's renowned Goldsmiths' College; Christopher went to Magdalen College School, and read mathematics at St Peter's College in Oxford, before joining the world of computers. Deborah attended Oxford High School and read physiology and psychology at St Anne's College. She was interested in 'whole people', and rather than becoming a 'bench scientist' she decided to study communication difficulties. Mavis was able to help Deborah with her choice of career as she had remained friendly with Joyce Mitchell who had travelled with her from Euston to Bletchley on their first day at Bletchley Park. They had spent their time on the train chatting and getting to know each other, and Joyce had told Mavis about her training as a speech therapist. 'It is amazing how things crop up,' Deborah said, 'because when I was at university Mother became friendly with an actor, George Benson, who was a descendant of William Gilpin. George had had a stroke and was receiving speech therapy for aphasia.' Deborah did some research about this and decided aphasia and autism would be interesting routes for her to follow.

Mavis gradually found time to enjoy still more activities as well as becoming further involved with the GHS and, still keen on working towards the conservation of the landscape, she kept up her membership of the CPRE. The 1960s were a time of comprehensive development and she felt they had to make a stand, as, of course, she was 'wife of the chest'.

Mavis devoted a great deal of her time to delving into garden history and was a frequent visitor to the stacks at the Bodleian Library. One day her daughter Elizabeth happened to be there too, and a porter pushed a trolley laden with huge volumes of *Country Life* along the gangway in front of her, and to her surprise she noticed they were destined for her mother. When Elizabeth told Mavis at dinner that evening that she had been working in the library on Floor J, Mavis immediately responded, 'Ten floors down.' Elizabeth was startled; 'How did you know that?' Mavis did not explain that corresponding letters of the alphabet and numerical order was something that came automatically to mind when working as a codebreaker. She quickly changed the subject – keeping secrets was another habit which had become automatic.

As Elizabeth got older she made up a code and she and her friend would write notes to each other. When Mavis looked over her shoulder and immediately transcribed her message Elizabeth was mystified. How could her mother have done that so quickly?

When young, the girls never discovered what their parents had done during the war years but they may have been suspicious and possibly made up little fantasy tales about this. Mavis had been given a small ornament by Dilly, a silver pepper pot, inscribed with the letters ISK, Intelligence Services Knox, that she treasured and which the girls came to understand was very important to her. Their reaction was to smuggle the pepper pot into the garden shed, and having raided their box of dressing-up clothes would make themselves look as they thought druids would look. They would then stand the little pepper pot on a bench and take on a ritual of worshipping it. That was their secret – Mavis never did discover what was going on – or so they thought.

Strangely when things started to become declassified the three teenagers were not really very interested in this strange world where their parents had spent the war years; they had other things on their minds. Elizabeth and Christopher were starting out on their careers and Deborah was at university. The first Deborah heard about it was in 1978 in an article in *The Oxford Times – Rara Mavis: An Ultra Good Code-Cracker* – but Mavis played it down; she was more interested in garden history.

Mavis and Keith were always very modest about the part they played and both felt it was people on active service who were the real heroes. Deborah recalls, 'They always stressed that the work done was always a team effort and they never wanted to make much of their own contributions.'[1] As an historian Mavis was anxious that the facts should always be recorded properly, and her book *Dilly, The Man who Broke Enigmas* which she wrote late in life gave her the opportunity to do this. However *The Oxford Times* article says: 'When all the excitement over Ultra began, with the public release of the wartime signals by the Public Record Office, Mavis became rather impatient with interviewers who earnestly enquired what it had been like to be possessed of the greatest secrets of the war. Her answer was, "Well really, I never thought about it like that at all, in real life you don't live on that sort of serious, dramatic plane. We knew, of course, that what we were doing was top secret, so was a great deal else that was going on in wartime. Even talking about someone coming on leave could be disastrous. So one just accepted that you didn't talk about your work. We knew that our work was urgent and important and we worked very hard and for very long hours – until we were pink-eyed often. But we were young and frivolous too."'[2] Deborah commented that, 'What she said makes me realise she did not know the significance of her work until years later when the facts started being put together.'[3]

Mavis was forever reading and scribbling – she had numerous articles published and was writing a book about the gardens of Oxford and Cambridge. There was paperwork here, there and everywhere around the house – every available drawer seemed to be filled – even in the kitchen, and once, on just a single occasion, she stored some papers in the warming drawer below the oven. However, Mavis deserved to be praised, for she somehow knew, at any given point, exactly where to lay hands on the papers she required – nevertheless, when they moved house, her mass of papers did become something of a problem.

Naturally, Mavis wanted to know the history of their own garden. When she and Keith arrived in the 1960s the house was still occupied by Lady Douie who had two undergraduate lodgers from Lady Margaret Hall, whom Mavis would later meet up with as garden historians and friends – Joanna Matthews and Eileen Stamers-Smith. The Bateys knew the Douies had been in India before they retired to Charlbury Road and were intrigued when they found a huge humpback trunk in the attic with POONA stencilled on it. There were at least ten Douie family members; the daughters had scholarly interests and were emancipated, well-educated North Oxford women. When the Bateys moved in they were advised not to do any weeding until they knew what was in the garden as there could still be interesting Himalayan seeds lurking in the undergrowth; however, they were to be disappointed as it soon became apparent that there were only good English weeds, except for a few suspicious poppies.

The drawing room opened on to a conservatory with large pipes heated by a small stove outside, but not being interested in tender plants they never felt the need to light it. Mavis was not a particularly keen gardener although she always had ideas as to how their gardens should look. She was especially renowned for being hopeless with houseplants, and when she was first pregnant her mother joked that she hoped she would look after her children better than she did her plants!

For her report on the Victorian gardens, the large scale OS maps of North Oxford made in the 1870s, together with the estate agents' advertisements and photographs, gave a detailed picture of the layouts of the gardens. There were carriage sweeps flanked by ornamental flower beds enclosed by brick walls and iron palisades, and there were indoor ferneries and conservatories galore. Flowers were confined to shrubberies, herbaceous borders or the popular island beds; these were usually semicircular or arabesque in shape and edged with low box or hooped wire framing. Flowers were graded from small plants to trees, usually weeping, in the centre of the beds.

Mr Gee was the local nurseryman whose splendid greenhouse still existed in the late sixties, albeit as a restaurant, set up in Banbury Road to supply the suburb, and some of their bills had survived. Victorian ferns and spiky plants in pots to echo spiky pinnacles and gables were much in demand. There was no lack of scientific interest with Dons exchanging notes about soil analysis, the carbon content of the North Oxford atmosphere and the best contrivances for heating greenhouses.

The Wayneflete Professor of Chemistry laid out his garden at 15 Norham Gardens with the help of his father-in-law, Dr Alfred Smee, F. R. S., the eminent eye surgeon and ecologist. It was divided into sections – a fern glen, a saxifrage, sempervivum and sedum garden, an American garden and an alpine mound. He was careful to leave room for the croquet lawn which his eye of authority told his daughter must be a parallelogram, 'as the hoops of the game are placed geometrically, it is offensive to have curved lines in relation to them'. Croquet was comparatively new to Oxford when Lewis Carroll introduced the croquet scenes in *Alice's Adventures in Wonderland*, but was soon to become a fashionable family game.

Mrs Humphry Ward, the author of the acclaimed novel *Robert Elsmere*, granddaughter of Thomas Arnold, niece of Matthew Arnold and wife of a Brasenose Don, was thought the best chronicler of Victorian life in the Dons' suburb. In *A Writer's Recollections* she wrote, 'Most of us were very anxious to be up-to-date and in the fashion whether in aesthetics, in housekeeping or education.' She admitted that initially housekeeping had its difficulties, particularly with inadequate help, and especially in the preparations for dinner parties when the average income of 'the new race of married tutors' was then little more than £500 a year. With practice, however, she thought on the whole they became 'very fair housekeepers and competent mothers' as well as keeping up with aesthetics.

The Women's Movement coincided with the cult of aestheticism in Oxford, not surprisingly with Walter Pater, its high priest, living at 2 Bradmore Road on the Norham estate with his two sisters, who with Mrs Ward were members of Mrs Creighton's original women's rights committee. The emancipated North Oxford women wore aesthetic colours of sage green, peacock blue and ochre, the 'Greenery Yallery' satirised by Gilbert and Sullivan. 'We used to sew sunflowers in crewel on our blue-green serge dresses,' recalled Mrs Ward. 'They did not want to be upholstered as their mothers had been, but wore slim Liberty gowns to portray the beauty of motion, which was seen to advantage on the croquet lawns.'

They read the gardening magazines and gardened themselves in Arts and Crafts fashion. A few who were still imbued with Ruskin's ideas indulged in exotic gaudy bedding-out schemes; but the North Oxford women grew the old-fashioned flowers that greeted Tennyson's Maud or Carroll's Alice in the *Garden of Life* flowers, and they cherished the larkspur, the lily, the musk rose, jasmine and the passion flower. Their houses were furnished with Morris wallpapers, spindle-legged chairs, cold chests and cabinets in hand-worked oak on which they stood blue pots – materialism was frowned upon. House and garden were united as never before. The garden came into the house with its Morris wallpapers and fabric, often literally, with ubiquitous creepers; a very few well-chosen flowers were arranged in vases with simple, yet new, oriental artistry. Pampas grass was particularly favoured, not only as a feature for the centre of the island bed, but in a tall vase against a green wall decorated with William de Morgan tiles.

It was the Paters who were the first to have Morris wallpapers in Oxford, followed by the Wards, and there were soon very few North Oxford houses without walls covered with his flower designs of marigolds, blackthorn, honeysuckle, corn-cockles or sunflowers. The name of William Morris, the founder of The Society for the Protection of Ancient Buildings (SPAB), is as much linked with campaigning as with his Arts and Crafts ideology. Mavis liked to think of this when having Oxford Civic Society, CPRE, or GHS meetings in their dining room with its blue willow Morris wallpaper, which in the 1970s she feared must have only been reproduction.

When working at Bletchley Park Mavis had become very friendly with the author Penelope Fitzgerald who was Dilly Knox's niece. He had always wanted her to work at Bletchley Park and he had asked her over to his home at Courn's Wood to talk about it, suggesting she dropped journalism and the BBC, for whom she currently worked. As Penelope and Mavis were friends, when Penelope did not agree, Dilly asked Mavis to persuade her to join, but this was to no avail as

Penelope had made up her mind not to work at Bletchley Park. Dilly made this suggestion shortly before his death; he knew he was dying and it was as though he wanted the two young ladies to keep in touch, but he need not have worried because they always remained friends.

Penelope Fitzgerald visited Mavis in the early seventies when she was researching for her biography of the Victorian painter and designer, Edward Burne-Jones. She had immersed herself in Arts and Crafts and was attracted by all its features, such as those to be found in the domestic setting of the people of the Norham Manor Estate. Penelope too wore Liberty prints, and she also carried a capacious William Morris bag.

The two friends went to Keith's rooms at Christchurch to have their tea and Penelope told Mavis she had also embarked on yet another book, *The Knox Brothers*. Mavis was pleased to hear this and they went around the college together discussing *Alice in Wonderland*, Lewis Carroll and the *Alice in Wonderland* illustrator, John Tenniel.

Penelope's research of Burne-Jones' stained glass had taken her to churches and cathedrals in various counties. When she and Mavis were in Christchurch Cathedral Mavis thought they made what seemed an amusing search: Penelope was keen to look for Burne-Jones' trademark wombats in the stained glass windows.

As well as Burne-Jones, Penelope's heroes were Ruskin and William Morris and she was inspired by what they called 'useful arts: work drawn from nature', and Penelope had a copy of John Ruskin's treatise *The Seven Lamps of Architecture* that her publisher Stuart Proffitt considered an emblem of her life's values.[4]

Mavis was very happy at Charlbury Road. Her family was happy and she found the community, past and present, inspiring. It was a friendly environment and she relished the constant flow of visitors who called upon them – friends and relations who came to stay, children from school who called in for tea and a cake, various committee members, or even whole committees who came for meetings. Mavis appears to have been in her element. She found time to write and she enjoyed working with various committees, particularly the CPRE and the GHS.

CHAPTER THIRTEEN
Mavis Becomes a Campaigner for Conservation

Having witnessed so much destruction during the war years, it is logical that when peace came there was an undeniable trend in favour of conservation. Britain was now looking to the future, but there was no reason why some things of the past should not be saved and appreciated; Britain's rich cultural heritage, which included historic buildings, gardens and landscape, did after all foster continuity and stability, identity and pride, and Mavis's pet interest, the sense of place. Some public bodies were keen to make a clean sweep and demolish architectural treasures spared by Hitler's bombs, and were also prepared to ruin vistas by traversing treasured landscapes with a web of roads and railways. However, conservation became a burning issue, and there were those such as Mavis who set out to preserve countryside and landscape, and her colleague of Bletchley Park days, Jane Fawcett, who spent her time saving St Pancras Railway Station from demolition – neither could see sense in artless destruction.

The GHS was originally founded to become a learned society for the study of garden history, but it rapidly became apparent that this was inseparable from a commitment to the conservation of historic gardens and landscapes. The Georgian Group, the National Trust, the Council for the Preservation of Rural England and the Civic Trust were allies of the newly founded GHS which was becoming well known for its conservational interests. When Mavis became secretary of the society she led a campaign for the recognition of historic parks and gardens as a national asset, and played a key role in promoting a greater public awareness of their importance, whether private or public, large or small. The impact of development on the wider environment, landscapes, views and vistas too, was also to be considered.

In the 1950s the new technological age called for a non-historical approach to landscape. By the 1960s the conservation movement had gathered strength, but garden designers and landscape architects who were influenced by past traditions, and the authentic restoration of gardens, were dismissed by the newcomers, the landscape architects influenced by the Modern Movement, seeking freedom to develop a site without restrictive measures being forced upon them.

When asked about the early involvement with conservation by the society, Kay Sanecki remembered Frank Clark, founding president of the GHS and a past president of the Institute of Landscape Architects, who had played a leading role in reconciling the 'new lives, new landscapes' attitude with a respect and understanding for the past, particularly the eighteenth century. At a committee meeting he excitedly 'waved a newsprint cutting about Studley Royal and the Duncombe Park terraces'.[1] The leading article, in the first newsletter, made the important announcement of the impending sale of the Fountains Abbey Estate and Studley Royal Garden, near Ripon in North Yorkshire. Subsequently he and Kenneth Lemmon, another committee member, took local action on behalf of the GHS. Clark wrote to the county council of West Riding imploring them to preserve the gardens of Studley Royal for the nation. When the planning officer for Studley Royal praised the lovely heritage gardens and said that he would recommend some action to further improve them over a period of years, Clark offered the assistance of the GHS with any restoration work.

Influenced by her guru William Hoskins and her obsession with Nuneham Courtenay and its 'deserted village', Mavis's interest in garden history as an academic subject expanded to include the conservation of landscape as well as gardens, and as secretary she led the GHS to develop as a campaigning conservation body, and was later proud to confirm that Clark's letter concerning Studley Royal was the first conservation letter written by the society. Other early conservation work included a request for help from the National Trust with Westbury Court,[2] and then there was work to be done at Levens Hall Park, Cumbria.

The practice of allowing historic gardens and landscapes to be divided by roads, or ruined by housing development, was frowned upon, and a series of principles were set out for the future of the society's participation in the campaign for conservation. Its first action in 1969/70 was to present evidence at a public enquiry when the Ministry of Transport threatened to build the dual carriageway M6 link through Levens Hall Park. This would require an avenue of oak trees to be felled, causing not only loss of the trees but also important views.

Arthur Hellyer and Peter Hunt visited Levens Hall to walk the park. It was established that the French gardener, Guillaume Beaumont, a pupil of André le Notre at Versailles, was brought in by the owner, Colonel James Grahme, in 1688, to plan a fashionable garden at Levens Hall Park. Beaumont had 'borrowed' the vista at the head of the avenue by using the bend in the river – an early example of landscaping. In 1810 a new head gardener was appointed who undertook the restoration of the late seventeenth-century scheme which went on to survive for over one hundred years.

The current owner, Oliver Bagot, employed two Queen's Counsels to take up the enquiry. Representations were given by Denis Thornley of Manchester University, in collaboration with Diana Uhlman of the GHS, their cause based on historical research and an appraisal of the scenic value of the landscape, so establishing a claim for the protection of the site. The intervention proved persuasive and the Ministry of Transport offered an alternative route – one hundred oak trees were saved from demolition. The Levens Hall public enquiry of 1971 was the first real battle and national success with which the GHS had become involved, and considerable publicity was garnered.

Until that time their cause had been chiefly academic, giving expert advice on restoration, but now there was an important move away from this role to become a campaigning force in the protection and conservation of gardens and landscapes; the society expanded and its status grew. Help was frequently given to local authorities by providing the historical background to various sites, and also to local societies by helping prepare their cases for designation. However, 'although this established a claim for the protection of one historic landscape there was as yet no national policy'.[3] Kay Sanecki wrote that 'the success at Levens Hall Park was owed to the determined efforts of The Hon. Diana Uhlman who was the committee chairman at the time; without her the society would not have been represented'.[4]

This was the year that Mavis took over from Kay Sanecki as secretary; she was very aware of what was happening and would have learned from the experience – even without being directly involved she found it all very interesting and no doubt, enjoyed the battle which fired her enthusiasm, and she never looked back as far as preserving the landscape was concerned.

Success at Levens Hall Park was followed by campaigns at Audley End, Petworth, and Beckley Park in Oxfordshire, when its splendid topiary garden of the 1920s was saved from encroachment by the proposed new M40 motorway. This was the tip of an iceberg, and in 1973, encouraged by Mavis, the GHS set up its first Conservation Committee, a driving force including John Anthony as chairman, Mavis as secretary, David Lambert as conservation officer, who, with their supporting team of Marcus Binney, Ted Fawcett, Peter Goodchild, Peter Hunt, Susan Jellicoe and Dorothy Stroud, pushed ahead with many more campaigns. Mavis reported at the Annual General Meeting in 1974:

> The main concern of the committee has been an attempt to secure a national policy for the protection of historic gardens and landscapes.

Simultaneous threats to the three Brown parks at Audley End, Chillington and Petworth, highlighted the risks to which landscape parks were subject in the increasing pressures on the countryside due to road-building and industrial intrusion. A letter expressing these views was printed in *The Times* on 21 October 1973…[5]

The GHS was heavily involved at Audley End, Essex, in opposition to proposed new sewage disposal works; it gave restoration advice at Shireoaks, Nottinghamshire; at Summerhill, Bath, representation was made at a public enquiry regarding proposals adversely affecting a Repton garden; and at Vanbrugh Castle, Greenwich, development spoiling the vista was successfully opposed.

From that time forward the GHS played a leading role; campaigning proved to be a great step forward with its achievements. 1975 was European Architectural Heritage Year and the society felt it could join forces with Architectural Heritage enthusiasts. A symposium was held at Imperial College, London on the treatment of the grounds, gardens or parks of historic houses, and it was agreed that such buildings should be enhanced by appropriate settings and so encompass a sense of place. Mavis, together with the Civic Trust, had effected a major achievement: this consideration was first introduced in the Town and Country Amenities Act (1974), and official recognition was received when an amendment was made to the Historic Buildings and Monuments Act (1953) and grants were made available for gardens as well as historic buildings.

The GHS was invited to speak at the Schwetzingen Conference (1975) held by the International Council on Monuments and Sites (ICOMOS), in conjunction with European Architectural Heritage Year, on the conservation of historic gardens. Mavis was pleased when she read the invitation; it was acknowledged that England had always led the way in gardening so should be in the forefront of garden conservation. In 1977, the GHS was prompted to set up a pilot survey of historic gardens and landscape parks of six counties which Mavis believed might form the basis of a register. When living at Nuneham Courtenay Mavis had already worked hard on this project and, entirely alone, she had surveyed Oxfordshire; over a period of five years she covered forty gardens and landscape parks. She believed she was 'sitting pretty' living quite close, as she did, to many interesting gardens and landscape parks; Blenheim, Foulsham, Shotover, Stonor Park and the Oxford College Gardens were all nearby.

In 1985 there was another move forward when Mavis's idea for a National Register of Historic Parks and Gardens came to fruition. The aim was to protect gardens and parks – in addition to houses – of historic importance, to increase public awareness of the value of garden heritage and to ensure their protection wherever possible. Lists were issued for the first ten counties and Mavis recruited and led the research and recording teams for nine of these.

To do this in an orderly fashion, Mavis approached Anthony Crosland, then Secretary of State at the Department of the Environment, and she reported, 'Of course, I got the usual answer. "No money, no staff." So I said to him, "Shall we do a pilot scheme, if you haven't got the money? We are all volunteers." He was slightly taken aback, but he agreed.'[6] Consequently, Mavis was put in touch with Jennifer Jenkins, wife of Roy Jenkins whom she had known at Bletchley Park; they held the same values and they worked well together. '"She was among the first to see conservation in the round, as a matter of whole areas and villages and towns and cities, rather than solely as a matter of grand old houses," [Max] Hastings declared. "She said briskly from the beginning she was not in the business of handing out money to impoverished aristocrats."'[7] Roy and Jennifer Jenkins were a hard-working couple and Mavis found them easy to get along with. Roy Jenkins had joined Bletchley Park in April 1944, following three months' training at a cypher school in Bedford, where he was taught the Baudot code by a young man from Balliol College, Oxford; he then transferred to Bletchley Park where he stayed until the end of the war. 'He found the work gruelling and many years later he confessed to being out of his depth and the memory of this still scared him.'[8] However, serving in the Labour Government, Harold Wilson cultivated a respectful partnership with Jenkins, enabling him 'to achieve a sweep of path-breaking reforms at the Home Office'.[9]

During the year that Jenkins was at Bletchley Park, due to a travel ban it was difficult to meet up with Jennifer; however, they were able to arrange to spend some weekends together when she would join him between shifts and they would stay at Woburn Sands and Roy and Jennifer would have some time for discussion and Jennifer would sometimes manage a chance meeting with Mavis.

Jennifer Jenkins and Mavis set up an unofficial advisory gardens committee which Mrs Jenkins chaired, so that the lists of historic gardens could be graded in a way acceptable to the Historic Buildings Council: 'The minutes were written up after hours, and we didn't even get an official cup of tea!' Mavis complained. 'But we must always be grateful to Jennifer Jenkins for the encouragement she gave to getting historic gardens into mainstream heritage,'[10] she said, as ever showing appreciation of those who gave their help.

Mrs Jenkins and Mavis achieved their goal by the initiative taken to promote this unofficial garden listing, and, when the National Heritage Bill was in preparation, historic gardens could be discussed with better understanding than previously. Mavis was delighted that there was another successful outcome, for they achieved a resolution that historic parks and gardens should be recognised as essential components of European culture. And it came as no surprise that Mrs Jenkins eventually became chairman of the Historic Buildings Council (now English Heritage), and later chairman of the National Trust.

There were further achievements, and in 1983 the National Heritage Act set up a new body, the Historic Buildings and Monuments Commission for England, which would compile the official Register of Gardens and Parks of Special Historic Interest. The name was not thought to be very 'snappy' by its first chairman, Lord Montagu of Beaulieu, so it became known as English Heritage. This move ultimately led to the National Register of Historic Parks and Gardens of Special Historic Interest in England, designed to afford some degree of legal protection to historic gardens in the planning process.

Mavis was enthusiastic about the protection of historic gardens and landscapes, but realised that because of their organic, ephemeral nature they should not be dealt with in the same way as historic buildings. She felt it important that everything should be looked at on its own merits, and appreciated that much could be done to retain the atmosphere, and the designer's intention.

When a symposium was held in association with the Ancient Monuments Society in 1984, on the conservation of historic gardens, Mavis knew there would be a tussle and saw to it that speakers from all the garden heritage bodies were invited, enabling them to work together for their common aim.

Mrs Jenkins, who chaired the meeting, had on a previous occasion been instructed that no official in the Department of the Environment was to spend his time on such a frivolous activity as listing gardens. That had not pleased Mavis, so there was delight at the positive outcome that not only gave status to the GHS, but established which parks and gardens were to be listed as of historic interest. Owners, as well as public bodies, would now be able to access information, and English Heritage was authorised, by Parliament, to prepare a Register of Gardens, and Other Land of Historic Interest, with listing Grades I, II*, II, but no statutory powers were authorised regarding planning for registered gardens. Government grants were to be allowed for repair and improvement, but not for maintenance.

The registers were originally the brainchild of Mavis; she had organised her team and together they had surveyed the gardens. The first registers were compiled and brought to the attention of government, and registers and listing grades became worthwhile tools. The undertaking proved to be an enormous success for which Mavis reaped a fair reward when she was appointed a member of the official English Heritage Historic Parks and Gardens Advisory Panel, a position which she enjoyed and retained for the next ten years. Dr Christopher Thacker, who had been founder-editor of the GHS, became the first inspector and registrar of gardens.

One site which was soon to benefit from being listed on the register was that of Mount Edgcumbe on the Devonshire coast. Margaret Campbell-Culver, author and GHS member, praised the scholarly enthusiasm and energy put into the Garden History Report for Mount Edgcumbe by Mavis, which was presented to the organising committee in 1985. Mrs Campbell-Culver offered appreciation saying 'the impetus for all the successful garden and landscape restoration was largely due to Mavis'.[11] On this occasion the councillors and their officials were unexpectedly wooed by her with the poetry of John Milton and James Thomson, to help explain the landscape and the vision! – a vision which was accepted, and Mount Edgcumbe was given the designation of Grade I on the register. Numerous further sites appropriate for inclusion continued to be brought to the notice of the committee. The registers, which have become the backbone for any subsequent work on research or conservation, have earned themselves an official status and are regarded with respect.

The GHS also set itself the task of fundraising for those gardens requiring financial help. There was little money available for historic buildings – and none for independent designed landscapes – although this did change with the coming of the National Memorial Fund.

In 1944, a conference concerning future war memorials was organised by the Royal Society of Arts. It was agreed that unlike the edifices of World War I, when it was more frequently the practice to commemorate sacrifice with an emphasis on stone monuments, World War II presented an opportunity to dedicate scenes of natural beauty. The purpose was to enhance the happiness and health of the living, rather than build sad monuments in gloomy places. The public would then be encouraged to look forward to a happy life and the certainty of peaceful and beautiful landscapes as dignified war memorials.

The idea was not completely new. In 1919 Lord Leconfield gave Scafell Pike, at 3,210ft the highest point in England, to the National Trust in memory of the men of the Lake District who had given their lives in World War I. The fellow countrymen of the fallen, members of the Lake District Fell and Rock Climbing Club, followed in this vein and acquired twelve mountain peaks in the Lake District, each more than 1,500ft high, 3,000 acres in all, as a memorial to their fallen. Surely there was no better way of remembering those sacrificed than by the mountainous terrain they had once climbed together, and on Scafell Pike on 8 June 1924 a bronze tablet was unveiled:

> In glorious & happy memory of those whose names are inscribed below… members of this club – who died for their country in the European War 1914-1918, these fells were acquired by their fellow members & by them invested in The National Trust for the use and enjoyment of the people of our land for all time.

When Mavis heard that Painshill Park was derelict and the Painshill Park Trust was desperate for money, and also that people were growing Christmas trees on the site commercially, she felt something had to be done. She set to work and discovered that after World War II, Chancellor of the Exchequer, Hugh Dalton, had in 1946 inspiringly set up the National Land Fund. Rather than the usual war memorials he felt that acquiring scenic land in perpetual memory of the fallen would be more fitting. The fund would use £50 million raised from the sale of war surplus goods. Dalton's Budget speech on 9 April 1946, announced:

> We shall dedicate some of the loveliest parts of this land to the memory of those who died in order that we might live in freedom… let this land of ours be dedicated to the memory of our dead and of the use and enjoyment of the living forever.[12]

Painshill Park was saved by a grant from the National Memorial Fund from becoming a permanent commercial site for the cultivation of Christmas trees. However, when held by the Treasury the money allocated was never separately accounted for, and was overlooked. This meant that Dalton's wishes had not been carried out. Undeterred, believing Painshill Park could be eligible, Mavis contacted the Treasury and there was a subsequent government inquiry into the suppression of the fund; the Treasury denied ever being asked about it. 'Then I appeared with my number, and date, and time, and name!'[13] chirped Mavis, her laughter betraying a little pride. She was overjoyed when Painshill Park became one of the first landscapes to receive grant aid from the new National Heritage Memorial Fund, notification of which she received by special messenger ten minutes before it was allowed to be made public. Many years later Mavis recalled that Painshill Park Trust brought the landscape back to life. They did a wonderful job although many people do not realise it is an historic park.

'As well as developing a "National Estate", Dalton envisaged that the reserve fund would also be used to help not-for-profit organisations such as the National Trust, the Youth Hostels Association, and the Ramblers' Association to provide sites for recreation, open-air sport and physical fitness.'[14] Many other institutions followed, receiving grant aid, but unfortunately it became something of a 'rescue service' for works of art, houses and furniture. This was not what was intended by Dalton, and the National Land Fund was renamed the National Memorial Heritage Fund (1980) and continues to offer grants for historic parks, gardens, landscapes and other heritage assets.

In 1985 Kay Sanecki wrote:

Mavis has taken the society's work on conservation to the highest national level, to meet the challenge of the times. While it is splendid to see the society flourishing in this way and to know it is a power to be reckoned with, I wonder sometimes if Peter Hunt – who died eight years ago – would still hanker for his learned society which is what he planned. Conservation barely came into it.[15]

However, Kay Sanecki had no need to worry – although sometimes appearing to take second place, interest in garden history has continued to flourish alongside conservation, and the GHS continues to inspire first-rate academic study and have a worldwide following.

CHAPTER FOURTEEN

The Garden History Society Spreads its Wings

Along with the society's aim to become international, the GHS made many visits to countries abroad to see their gardens and learn something of their culture. Edward Fawcett had arranged the first foreign tour to France in 1971 when fifty GHS members visited fifty gardens over four days. This was so successful that many future tours followed, including trips to Switzerland, the first European country to have a garden history society, Portugal, Poland, Hungary, North and South America, Japan, China and Russia.

Mavis did not travel herself, but she always took a great interest and gave help if it was needed. It warmed her to think that friendship with Poland was being sustained by an interest in gardens. As a codebreaker working with Dilly Knox, Mavis became familiar with the contribution the Polish codebreakers had made to the British success in breaking the Enigma code more quickly. She believed the help Britain had received from the Polish at the beginning of World War II had not been sufficiently recognised. Mavis felt ties with these Polish mathematicians and was glad when later she learned that in July 2011 a memorial commemorating three Polish men, Marian Rejewski, Henryk Zygalski and Jerzy Rozycki, would be installed at Bletchley Park.

Reciprocal visits were sometimes made by foreign garden societies and those between Russia and Britain were particularly popular. Perhaps having had connections with Russia during her time at Bletchley Park and when she started to learn the Russian language, followed by a spell at Eastcote post war, Mavis became enthused to take an interest in Russia and its people. The USSR welcomed visitors from Britain, feeling it would be an advantage for connections to be established with the GHS which seemed keen to help them with conservation issues, restoration and re-creation of their gardens, and in this way each country would be able to share their knowledge.

The first GHS trip to Russia was to Moscow in 1984 when it visited many parks and gardens as well as enjoying Russian culture, especially art and architecture. The group had a very full programme and was given support by Intourist, the official national tourist agency. It was received by the Union of Architecture and addressed, in excellent English, by Dmitri Shvidkovsky. He spoke about Charles Cameron (c.1743-1812), British decorator, architect and landscape designer for Catherine the Great, whose work around Saint Petersburg shows the influence of the English landscape garden movement. This was followed by a talk given by Michael Symes on Painshill Park, and finally their chief landscape architect spoke on the projected plan for parks and gardens to encircle the city of Moscow, where 'eventually thirty-five per cent of the area would be green space'.[1]

The group had visited the ten-mile-long 'garden ring road' earlier that afternoon when making the city tour. This was, of course, of great interest to the GHS which, since the symposium held in 1975 at Imperial College, London on the treatment of the grounds, gardens and parks of historic houses, had had an even greater interest in landscape and in greening British cities.The following two days were spent in the country, and at Vladimir where the city architect spoke of another project – landscaping the river and blending river and landscape. This was of particular interest to anyone concerned with landscaping the River Thames with which Mavis was soon to be involved.

In the 1980s Mavis's friend Penelope Fitzgerald's public activities centred on PEN International, the prestigious association of poets, playwrights, editors, essayists and novelists. It was founded to promote co-operation between writers from around the world in order to promote international goodwill. Penelope Fitzgerald took part in organising many varied events including inviting people to give talks; Mavis was one of her guest speakers and, when requested to talk about Dillwyn Knox at Bletchley Park and Room 40 – their pre-war establishment in the Admiralty building – she was glad to accept.

Mavis was proud to have been asked to speak at PEN, whose Writers' Days always included top-class writers and celebrities, and she felt it to be a privilege. She no doubt made the most of the occasion, taking the opportunity to network with members and leaders of PEN and to bring to their notice the GHS, as they were also in the business of promoting international goodwill, and tell them of GHS's travels to other countries and the society's enthusiasm for encouraging international friendships.

Dmitri Shvidkovsky was soon to make a visit to Britain and Mavis would, of course, tell him about the aims of PEN which might also be of interest to him.

In May 1987 Dmitri Shvidkovsky made a visit to Britain, his hosts being members of the GHS who escorted him around many gardens and places of interest in Edinburgh and London, with a broad radius of gardens in the south of England. He and his wife, Katyia, were guests of Mavis and Keith, who accompanied him on a number of visits, mainly in Oxfordshire, including the Bodleian Library in Oxford, where he was pleased to see a copy of a Repton's Red Book. They had dinner at Christ Church College, and also visited Magdalen College. Shvidkovsky was charmed by country pubs; being particularly English they were often the choice of venue for lunch and certainly became favourites of Shvidkovsky and Katyia. Mavis enjoyed the time she and Keith spent in their company and formed a lasting friendship with the couple.

Shvidkovsky followed up his visit, writing an interesting letter of thanks to Mavis saying the impression made by the landscape parks was important because it helped him to understand Charles

Cameron's works in Russia and to put forward the idea that Cameron's designs showed the park had the 'grandeur' of Brown's nature. He was charmed with the '"impression of youth" in Rousham; there I received the feeling of the spring of landscape style.'[2] 'In Blenheim I was astonished by the difference of Kent's picturesque style and Brown's theatre of landscape, more beautiful than Nature.'[3]

Shvidkovsky went on to say that it gave him enormous pleasure to meet Mavis and Keith, remarking on how much he enjoyed Mavis's comments on the parks they had visited in Oxfordshire – and Wonderland. One cannot but smile as he finishes his letter, 'The views of the English parks will remain with me as the grin of the Cheshire cat, even when they'll be far from me.'[4] They obviously enjoyed a great rapport.

The fifth GHS visit to Russia was in July 1987, and Intourist arranged a tour which took them to parts of the country rarely visited by people from Western Europe. They did not visit the spectacular gardens maintained largely for the benefit of the tourist, but mainly lesser gardens and parks. Their last day was spent in the depths of the countryside and it was remarked that, 'The profusion of wildflowers in the Russian countryside was brought home to us, a reminder of how impoverished the British countryside has become in this respect, since the widespread use of herbicide.'[5]

The mention of wild-flowered meadows pleased Mavis. She was interested in garden design and how it had changed through the ages, but said that she was not at home with the pristine gardens so often to be found at the Chelsea Flower Show. She found the relaxed style of William Robinson's (1838–1935) wild gardening more satisfying; in public parks and green spaces she would like to see wild-flower meadows with plants for butterflies. The prairie style she found interesting and thought it would become more popular in Britain in the future – and so it has.

Public parks were once the province of the elite and some squares were 'key gardens', so called as entrance keys would be available only to the people occupying the properties around the squares where they lived. After the Reform Act 1832, which was perhaps the inspiration behind many philanthropic gestures, many squares became open to everybody. Unfortunately they became run-down, but partly due to campaigning by the GHS, and later London Parks and Gardens Trust, the Heritage Lottery Fund has made money available to bring them back into order. Mavis considered that public parks should be parks for the people when restored, with walks and green spaces where people could relax and, as well as children's playgrounds, there should be areas provided for recreational activities such as tennis and netball.

In September 1989 after arriving in Moscow, the group enjoyed a tour around the city, and the following day they flew to Lvov near the Polish border and visited a village of reconstructed houses, but sadly living conditions were very poor. A visit was made to Striiski Park, created in 1822 by the architect Rering. They admired the many good buildings in the park and in particular praised a fine natural setting of trees to which had been added many fine and rare species. Reconstruction was in progress, especially of the lakes and fountains. On an unheralded visit to the University Botanic Gardens led by the city's chief engineer, it was noticed that they were having difficulties. 'We found the plantings by which the staff set store neither impressive nor well maintained, but their research may well be very good – we had no way of telling. The glasshouses, in course of reconstruction, were better, with collections from Australia, New Zealand and Mexico. It is sad that these enthusiastic people do not have better facilities.'[6] It was a fantastic tour and not another thing could have been packed into the crowded programme.

Mavis saw that a friendly relationship had been building up between the GHS and those interested in garden history and conservation in Eastern European countries. Listening to their stories when they returned home Mavis felt that a conference, open to all interested people, particularly those from Eastern Europe, would be a good way of encouraging future links between the countries. In May 1991 a conference, *The English Gardens Overseas: Eastern Europe,* was held in Oxford with the Oxford University Department for Continuing Education, and Tony Baggs was responsible for the considerable organisation involved. The range of speakers from home and guest speakers from Eastern Europe was admirable: Andrzei Kostolowski from Poland, Dmitri Shvidkovsky from Russia, Jozsef Sisa from Hungary and Olga Basceova from Czechoslovakia, and it was pleasing that connections with these delegates continued.

One theme was the *Influence of the English Garden in Eastern Europe.* It was a full programme and a visit to Rousham was included. When writing a review of the conference Mavis brought attention to the way historic gardens had often been destroyed to make way for English ideas and 'restoration schemes had got underway, even under Communist rule, by playing the system and maintaining that the cost and effort was a tribute to the original workers who had laid the gardens out'.[7] The progress of English ideas across the Continent was followed, pointing out that many made the Grand Tour in reverse and tried to emulate in Eastern Europe what they had seen in our landscaped gardens.

Each of the Eastern European countries had been affected by the English style: Kostolowski explained that Poland was quick off the mark and this was through direct contact; in Hungary the English style arrived at the end of the eighteenth century and was a greater understanding of the principles behind the English garden. The picturesque was apparent and an illustration was shown of a cottage orné with a smoking chimney in a woodland scene straight out of Repton. In the Czech lands of the Habsburg Empire, the landscape movement moved more slowly than in Poland and became most prevalent in the early nineteenth century when the magnificent baroque garden at Lednice with its sculpture gallery and fountains was naturalised. In Bohemia and Moravia spa resorts were laid out in the English Regency style.

There was a discussion about books and their influence on promoting the style, and importantly Mavis pointed to the wealth of information still to be tapped in untranslated journals and letters.

The visit to Rousham was rewarding, giving the opportunity for the GHS to bring the English garden into sharper focus. It is interesting to see what is original about the style through the eyes of Eastern Europe with its different traditions and history.

Mavis brought the conference to a close, saying:

The conference gave us a real opportunity to bring the English garden into a sharper focus by seeing what is original about the style through the eyes of Eastern Europe with its different traditions and history… Our weekend study of a shared cultural heritage in the English garden left us with a new sense of friendship and desire for co-operation with our Eastern European partners, and we are delighted that our guest speakers were so grateful to be made honorary members of the society.[8]

This was a conference that sealed friendships.

The GHS made a further trip to Moscow in 1991, and Marion Waller, the society's publicity officer, was able to contact Russian members of the GHS and take them more books together with a small grant from the Silver Jubilee Fund, as approved by its trustees. The grant was given towards the founding of a Russian Garden History Society and the publication of the successful journal, *Public Prospects*. The members of the new society were delighted, and Mavis is reported as having received a letter from Dmitri Shvidkovsky, now chairman of the Society of Architectural and Garden History, Russia, expressing extreme gratitude for the help given to establish studies and to begin publications in the field of garden history. Further grants followed, enabling the translation of Eastern European journals.

Visits to Russia continued and Mavis and the Shvidkovskys enjoyed further correspondence and it was hoped that Dmitri and Katyia would visit again in 1994.

When being interviewed for the National Sound Archive in March 2003 Mavis revealed that Shvidkovsky had told her that he had become interested in Hoskins and would have liked to look at the Russian landscape in the same way as Hoskins had looked at the English. However, he pointed out that England was so tiny that when coming out of Oxford the landscape changed every half hour, and he felt that Russian landscape was too big for it to be examined in the same way as by Hoskins. He thought Hoskins' method was more suited to England.

One of Shvidkovsky's reasons for visiting England was to see how our 'volunteers' and 'friends' worked and how such an organisation could be started. Mavis told him he had a problem:

> Under communism you could not even form a group. Volunteers could not be coped with. We started with amenity societies and it has been going on for centuries – started by people like Ruskin, Octavia Hill, Morris and the National Trust. The idea comes from something small, but stage by stage it works. You can't just legislate and hope it will happen because half the time it won't. It will come, no doubt. You must do pilot schemes to show it will work. Things are different now – there is too much media.[9]

Mavis never did travel to Russia, but her interest was intense. She thoroughly enjoyed the conference and entertaining visitors and was proud that GHS international relationships were continuing to develop. The Shvidkovsky family remained her friends and correspondence continued to go to and fro.

CHAPTER FIFTEEN
A New Home:
Living on the South Coast

In 1985 Keith retired from Christ Church and in 1987 he and Mavis moved to a Regency cottage orné, West House, Aldwick, near Bognor, West Sussex. '... we were looking around for a house when we saw this "For Sale" notice. It was an absolutely charming cottage with picturesque Gothic windows and we couldn't believe our eyes.'[1] There was no hesitation, it was immediately decided that this was the place for them and purchase was arranged.

Keith was able to keep his flat in Oxford, which was near the railway station and convenient for all the family to use on various occasions, but he also wanted the opportunity to be near the sea. Mavis was enthralled with the architecture; the cottage was built with brick and flint and covered with Regency stucco – there was a balcony and low ceilings, and the pretty Regency Gothic windows delighted her – and she claimed they were straight from Jane Austen.

Mavis, as usual, was quick to start delving into the history of the house and, many years later, among her papers a charming note was found with a description of West House which she had obviously lost no time in writing:

West House was a Sussex farmhouse with cornfields stretching down to the sea in the 1760's. In the Napoleonic Wars there was a camp nearby, hence the name Barrack Lane… After the war a sailor bought the house with some prize money, and converted it into a picturesque seaside *cottage orné* with Strawberry Hill windows, and fashionable Roman Cement to cover the brick and flint, and it was re-named West Cottage. The ever observant Jane Austen, who had an eye for such foibles, commented in *Persuasion* that a farmhouse had recently been elevated into a cottage with a verandah and pretty windows. We have had to revert to the name West House as there is now another West Cottage in the lane – it was formerly the stables for our 'cottage'.

Following her usual practice Mavis researched the previous owners of the cottage. She discovered there had been several previous owners and it had more recently belonged to Duff Cooper and Lady Diana Cooper, née Manners. They had made changes to the house when it became their retreat from the horrors of London during the war years and Lady Diana's mother, the Duchess of Rutland, stayed with them. The duchess did not like low ceilings; rooms in the cottage were not quite like those of her home, Belvoir Castle, where she usually lived – so they added a master bedroom with a high ceiling from where she was able to see the sea.

Duff Cooper had been chairman of the Cabinet Security Committee at the time of 'Operation Mincemeat' at Bletchley Park and he wrote a novel about it, *Operation Heartbreak*. Ewen Montagu, who had taken part in the deception, wrote an officially sanctioned account in *The Man Who Never Was* (1953), which sold nearly two million copies, but of course the real truth could not be told.

Noel Annan described Lady Diana as a '*declasse aristocrat,* one of a set of spirited women including Nancy Mitford, [and] Ann Fleming who had broken out of the suffocating embrace of eligible matches and estates'.[2] Diana Manners was the reigning beauty of the Asquith and Grenfell set when being courted by Duff Cooper in the early twenties, and she was setting a new style in upper-class circles. 'To drink whisky and soda in public would have been thought common, but she drank vodka and absinthe in private and asked openly at parties which would be the soporific for the night – morphia or "jolly old chlorers".[3] However, there was a refined side to her character and as a member of the *Souls,* who Lady Bonham Carter considered 'unconventional but neither fast nor loose',[4] she encouraged playing bridge or party games as evening entertainment, and it became considered an accomplishment to be able to 'turn a set of light verses'; they should be well read and able to quote from the poets. Lady Diana Cooper went along with this trend, and there must have been wonderful beach parties at West House which would surely have appealed to the romantic imagination of Mavis and her young daughters.

Once there had been a front garden to the beach, but previous owners had sold the access and the view was blocked by a bungalow. However, the path to the beach was just along the road and the whole family spent many enjoyable days playing and picnicking on the sandy shore; it was beautiful, and empty, and clean enough for a crop of kale to grow. Another advantage was that Mavis and Keith were nearer to their children and seven grandchildren. Their son was at Brighton, and Elizabeth, their elder daughter, was married to a general practitioner and living at Worthing.

The family must have been pleased to have a house by the sea, but they had been at Aldwick for only a year when they had quite a shock. They had been kept awake all night by a very fierce gale: it was exciting, but also sad, for when they looked out at dawn and saw all the trees lying down they just could not believe it and they must have felt relieved that there was a bungalow between their house and the sea. Mavis remembered this later when recording for the National Archive:

Here we are choosing leafy Sussex to come to, and here we are, all the roots standing out like huge giants with white chalky soil on them. They looked absolutely grotesque on the chalk downs… Pines did not go as quickly as the deciduous ones which were very heavy;

because the leaves were still on the trees you did not hear bangs. They swayed and swayed and they were cushioned by all the leaves. We didn't hear the bangs all around. So you could not understand how it had all happened.[5]

Mavis became a member of the English Heritage Storm Damage Committee and was asked to go to a committee meeting in Arundel. The castle grounds were badly damaged and in some places the walls were down. The deer had escaped and one animal was found wandering around a supermarket.

The great storm of 1987 had been so ferocious over the south and south-east of England that complete plantations of fir trees lay like matchsticks across the landscape. However, this did provoke a catalyst for change, and for the first time a system of grant aid was administered by English Heritage and the Countryside Commission towards the cost of dealing with storm damage. So bad was the destruction it was a difficult task to allocate the funds – most of the money could have been given to Arundel alone, nevertheless, the late Jeremy Benson, chairman of the English Heritage Garden Committee, was said to have done a very good job.

Grants... were not only conditional on well conducted surveys and researches but also on the production of 'management plans' to provide a rationale for restoration and replanting; crucially the grant also paid a high proportion of the cost.[6]

Every application had to be considered and, although the south was the worst hit, funds had to be eked out and allocated towards rectifying damage countrywide.

Mavis was concerned when she heard that two of her favourite gardens had suffered. A great deal of Mount Edgcumbe was dominated by large trees which had fought against the elements; there was a fierce and prevailing south-west wind, and Nuneham Courtenay also suffered a great loss of trees. Unfortunately, the destruction caused by native trees and large exotics being brought down was succeeded by other problems when large trees fell upon small. The many millions of trees believed to be lost presented a difficult situation, and as time went by the number increased. Fortunately, the result of the grant system brought a change in attitude towards the preservation and maintenance of historic parks and gardens and stimulated the development of expertise in areas of conservation work by putting more emphasis on research and education and providing grant aid. The grant system resulted in a change in attitude towards the preservation and maintenance of historic parks and gardens and was a stimulus to the development of expertise in these areas of conservation work.

'There were so many trees brought down that views and vistas were changed and it was amazing how many people were heard to say "Oh look, I can see the sea." That remark was to be heard over and over again,' [7] Mavis recorded. 'It was a sad scene for miles around, and although natural regeneration was much quicker than expected, it involved a great deal of hard work with the clearing of debris, building new walls, repairing roofs and planting new trees – the list was endless – but it was not too long before the countryside was green again,'[8] Mavis recalled.

West House proved to be an ideal place for family gatherings, and there was an endless stream of visitors from Bletchley days who still kept in touch. Of course, Margaret Rock came to stay. Mavis and Margaret always remembered their favourite quote of Dilly's when he referred to Margaret and Mavis working together: 'Give me a Rock and a Lever and I can move the universe.' After the war, Margaret and Mavis went to Eastcote with GCHQ to work on Russian codes. Margaret was appointed an MBE and continued working at GCHQ until her retirement in 1963. She always remained a close friend of the Bateys.

Peter Twinn and John Herival, chess-playing friends of Keith, both came with their families. Peter Twinn and Keith had become firm friends and it was Peter who had been Keith's best man at his wedding. John Herival had been recruited from Cambridge by

Gordon Welchman in January 1940 and all three had worked together at Bletchley Park.

When this little group of friends came together they did not often refer to their past life at Bletchley Park, but would be open to talk about anything new that was currently happening there, particularly if it was news about other people they had all known.

Mavis and Keith seldom discussed their war years at Bletchley Park, but they were surprised when they heard that James Bamford, who they had known whilst working there, had written a book called *The Puzzle Palace* – it had been published in 1974 but could not be released until 1982. The National Security Agency (NSA) in America had evidently been trying to put a halt on publication as it revealed a lot of inside information, but they were unsuccessful.

One man they all knew well and admired was Gordon Welchman, and in 1982 it was his turn to be in the news. Gordon had written his book *The Hut Six Story* which he had been working on for a considerable time, but hindered by the Secrets Act he had delayed until officially allowed to publish. The British were also against publication of any book revealing information about activities of the NSA or their own SIS, also any technical information concerning machines at Bletchley Park.

Gordon Welchman had always observed the rules and never spoke of Bletchley Park to his friends and family, but *The Hut Six Story* which he started in 1974 was a complete technical account of activities in Hut 6. The British and American Governments did not want these details discussed and he met with pressure to remain silent. It is unlikely that he found this difficult as he even refused to contribute to a film, broadcast by the BBC in 1977. He was conscientious and never discussed his work at Bletchley Park, refusing to participate unless he had official written permission. However, although he did have his reasons for feeling anxious to publish, he waited a while, and his book did not appear until 1982. Welchman was popular with his group of friends and all were pleased to hear that the book had eventually been published.

'Government Communications', was the announcement made on the gate at Bletchley Park; an ambiguous statement that did not give much away. It was unlikely that the townsfolk, or the enemy, would link this to codebreaking or telecommunications, but there really were carrier pigeons in the stableyard. Mavis said they supplied the perfect alibi for the work being carried out at Bletchley Park and pigeons became yet another of her interests.

In 1937, with the threat of war lurking, realising the importance of the part that could be played by pigeons, the National Pigeon Service was set up. The Army, Royal Air Force and Royal Navy all held sections of the NPS and 'by the end of World War II nearly 200,000 pigeons had been given to the war effort by private fanciers'.[9]

Pigeons were kept in the stable loft at Bletchley Park during WWII, and were managed by a local man, Charles Stevington, from Newport Pagnell. He worked for a corn merchant, and as a keen pigeon fancier it became his duty to tend the pigeons at Bletchley Park. This was important work, and classed as a 'reserved occupation', so excusing him from military service.

Stevington trained the birds, some playing a vital role during the war when they would be collected by special agents who flew them out to a venue in Europe where they would be dropped by parachute. It was important that they should be securely wrapped to prevent injury – but nevertheless, they might sometimes be killed or injured in the drop, or attacked by predators such as peregrines or sparrowhawks. For a while Bletchley Park had its own agents' traffic coming in, but that was brought to an end when in order not to attract too much attention the wireless was taken down from the huge wellingtonia tree Station X, which supported it.

It was not unusual for pigeons to be dropped behind enemy lines to resistance workers or spies, and on some occasions double-cross messages were sent out to them by pigeons. Messages would be attached to the pigeons' legs before releasing them to fly back to their British base. They were usually released in pairs, two males or two females, to avoid any promiscuous distractions and, when they returned carrying their messages, as they approached their loft the cooing of their mates could be heard – a welcoming sound. Most British bombers carried pigeons; if the plane should be put out of action and the radio damaged, the pigeons would be there to carry a message back to base.

The pigeon loft at Bletchley Park was close by the Cottage. Mavis enjoyed simple pleasures and liked to visit the birds, and sometimes she would hitch a ride when they were being driven to their point of release. Her voice betrayed her pride as she thoughtfully remembered these occasions:

> … he was a very nice man in charge of them. They weren't let off at Bletchley – it was quite near London, in a park, and we used to get lifts almost into London with the pigeons sometimes, because obviously we could then get a Tube into London. I don't know where it was, but I have actually let the pigeons off… and they came back… Some of them got awards; you can get awards for bravery if you are a pigeon, too. There was everything. We were a real spy world even down to the pigeons.[10]

The bravery of pigeons has long been remembered, and after WWII thirty-two pigeons were honoured with the Dicken Medal donated by the People's Dispensary for Sick Animals. In 1922 a section of the grounds of the Beach House estate, Worthing was purchased by Sussex Borough Council, and after World War II a memorial was commissioned by the actress Nancy Price in honour of pigeons who had given their services during the war years. The sculptor was a local man, Leslie Sharp, who worked on it in the late 1940s, and the memorial was unveiled on 27 July 1951 by the Duke and Duchess of Hamilton.

Two stone pigeons once stood on a small rockery in the garden of the Beach House estate, with shrubs, streams and pools of water – and two boulders were carved with the words:

IN MEMORY OF WARRIOR BIRDS WHO GAVE THEIR LIVES ON ACTIVE SERVICE, 1939-1945, AND FOR THE USE AND PLEASURE OF LIVING BIRDS

The second stone bears a quotation from the Book of Ecclesiastes:

A BIRD OF THE AIR SHALL CARRY THE VOICE AND THAT WHICH HATH WINGS SHALL TELL THE MATTER. THIS MEMORIAL IS PRESENTED BY NANCY PRICE AND THE MEMBERS OF THE PEOPLE'S THEATRE, LONDON.

Many years later, when Mavis's grandchildren visited her at West House, if they took a trip into Worthing they would stop at the garden and Mavis would tell them tales of the adventures of the pigeons during the war years. It is sad that the two stone pigeons were stolen, but Worthing Borough Council kindly arranged for the upkeep of the two boulders, and a fence has been installed to discourage further vandalism.

West House was cosy, with the sound of the sea ever present, and with a beautiful seaward view from the top floor. There was a nature reserve nearby that Mavis would visit; she would watch the wintering birds in Pagham Harbour and was thrilled by the storms that hurled pebbles horizontally from the beach towards the house. She was able to cast her eye around the landscape and find the picturesque, the beautiful and the sublime; all were there to please her.

They had a tiny garden and, in keeping with the Regency style of the house, Mavis decided it should have 'Regency flounces' such as William Gilpin would have recommended at the Royal Pavilion, Brighton, before John Nash made an entrance. 'Then you can put in whatever you like as long as the flounces are retained,'[11] said Mavis. That would be easy for Mavis as she never pretended to be a practical gardener, but Keith would often oblige and meet her requests. She thought of herself as a theorist, never really a garden designer and Mavis loved to visit other gardens, particularly if there was history trailing behind.

There were also happy family holidays when they might be joined by the Herivals. They sometimes went to Cornwall, and there was one memorable holiday in Ullapool, Scotland. It was the height of the midge season and poor Mavis was bitten to shreds – perhaps another reason why she did not indulge in practical gardening. Keith was more fortunate; the midges gave him a wide berth.

When Mavis and Keith decided to move for the last time, the estate agent called and was quite overwhelmed by their presence. He had summed them up as the average 'Mr and Mrs Pepperpot', but he had most certainly got his sums wrong on that occasion. Nevertheless, this did give Mavis and Keith a reason to laugh, when they remembered the pepper pot Dilly had given Mavis and that the girls used to play with when they were little.

When the agent arrived Mavis was sitting with a large pile of dusty reference books around her and gave him a brisk talk on the history of the house, spattered with historic and literary references that he pretended to recognise, and he is later to have been known to say, 'She demanded to know if I knew my Jane Austen'. He had learned that Mavis had made what he called a 'myriad of achievements' and she had written a book about Jane Austen. He felt glad that he did not have a lot to say, as Mavis and Keith continued telling the long history of the house, 'and they knew it all, down to the early-nineteenth century building methods used to create the front garden wall'.

He tried to compete and rattled off the guest list of Duff Cooper and his wife that included people like Winston Churchill and Ian Fleming and most were known to Mavis and Keith. 'They all used to drop in' he told them '...It is amazing to think that those people looked out of the same windows you are looking out of now. Very glamorous and all. But not half so glamorous as the very different geniuses who've been looking out of those same windows since 1986.'[12]

He was pleased to have the last word and added that Lady Diana Cooper spent much of the war at West House 'keeping cows, in her charming way, and entertaining her snazzy friends... the house once *throbbed with fashionability*'.

CHAPTER SIXTEEN
Two Regency Gardens

Whilst living at Aldwick, Mavis remained very active in garden history and conservation work. She became involved in teaching a number of courses at West Dean College, in West Sussex, which she found particularly rewarding as she had a number of foreign students who were appreciative of the landscape and this, she said, 'spurred one on'.

Mavis had become interested in Regency gardens when leading the team of GHS members and giving advice on a contemporary layout for the garden of Keats House at Hampstead, North London. Local people were consulted and Mavis learned a lot, particularly about Regency planting, including the flora available in the Regency period, both garden and wild flowers, and newly introduced plants and shrubs from North America and the East. Through her involvement with various Regency projects a Regency file was established, and this was to prove useful in the future with other Regency gardens and assisting those producing films set in Regency gardens.

Another project with which Mavis was personally involved came about in the late 1980s when the idea of restoring the grounds of Brighton's Royal Pavilion was mooted by the newly formed Sussex Historic Gardens Restoration Society. Supported by Marion Waller, deputy director of the Royal Pavilion, Mavis started to explore the possibility of recreating the gardens, although at that time there was no definite evidence that an original design for the garden had been created. Mavis was enthralled by the oriental grandeur of the architecture of the Royal Pavilion which would form the backdrop of the garden. It would be enchanting.

Mavis had no doubt heard of this beautiful building being used as a hospital for Indian soldiers at the close of World War I and would have agreed with the journalist Michael MacDonagh, who wrote that 'for once its ridiculous Regency oriental fantasies are "harmonised. A thrilling experience to see in the grounds dusky and turbaned Oriental warriors".'[1] Mavis would not have thought the architecture to be ridiculous but many have considered it to be. It might once perhaps have been 'the shock of the new' that allowed the pavilion to be described as in bad taste, but gradually the grace and subtlety of the curves of its domes and arches became thought harmonious and undeniably beautiful. Bathed in the day's ever changing light this architectural fantasy of Eastern mystery could not fail to kindle a desire in the 'Romantically' inspired Mavis to re-create the gardens, and to persuade the pavilion's director to grant her wish that a re-created Regency landscape would be the ideal setting for the building which was about to undergo intensive restoration.

The Regency style of gardening was popular in its heyday, but few examples can be found today, however Mavis and Marion were excited to take up the challenge of designing the flower beds at Brighton Pavilion. Once approved, there would be extensive research to be carried out and this would most certainly please her.

Virginia Hinze, a member of the GHS, was chosen as the landscape architect whose role it was to design the restored garden layout and the detailed planting schemes for the fifteen or so beds and to manage the contract for the works. There was soon a bond between the three women, each enthusiastically striving to achieve the best possible results, and when pooling their knowledge they made a successful team.

Virginia praises Mavis and Marion, saying they gave her invaluable research advice and information which she was able to capitalise on.

Together with her additional research into plant introductions and the detailed study of various historic maps of the pavilion estate which were brought to her attention, this pool of information enabled Virginia to design the restored garden layout and planting schemes.

The boundaries of the gardens had changed over the years and some alterations to the landscaping were necessary, but unlike many other projects which Mavis had worked upon these gardens were not under threat of development of buildings or roads. This was a more romantic task, and they found themselves researching Regency gardens, from cottage gardens to flowery shrubberies and early plant introductions, as well as new styles in planting.

It was an extensive undertaking. Paintings, prints and drawings were discovered, and among one of the most valuable finds was the Prince Regent's architect, John Nash's *Views of the Royal Pavilion* (1826) which gave a good idea of what he had envisaged and the vision to which Mavis, Marion and Virginia were striving. The catalogues of nurserymen of earlier times were searched, including the books of the Regency gardener, Henry Phillips. He was a Sussex man who had probably witnessed the planting of the pavilion's pleasure gardens, and had published *Sylva Florifera* (1823) and *Flora Historica* (1824) which were particularly useful. It was in 1823 that Phillips spoke of the popularity of floriferous shrubberies, which were part of the Regency garden design that could be found in spa gardens, public parks, college gardens, botanical gardens and private pleasure gardens, and the style often used in the garden of the cottage orné.

That same year Phillips drew up a design for a floriferous planting plan to be used in a garden in neighbouring Kemp Town, and his books gave suggestions for planting schemes. When writing about shrubberies he recommended that evergreen shrubs should be planted first, with attention paid to their various hues. Hollyhocks, martagon lilies, peonies, foxgloves, day lilies, sunflowers and Michaelmas daisies to be planted in recesses, with climbing shrubs ornamenting bare trunks of small trees also to be included. North American plants accompanied by new plants from the Orient brought colour – always a consideration of Phillips.

The final stage of the restoration of the Royal Pavilion grounds began in 1991. The purple pansies of Victorian-style bedding schemes were swept away; the tarmac service road which had been allowed to cut off the pavilion from the lawns was ripped up and grassed over, and Nash's turning circle in front of the *porte-cochère* was reinstated by arrangement with the Hove and Brighton Urban Conservation Project. Curving paths were introduced to wend their way around the newly created picturesque, floriferous shrubberies, and the strolling public were treated to glimpses of the strange beauty of the domes and minarets of the Orient.

The Royal Pavilion, enhanced by its fantastical garden, has become a special place; Virginia Hinze is responsible for the authentic planting on the approach lawns, as seen in Nash's views, which were particularly successful and went on to be maintained by a team of volunteer gardeners. The re-creation of the garden and grounds of the Royal Pavilion is outstanding and, listed Grade II by English Heritage, they were added to the Register of Parks and Gardens for East Sussex.

The glorious Royal Pavilion is greatly admired by the people of Brighton. The Red Drawing Room of the original marine villa, where the Prince of Wales had lived clandestinely with Mrs Fitzherbert 200 years earlier, is now a favourite choice for romantic weddings. Indeed, no grandmother was so excited as Mavis when in 2006 she attended her granddaughter's wedding there, and photographs were taken in the gardens of the Royal Pavilion.

The upkeep and maintenance of a garden after its original creation or re-creation is something that is frequently neglected, but this was not so with the pavilion garden. For several years Virginia remained as an advisor and ensured proper maintenance by helping to set up a volunteer group (and at the time of writing), a surviving and still thriving gardening group.

Mavis always enjoyed meeting people, particularly those involved with local projects, so she was delighted when the idea for a new Regency garden at Alverstoke, near the seaside town of Gosport, was brought to her notice and she agreed to make a visit.

When moving to Alverstoke Crescent the artist in Wendy Osborne was quickly alerted and she pondered over her dream to recreate a Regency garden there. In 1991 she became involved with a group of local people preparing for the restoration of the neglected park opposite her home, and had sketched a design for its possible restoration. Knowing nothing of garden history, she was amazed to learn her gardening friends had forwarded her plan to the GHS. When she heard that Mavis Batey would be paying her a visit she was overcome: 'I made cucumber sandwiches and expected a grand formidable lady,' but Wendy was surprised when Mavis arrived 'laden with carrier bags, an un-intimidating, smallish lady. Research notes and copies of plans (mine included!) tumbled out of the bags, and a new field of learning was opened for me,'[2] explained Wendy, who considers herself very fortunate to have met Mavis.

The two ladies got to know each other over tea and it was a friendship, linked by garden history, that continued over the years. Wendy valued Mavis's help and Mavis too was very happy and enthusiastic about helping. And she must most certainly have been overjoyed when she discovered there were links with the Austen family. Jane Austen's younger brother, Captain Charles Austen of the Royal Navy, and his young family, lived nearby in the early 1830s and, when visited by his sister Cassandra, they would surely have enjoyed a stroll around the crescent gardens to take the fresh air and admire the view over the Solent to the Isle of Wight beyond.

The garden had an interesting history. Robert Cruickshank was a well-known Gosport entrepreneur who wanted to create a fashionable new Regency spa such as that at Brighton. His plan encompassed a 1.36-acre plot, a semicircle of land situated before a crescent of semi-detached and individual neoclassical houses.

Cruickshank commissioned a twenty-one-year-old local architect, Thomas Ellis Owen, to carry out his scheme, but unfortunately it proved to be too ambitious and not all the proposed buildings were achieved; only the first half of the ornamental garden was built. Nevertheless, there were views to the Isle of Wight from the raised terrace, and a ha-ha was constructed to prevent cattle straying from their grazing area between the garden and the sea. The garden was enclosed by railings and at the centre was a small neoclassical building, a curved reading room with bath houses on each side where warm and cold sea water baths could be taken. It is interesting that there was also a similar bath house with a reading room at Kemp Town Spa neighbouring Brighton Pavilion.

Alas, over time there have inevitably been a few changes made to the garden; the marine terrace promenade with its beautiful views and long, straight flower bed was swept away when a new road and houses were built. Nevertheless, there is always a bright side, and the owners of the later houses came together with the people of the crescent to contribute their comments on the plans for a new garden and it was, of course, the Regency style that was chosen.

It was once a 'key garden'; subscribing tenants met the cost of the gardener, Henry Cooper, who lived under the reading room and paid a fixed rent of thirty shillings a week, but gradually costs increased and, after World War I, the rise in the cost of labour became prohibitive and the gardener could no longer be employed. During World War II the iron railings, as throughout the country, were compulsorily donated as scrap metal contributing to the manufacture of munitions. The visual impact of the garden changed completely and it became a wilderness. However, in 1949 Cruickshank's great-great-granddaughter handed over control to the Gosport Borough Council as an open space for the enjoyment of the people of Gosport. Sadly, the reading room and bath houses were demolished in 1950.

At the end of the 1980s the Hampshire Gardens Trust was approached by the chairman of Gosport Borough Council, Freddie Emery Wallis, who liaised with the trust's chairlady, Gilly Drummond, over matters concerning the garden crescent and together they made useful decisions.

With the help of English Heritage they carefully perused the original plans drawn up when Angleseyville was evolving and were soon smitten by the potential of this now derelict area. English Heritage gave substantial grant aid for restoration of the railings and the original path layout, and together with Gosport Borough Council the Re-Generation of Older Areas Programme began.

The railings were restored and the Anthemion heads which had survived were reinstated, and the original path layout was re-created in Breedon gravel. This layout was copied from maps of the period when Angleseyville was evolving. Maintenance is something that is frequently forgotten, but fortunately Gosport Borough Council agreed to cut the grass and donated some shrubs. Wendy and her gardening companions in the crescent formed a group – Friends of Crescent Garden.

Wendy had become friendly with Mavis, who was so generous with her knowledge and together they decided to adapt a plan for a villa garden in the picturesque manner from J. C. Loudon's *The Suburban Gardener and Villa Companion* (1838). There was no place for rigid garden beds of the Victorian era; and the more natural and fluid, flowing style with the floriferous borders of Henry Phillips was introduced, reflecting that of the Regency garden of the Royal Pavilion. The Friends were meticulous in their planting; they took trouble to locate specialist nurseries prepared to supply them with plants of the chosen period, and it was agreed there should be no plants included that were introduced into this country after 1850.

Gilly Drummond recommended to Wendy that Hazel Le Rougetel should be approached as old-fashioned roses were her speciality. Wendy wanted to be sure that everything was correct, so went off to meet Hazel, who was extremely helpful with her advice. 'I went home and thought of little else… But I tried to think like Loudon – I drew a draft suggestion for the garden's central area and sent it to Hazel.' Hazel telephoned Wendy at eight o'clock the following morning and asked if she could send Wendy's plan to her friend Mavis! 'That is how it all began,'[3] remembered Wendy, and the two ladies remained friends for three decades, with Mavis always on hand to give support and encouragement.

There was an almost impenetrable thicket bordering the Terrace Walk which held little evidence of the original planting, but the Friends were undaunted, and the overall design gradually emerged and was said by Wendy to be influenced strongly by Regency garden writers Henry Phillips, Charles McIntosh, William Sawrey Gilpin and J. C. Loudon. The deep bays and indentures of the central beds were continued more shallowly in sinuous and grassy curves, regulated by existing trees and shrubs which formed a backbone of evergreens: 'Hollies, bays, Arbutus and *Prunus lusitanica*... A walk was formed giving interest and variety,' wrote Wendy. 'Henry Phillips' dramatic touches, Laburnum, waving its golden treasure over the snowy Guelder Rose, against the sombre evergreens... "splendid ornaments" of flowery climbers, are all beginning to add excitement and colour.'[4]

The creation of this Regency garden is just one of the achievements of the Friends of Crescent Gardens. Just as commendable as the effort put into the re-creation of the garden is the pleasure given by the many organised activities, including gardening, visits to other gardens around the south of England, open days and fundraising events. The garden is enjoyed by all those in and around the community who raise funds for its upkeep as well as money for charitable causes.

The hardworking Friends earned a very well deserved reward when they received the Green Flag Award – and a Green Heritage Award – for this historic garden.

Mavis was excited by the various Regency gardens that came to her notice and she hoped her small book entitled *Regency Gardens* would encourage the restoration of more gardens of this period.

In June 2004 the GHS and the Friends of the Royal Pavilion Art Gallery and Museum held a study day on Regency gardens at the Royal Pavilion. Participants who had come from far and wide were enthralled and, as vice president of the GHS, Mavis gave a talk on 'Regency Gardens' and Wendy Osborne an illustrated presentation on 'The Crescent Garden at Alverstoke, Gosport'. A guided tour of the gardens of the Royal Pavilion was also arranged and led by Virginia Hinze and proved extremely popular. The Royal Pavilion has perhaps played a wide role in making Brighton once again a popular seaside resort.

CHAPTER SEVENTEEN

Thames Landscape Strategy: Hampton to Kew and The Garden at Strawberry Hill House

Interest aroused by the Thames Connection exhibition at the Royal Fine Art Commission in 1991 stimulated a full study of the River Thames from Hampton to Kew which led to the launch of the *Thames Landscape Strategy* by the Minister for Local Government and Planning.

Mavis had first got to know this stretch of the Thames in her early years, for this was where her youngest daughter, Deborah, had lived. 'Deborah had a villa in Twickenham, not Palladian by the River, of course, but William IV by the station, and I used to pram push [my grandchildren] along the towpath.'[1] As this was her favourite part of the River Thames Mavis was full of enthusiasm, particularly because she had firm links with Strawberry Hill House and Garden which she knew were considered to be of major importance in the enhancement proposals. Mavis was a regular visitor to Strawberry Hill House and, although it had become in need of attention, she was still very fond of the garden. When her pram-pushing days were behind her Mavis remained an admirer of Strawberry Hill House and, of course, the garden, and became an active supporter and patron.

Kim Wilkie, landscape architect and urban designer, presented his vision for the future of the River Thames based on his ideas for the restoration of the network of historic vistas, avenues and landscapes linking the great houses and palaces along and across this stretch of the Thames. Through his work, local residents became interested, the community became involved, and the Thames Landscape Strategy was launched on 14 June 1994. This was a professional report, an approved background policy document guiding planning strategy with support from central and local government bodies.

Kim Wilkie first met Mavis Batey when she was peering over his drawings in the exhibition:

'So when are you going to start?' she asked and before I knew it, she had mobilised south-west London to support the abstract ideas and they had become a project. This was the beginning of the Thames Landscape Strategy and the start of my friendship with Mavis and [her husband] Keith.[2]

There was a successful Heritage Lottery Funded bid, and the strategy was also funded by The Royal Parks; the Royal Botanic Gardens, Kew; the Port of London Authority; the Father Thames Trust; the Countryside Agency; English Heritage; the National Trust; and Elmbridge, Hounslow, Richmond and Surrey Councils.

Mavis had kept up with what was going on, and when walking along the Thames she saw there were many vistas which needed to be kept open, but there was a problem; she learned that both sides of the Thames would be affected – one side was under the jurisdiction of Middlesex and the other, Surrey – and they had obviously never communicated. Mavis recorded:

It all began because there was a planning application at Twickenham by Marks and Spencer, and this was followed by another by the old deer park, again for further development. It was obvious that this was going to happen all along the line if something was not done to give it some real protected designation of some kind...'[3]

Mavis had also become very knowledgeable not only on the history of Strawberry Hill and its garden, but with most of the characters who had connections there. She chatted to Kim Wilkie about the Thames Strategy and agreed that she would be prepared to give help if needed.

On behalf of the GHS Mavis devoted a great deal of her time and expert knowledge to persuading official bodies to give grants, seeking wider support for the project, and she would frequently join Kim Wilkie and David Lambert for meetings, as well as focusing on Strawberry Hill which she knew would also soon be undergoing refurbishment.

Mavis had built upon her knowledge of Strawberry Hill over the past few years and had learned that Horace Walpole (1717-1797), son of the first British Prime Minister, Sir Robert Walpole, was an art historian and had Strawberry Hill House built as what he called 'his little Gothic Castle'. His 'Twickenhamshire' had been alive with men of letters, celebrities, artists, actors and actresses, not to mention the poets, including James Thomson at Richmond, and the Harcourts and their poet gardener, William Mason, who Mavis so much admired, and whose friendship with Walpole had perhaps originally drawn her attention to this unique place.

In September 1985, no doubt prompted by Mavis's knowledge and familiarity with Strawberry Hill Garden, the GHS decided it would hold a one-day conference at Twickenham and the chosen topic was the influence of poets on landscape. The well-chosen venue was St Mary's College, Twickenham, once part of Strawberry Hill House, but which had been occupied by the college since 1923.

The morning session was on 'Twickenhamshire: Men of letters and their contribution to landscape gardening'. Things got off to a good start with Peter Martin giving new information about Pope's villa. This was followed by Michael Symes speaking on David Garrick, who in 1754 moved into his villa, just along the River Thames, where he built a temple to Shakespeare; the audience then enjoyed hearing a passage from his *Clandestine Marriage*. Next there was a tour of Strawberry Hill House which at the time was shrouded in scaffold. The garden was not mentioned in the report on the conference in the *GHS Newsletter*, so perhaps nothing of importance was happening there at that time.

The group next went along the road to visit Pope's Grotto, passing by the pub of the same name. On returning from their walk Mavis had interesting things to say about Mount Edgcumbe, Cornwall. The garden at Mount Edgcumbe had been strongly influenced by 'Twickenhamshire' ideas, and Mavis reminded the audience that it had always been said that the Edgcumbes were their own gardeners. However, along with the Harcourts of Nuneham Courtenay, and William Mason, the Edgcumbes had been great friends of Walpole, and they too ranked among the many friends of Walpole having an interest in flower gardens. So it was a surprise when Mavis announced that research undertaken by the GHS for Cornwall County Council had revealed a Nuneham-type flower garden, which had been given the name *The English Garden,* in honour of the poet-gardener William Mason who had advised on its creation.

The conference was an excellent day, pre-empting the refurbishment of Strawberry Hill Gardens which they knew would happen in the future. For many people it was their first visit and they were pleased to have the opportunity to get to know Strawberry Hill and its history.

In 1990 the GHS celebrated its twenty-fifth anniversary and it chose to have its celebratory meeting at Strawberry Hill, the home of Horace Walpole, as he had become recognised as the first garden historian.

The 'Thames Landscape Strategy: Hampton Court to Kew' was launched in 1994, and Strawberry Hill was among the properties, in that reach of the Thames, to be considered 'of paramount cultural importance in the enhancement proposals'.[4] The GHS therefore agreed to make a study of the existing gardens. They were fortunate that Walpole had written profusely about the gardens at Strawberry

Hill; however, it must be said that although he had written multiple letters each day on his work on the garden, the information given constantly changed, creating difficulties for researchers, designers and craftsmen. The refurbishment of the garden was not to be an easy task. The researchers were lucky that most items had been covered by Mavis and her fellow authors in their book *The Arcadian Thames*, which they were currently writing, and Mavis was also on hand to help. They were also fortunate that time was not an issue as refurbishment of the property could not commence without permission from various national heritage bodies and money would have to be raised.

However, works on the Thames Landscape Strategy were in hand. When the groundwork began thousands of trees and miles of native hedgerows were planted and laid according to traditional methods. Willows were introduced and reed beds were created to restore the almost lost environment of the riverbank; wildlife was encouraged to habitats created by managed water meadows, and a wild-flower meadow, an idea of Kim Wilkie's, was planted leading from Richmond Hill Terrace down to the river. The essential paraphernalia of street furniture was restored: steps, footpaths, bollards, benches and litter-bins of appropriate design were all addressed. Historic gates and railings were restored or replaced, and vistas overgrown for many years were opened up to reveal historic views for those walking the new towpath.

The remarkable view from Richmond Hill is perhaps the most well known and most treasured for it is the first view in England to be protected by an Act of Parliament. In 1902, the Richmond, Ham and Petersham Open Spaces Act was passed to protect the land on and below Richmond Hill from development, so preserving the views to the west and the south. This splendid panorama has attracted poets and painters, musicians and writers through the ages, including James Thomson, Sir Joshua Reynolds, J. M. W. Turner, John Gay and Sir Walter Scott, and it also served as an out-of-town retreat for a new cultural elite, including Richard Owen Cambridge, David Garrick and garden creators Horace Walpole and Alexander Pope. The garden in England and sensitivity to nature in poetry contributed to art in Europe.

Environmentalists believe that beauty must not be forced upon nature – beauty must be allowed to arise from the landscape. This is a belief that Kim Wilkie's practice is based upon, and it is certainly a belief to which Mavis also subscribed.

Writing was Mavis's first priority, but she loved to socialise. Throughout the following years Kim Wilkie and GHS Conservation Officer, David Lambert, and Mavis and Keith, got to know each other well. Mavis would travel from Bognor Regis to London almost every week to visit Kim in his little studio at the top of a house, at the top of Richmond Hill. David Lambert would come along too. He remembers pausing on Richmond Hill between Kim's flat and Richmond Station and looking down from Terrace Gardens at the famous view; this fired his enthusiasm to get on with the project. They would sit around Kim's table spread with maps and plans of the river dividing up the different reaches. Kim's beautiful model – with the views shown by lines strung tightly between pins – was hung on the wall. They each took around six reaches of the river and wrote a short history for incorporation into the strategy. David said, 'It was good fun as the history was so varied – from poets to boat builders, villas to tin shacks, and Cardinal Wolsey to Fred Karno![5] – and Mavis was just as interested in the rackety side of the Thames as in the elegant.'[6]

They took pleasure in working on the project together and, helped along by a bottle of sherry that Mavis had carried all the way from her home at Aldwick, West Sussex, they would have lively discussions. 'There is a well-known description of the view in Thomson's *Seasons*,' David remembered. '"Which way Amanda shall we bend our course? The choice perplexes. Wherefore should we choose? Tis all the same with thee?"' Did he mean he would walk anywhere with her, or that she didn't care much for the views? Their many successes might also be celebrated with Mavis's sherry, although it must be said that the bottle would occasionally be invited to keep spirits up when the going got tough. Mavis would sometimes take the last train back to Bognor Regis, and Keith was always there to meet her and see her safely home to West House. 'They made a wonderful, witty and enormously generous team,' remembered Kim. Keith was always very supportive of Mavis's work, but he was honest to his feelings and never hesitated to say he had little interest in gardens and garden history. Nevertheless, he would drive her to gardens and meetings and he was often to be seen, whilst waiting for Mavis, sitting in his car in a car park doing *The Times* crossword.

Kim Wilkie was the inspiration behind the complete project, designing the pastoral elements including Richmond Hill, Ham Avenue and towpath, working continuously with Mavis. David Lambert writes, 'The Garden History Society has been closely associated with the project throughout, thanks to Mavis Batey's eye for a visionary idea when she first saw the Royal Fine Art Commission Exhibition.'[7]

The GHS was delighted to play a part in the plan, and when they attended the launch on a beautiful summer evening in 1994, beside the river in Kew Gardens, Mavis and Kim thoroughly enjoyed the best possible introduction to the strategy – a boat trip from Hampton Court to Richmond under the expert guidance of Senior Countryside Officer for London, Henrietta Buttery.

Mavis continued to enjoy life, and in the summer of 1996 she was delighted to see, printed on the opening page of the *Garden History Society Journal: Volume 24: Number 1*, an announcement saying, 'ESSAYS IN HONOUR OF MAVIS BATEY, PRESIDENT OF THE GARDEN HISTORY SOCIETY, PRESENTED IN CELEBRATION OF HER 75TH BIRTHDAY.'

The journal contained a wide selection of essays written by her colleagues. The opening essay *The Genius of the Scene* is written by Ted Fawcett and gives a brief history of Mavis's work for the GHS and when asked about her thoughts on 'garden history', she replied, 'I hope that as many people as possible will visit and love gardens, and their history will become as much a part of our lives as poetry and painting.' Ted Fawcett finished his paper, saying, 'Insatiable curiosity, the scholar's desire for accuracy, the artist's for truth, we have indeed a remarkable president.'

The journal continued with a series of essays about all sorts of garden history topics. Committee member John Anthony writes of the trials and tribulations of conservation and planning; Margaret Campbell-Culver remembers the scholarly enthusiasm and energy of Mavis's Garden History Report presented to the organising committee when applying for planning permission for the garden and landscape at Mount Edgcumbe that brought a successful outcome; Virginia Hinze remembered with joy the time spent recreating John Nash's Regency Gardens at the Royal Pavilion, Brighton; Harriet Jordon, when writing of Skegby Hall in Nottinghamshire praises Mavis as the key player in the instigation and completion of the National Register of Parks and Gardens of Special Interest: 'Without her dedication, energy and willingness to attend meetings, which lacked the incentive of government-funded coffee, it is unlikely that the Register would have yet seen the light of day.' And so these splendid essays continue, all touching on some topic, special garden or landscape dear to Mavis.

The journal was brought to a close by Kim Wilkie who had spent a great deal of time with Mavis Batey and David Lambert when working together on the Thames Landscape Strategy. In Kim Wilkie's essay, the final essay in the journal, *History with a Future*, he writes about the Thames Landscape Strategy and how the project illustrates that 'Far from being narrow and backward looking, landscape history has a great future as the basis for inspiring new design'.

Mavis must have been overwhelmed to have been complimented by such a series of essays. It is a journal to be treasured by every garden historian.

During this period Mavis became friendly with Anna Chalcraft, a founder member of the Friends of Strawberry Hill, a group set up in the mid-eighties, and she soon persuaded Mavis to join her. It was the house that mainly captured Anna's attention but, as always, Mavis had an eye for the garden, and they both had a love for and shared interest in literary research.

Mavis would occasionally combine a visit to Richmond with a visit to Anna at her home and over tea they would talk about their families. When Anna mentioned that her son was a mathematician, she was interested to hear that this was also Keith's profession and they had a conversation about Bletchley Park.

When Mavis discovered that Anna found Charles Dodgson and *Alice in Wonderland* fascinating, she introduced her to people and places that inspired Dodgson, and gave her some of her own writings about them. Alice became a favourite topic of conversation and on many occasions they enjoyed discussion about Dodgson's logic and his books. There were frequent telephone conversations, often concerning *Alice in Wonderland*, and Anna came to believe that Mavis equated Alice with the garden at Strawberry Hill. Anna too became interested in the history of Walpole's garden, and it was probably these two ladies who helped inspire elements of the re-creation of this magical place.

Anna gardened at her home and they had endless discussions about Strawberry Hill Garden and, of course, Horace Walpole, who purchased the site for his retreat in 1747, the last available plot along this beautiful stretch of the Thames. Today the view to the river is interrupted by a housing estate, but a lot of thought has been given to the reconstruction of Strawberry Hill House and Garden, which is punctuated by a magnificent collection of trees, some planted by Walpole and others added by people who followed after him.

Both ladies kept busy and, while Mavis delved into the garden's history, Anna moved up the ranks of volunteers to become a guide showing visitors around the house. She then moved on to become head guide before making another step forward to encourage and train others to become guides. Anna became a patron of the Friends of Strawberry Hill, and later Mavis, along with the Duchess of Devonshire, was also invited to become a patron, and this she was proud to accept.

A trust was set up in 2002 with a mission to restore Strawberry Hill's Gothic villa and garden and to open them to a wider public. Horace Walpole had also opened his Gothic palace to visitors, but became inundated; numbers were restricted and entrance was by ticket purchased in advance. However, Walpole found his visitors so overwhelming that he had a cottage built in a far point of the garden

– no doubt where he could hide away with chosen friends, in a more tranquil situation.

As a patron of the Friends of Strawberry Hill, and representative of the GHS, on 12 July 2000 Mavis attended the launch of the Restoration Appeal by the World Monuments Fund; it was announced that Strawberry Hill Preservation Trust would be dealing with the restoration of the house, making it accessible to the public. The trust, assisted by the GHS, secured £8.9 million in funding for the restoration of the building, and later the garden, of course, and went on to be responsible for the campaigning and fundraising initiative, looking forward to the day when the garden, as well as the house, was once more open to the public.

Even before restoration works were put in hand, Mavis, anxious to bring some publicity to the project, offered to give a talk, probably the first garden talk to be given on the 'Garden at Strawberry Hill'. It was a new topic and very well received, arousing great interest.

When refurbishment of the house was well in progress it was time for a start to be made on the garden, and Kevin Rogers, Peter Inskip and Michael Snodin were involved in the planning. They each thought that Stowe had an influence, but to different degrees; Mavis was convinced that it had a great deal of influence but she held a firm belief that it was England that had inspired landscape parks and, in her opinion, this area of the Thames Valley was the cradle of the landscape movement.

Little remained of the original Strawberry Hill Garden, but after extensive restoration of the house was complete, and under the care of the Strawberry Hill Preservation Trust, work started on the garden. It was then that Mavis and her daughter Deborah made a visit. Mavis mentioned to one of the men there that she knew the architect Peter Inskip. 'I am Peter Inskip,' the gentleman replied. Mavis gave a smile, 'I'm always dropping bricks, but I just walk over them. I am not going to kick them.' 'She was quite unruffled and had a twinkle in her eye,' remembered Deborah, '… but I felt myself blush.' [8]

Once purchased, Walpole had begun immediately to convert the existing house into a splendid 'Gothick' castle. All that was Gothic was his passion, and after his grand tour of 1739-41 he made a Gothic tour of the abbeys, cathedrals and castles of south-east England. All classical aspirations were dismissed as he sought only to imitate the 'Gothick gloomth' of these buildings. The absence of light may have contributed to the gloomy atmosphere, but some spaces are illuminated with light filtered through the brilliantly hued stained glass. Gilding, papier mâché, carpentry, rich textiles, china, pottery, plaster and ironwork, wallpaper and decorative prints all enhanced the splendour of what became a fantastic wonderland.

In the Victorian period the house became the home of Frances, Lady Waldegrave, whose third husband was a Harcourt. She was charming and popular and endeavoured to create a sparkling, jewel-like setting for herself as hostess. She cleverly made several architectural changes, but did nothing that would eliminate any part of Walpole's original masterpieces.

Once, the garden covered fifty acres, and became a landscape park, but now it is much reduced in size and what has been re-created is a telescopic version, yet it continues to attract considerable interest. The Friars' Garden, near the entrance to the house, was one of the first specialised gardens to have been restored and it is thought to be an important symbol of Walpole's mediaeval vision. Views have now changed and some have been eliminated, making major differences. At one time visitors may have arrived by boat, but now the view to the river is interrupted by a housing estate and there is no access at that point.

On one side of the park where the ground rises along the boundary, a shrub border has been formed. A serpentine path meanders around the garden, passing the 'Chapel in the Wood', and then crosses open pasture before reaching a line of large trees, once the riverside path, and nearby a plantation of lime trees has again been introduced. The tour was once brought to a close by a large shell seat carved in oak, one of several objects placed around the garden to create an element of surprise, but now a replica has been introduced in a different position and can be used for photographic purposes when weddings are celebrated.

The discovery of the New World offered the possibility for a wealth of new American plants, shrubs and trees to be introduced to England and other European countries. Walpole is known to have taken advantage of this bounty and it is thought that some of these introductions found their way into his American border.

A considerable amount of thought has been given to the reconstruction of the garden and work is still in progress. When various plans and projects were under discussion Mavis never allowed the garden to be forgotten, and one of her favourite sayings was, 'If you don't understand the garden you cannot understand what was being done with the house'. Walpole felt there should be a romantic association between house and garden and in many places he endeavoured to link them. The china closet was united with the garden: there were blue and white imitation Dutch tiles on the interior walls and, outside, orange trees were arranged in Dutch blue delft pots; the ceiling was painted with blue and white convolvulus on poles and this was echoed in the exterior planting scheme. The trend continued in various rooms, which were also linked by bowls of fragrant potpourri and included damask roses and orange blossom from the garden.

All this information, and much more, appears in a seminal article, *A Romantic Garden for a Gothic Castle,* written by Mavis, which has influenced the restoration of the Strawberry Hill Garden.

As a tribute to Mavis's generosity in sharing her knowledge, and to preserve her memory through the works of succeeding generations of gardeners, an apprenticeship fund has been set up in her name, and since 2010 the Strawberry Hill Trust has taken on a garden apprentice each year, thus giving young people training or employment, and the opportunity to earn an NVQ qualification and enter the horticultural profession.

CHAPTER EIGHTEEN
Film, Theatre and Friends

It was a pleasant surprise for Mavis when she was invited to become the BBC's advisor for a serialised television production of Jane Austen's *Pride and Prejudice,* the first commission of this kind to be offered to a member of the GHS. It was celebrated when the front cover of the society's *Newsletter No.46* (Spring 1996) bore the first colour illustration in the history of the newsletter, and it was the last issue to be edited by Eileen Stamers-Smith, who had filled the role of editor for many years. The highlight of her editorial was Mavis Batey's part as advisor on the backgrounds of the landscape park and garden for the television serialisation of *Pride and Prejudice.* Scenes were set in a variety of gardens: Belton House, Lincolnshire; Sudbury Hall, Derbyshire; and Lyme Park, Cheshire; all featured. Mavis gave her utmost attention to these grand gardens and visitor numbers soared.

Eileen Stamers-Smith points out that Jane Austen's novels were meant to be read, not seen, but Mavis coped admirably. As meticulous as ever, she adapted the Regency setting of landscape and garden for a modern audience, advised by accurate historical sources. She also arranged for the producers to be given access to the GHS Regency File, thinking that this was 'surely the first time that a producer has become aware that getting the garden right was as important as researching costume, furnishings, dancing and carriages for any period film set'.[1]

When many people commented on how so much of the action in Austen's novel took place in the park or garden, Mavis explained in her article about the making of the television programme, that with the lack of privacy in houses of that era, shrubberies, walks, orchards and walled gardens 'must have provided welcome relief as outdoor rooms, and they were essential to the plot of *Pride and Prejudice* as places where confidential scenes could take place'.[2]

Mavis went on to say that there were, however, a couple of problems to overcome. In the book accompanying the film, *The Making of Pride and Prejudice,* she states there was not a busy Lizzie in sight at Longbourn; and she assures the readers of her article that the flower lists available in 1812, copies of which were provided, unfortunately caused some confusion as busy Lizzies never seemed to be in flower as film-shoots took place at different months of the year. However, shrubberies were flounced, bedding-out concealed, and climbing plants gave a Regency effect. There was also a lake that could not be obliterated, but nevertheless Mavis was delighted and it was a very worthwhile experience for the GHS.

Mavis again came under the public eye when she was selected to be a role model for Kate Winslet's character Hester Wallace, the star of the film *Enigma,* which was released in 2001. It was a thriller, centred on the intelligence work at Bletchley Park during World War II, and some romance was included when Hester fell in love with fellow mathematician codebreaker Jericho (Dougray Scott), presumably echoing the romance between Mavis and her husband, Keith.

Soon after production started, Mavis and Keith had tea with the producer, the director and leading man Dougray Scott to discuss the project. The couple explained that Keith favoured a technological approach while Mavis looked at the human elements and word patterns. 'It is just like driving a car,' she said. 'We can both do it, but Keith understands what goes on under the bonnet.'[3]

When they later saw the film they each found their different approaches brought different reactions: Keith was upset by factual errors, yet in spite of Mavis's addiction to thorough research she had no problem with accuracy in the film – she was reported as being 'enchanted by the way it captured the mood of Bletchley and her feeling of being very young and working on something of great importance'.[4] This was, no doubt, Mavis's romantic nature coming to the fore. However, she could not understand why the film had not been made at Bletchley Park, and was put out by the fact that the Polish role in cracking the Enigma was overlooked. Although no Poles worked at Bletchley Park, they did cast one Pole, and Mavis said she would rather they had not shown a traitorous Pole working on codebreaking – this, she said, added insult to injury.

These matters did not affect the role of Kate Winslet and Mavis was full of praise for her acting, although she was critical of her appearance, saying, 'She kept her attractiveness well at bay – though perhaps she *slightly* overdid the dowdiness.'[5] When Mavis and Kate Winslet met for tea in a Holland Park hotel, they were soon chatting away, and Kate confessed to Mavis that she was very anxious about her bump showing in the film as she was pregnant, but Mavis assured her that she looked fine, although she thought she looked a little scruffy. Nevertheless, when Mavis talked to the actress, telling her all sorts of tales about everyday life among the codebreakers at Bletchley – the concerts, nights at the 'flicks', and in a diplomatic way she explained that, without enough coupons to use for new clothes, they would 'do swaps' with their friends when going to a dance, and for 3/6d they could visit the on-site hairdresser – Mavis felt it important that this charming actress should know that at Bletchley Park everyone took care of their appearance.

When Mavis attended the premiere of the film she was greeted by Dougray Scott saying, '"Without you I wouldn't be here." Mavis shuddered with embarrassment, modestly protesting, "It was teamwork. I mean, what about all those Battle of Britain pilots?"'[6]

Mavis brought literature, music and conservation together in May 2002 when her idea for *An Arcadian Miscellany: The View from*

Richmond Hill in Words and Music was performed at The Royal Star and Garter Home on Richmond Hill. Mavis had put the show together to celebrate the completion of the first part of the strategy work on the Thames between Hampton and Kew.

Richard Morris and Douglas Pinchin of Richard Douglas Productions were approached by Jason Debney, co-ordinator of the Thames Landscape Strategy, to produce *An Arcadian Miscellany;* this told the story of the Arcadian Thames in words and music, celebrating the centenary of the act of Parliament, 1902, that saved the view from threatened development.

The two men were excited about the commission and enthusiastically read through the script. Unfortunately they encountered a slight, and what became a tricky, problem: Mavis's *Arcadia* represented a region of Greece which symbolised from early times an idyllic, pastoral landscape, as imagined, in the eighteenth century, by William Kent in his illustrations to the 1730 edition of the poet James Thomson's *The Seasons*, a eulogy to the matchless *Vale of the Thames*. Mavis's script consisted, almost totally, of somewhat academic material that, unless the audience shared Mavis's passion for the eighteenth-century concept of Arcadia, and also had her intellectual capability, would be lost.

Undaunted, Richard Morris and Doug Pinchin spoke to Jason Debney and with his permission they set about editing the script. They also introduced sections covering the history of relevant parts of the Thames prior to the eighteenth century and up to the present day, thus putting the story of the Arcadian Thames into context. They sent the refreshed script off to Mavis and cheerfully awaited her reply – but Mavis was less than pleased. 'She was angry, saying they had tampered with her work, and others in the past.'[7]

Initially strong words buzzed to and fro along the telephone wires. 'Mavis did not realise that not everyone shared her passions and was a little affronted when this was pointed out to her,'[8] said Richard, but her tone eventually calmed, and although she was a little frosty the show went ahead.

At the first performance at The Royal Star and Garter Home on Richmond Hill the audience was led through the history of the view.

Narrated by Timothy West and Prunella Scales, it was attended by the great and the good of the area, and the event proved to be a great success. Sir Roy Strong, President of the GHS at the time, was heard to say that it was an ideal way of presenting heritage and conservation to the public. The celebrations culminated with the launch of the £3.5 million 'London's Arcadia' Heritage Lottery Fund – a bid led by Sir Roy Strong to restore the delights of this world famous landscape. Mavis was placated and happy with the result.

Mavis had played an important role in the creation of the Thames Landscape Strategy, and when it became clear to the other participants that she was planning to reduce her involvement, and spend more time in Sussex, it was decided that there should be some sort of thank you and celebration of her work for the strategy – Richard and Doug were asked to write an entertainment in her honour and *An Arcadian Miscellany* became *A Garland for Mavis*.

Mavis may have thought her ties with the Thames Landscape Strategy had come to an end, but in the year 2004, although she knew a show was going to be put on at Ham House, what she did not know was that *A Garland for Mavis* was to be presented as a celebration and appreciation of all the work she had put into the development of the Thames Landscape Strategy. It was performed at the beautiful Stuart, Ham House, a country house that sits on the banks of the Arcadian River Thames at Richmond. Mavis was living at Aldwick at this time, and Deborah, her younger daughter, was able to accompany her on this occasion. Deborah was overjoyed to do so as, in the early years of marriage, her husband Jonathan's work had made it necessary for them to spend time in London and Washington DC, returning to London before going to Edinburgh and then back to West Sussex. Jonathan read natural sciences at college and became a scientist specialising in immunology. When he became a professor at Imperial College, London, Deborah was able to see Mavis more frequently and was particularly glad to be present at this event.

The entrance to Ham House is through its seventeenth-century gardens that surround the house; there is a kitchen garden boasting many heritage crops, and within the Cherry Garden stands a figure of

Bacchus, the god of wine, but it was in the great hall that *A Garland for Mavis* was presented.

Ham House is a National Trust property and the house manager at the time was Anne Partington-Omar, and it is said that she was not a typical National Trust person. She was somewhat relaxed – in a jolly manner she would allow rules to be broken slightly if she thought that even more fun would be achieved. There were a couple of difficulties. It wasn't easy lighting the stage, or for the cast to navigate their way through the labyrinth of the dark basement passages when on their way from the dressing-rooms to the stage at the other end of the building, 'but everyone had a great time at Ham House and staff, performers and audience enjoyed every minute of it', the producers recalled.[9]

The evening was loosely based on the old television show, *This Is Your Life.* Instead of conjuring up people from Mavis's past, it began by telling of her Bletchley Park days and continued with the story punctuated by her favourite music, poems, readings and characters from eighteenth-century Arcadia. And, of course, it included an excerpt from *Alice in Wonderland,* another favourite interest of Mavis.

Doug was happy to tell that, 'Much of the material deleted from the *Miscellany* was re-instated, so I think we were finally forgiven!'[10] It was first-class entertainment, lively music and pleasant poetry, a great deal of humour, and the players were dressed in the most flamboyant clothes that could be found. There was audience participation – particularly when they joined the cast, throwing themselves into the familiar chorus with newly adapted words.

Mavis and Deborah were delighted and enjoyed meeting the cast at the end of the performance when they were presented with a recording on a compact disc – and Mavis definitely thawed, no doubt helped by the joyful reaction by an appreciative audience singing this jolly song:

The New Lass of Richmond Hill

> There is a lass we know so well
> Her name is Mavis Batey

She does not live on Richmond Hill
But Sussex by the Sea
This lass so neat
With codes to break
Has won our right good will
With crowns resign to call her thine
Arcadia's garden queen
Arcadia's garden queen
With crowns resign to call her thine
Arcadia's garden queen.

This lass so sweet from Bognor town
(Or do we mean Aldwick – (Aside: that's the posh end)
Has charmed us so as years have gone
Her name's become unique
Prince Charles would say she's quite ok
And that's an understatement
We all agree she's quite divine
Arcadia's garden queen
Arcadia's garden queen
Prince Charles would say she's quite ok
Acadia's garden queen.

She's keen on lots of things
Including Lewis Carroll
Research has shown that Oxford was
Where Alice had her fun
The Duchess and the Queen of Hearts
The Dodo and the Gryphon
They all combine to be sublime
Among the dreaming spires
Among the dreaming spires
They all combine to be sublime
Among the dreaming spires.

Kim Wilkie brought the show to a close, saying:

> Whether making connections that illuminated a garden's history (her memory is far more capacious than the magic wardrobe where she files the carrier bags of notes) or writing the next letter of protest, the giggle at something that has tickled her is never far away. And still nothing seems to escape her. Only this autumn, she was on the 'phone disbelieving that people seem to have no knowledge of some of the heroic battles waged by the GHS and CPRE.'

It was a large and joyous crowd of garden historians that gathered in the grounds of Petworth House on 5 May 2011 on the occasion of Mavis's ninetieth birthday and to celebrate her long involvement with the GHS which spanned twenty-nine years, first as honorary secretary from 1971, until 1985, when she was elected president, finally stepping down in 2000. She worked hard and her hard work had been rewarded with the Royal Horticultural Society's Veitch Memorial Medal in 1985 for 'her contribution to the preservation of gardens which would otherwise have been lost' and, perhaps even more so, the award of an MBE in 1988 for services to the preservation and conservation of historic gardens.

Among the guests were Kim Wilkie, who remembered the time they had spent working on the Thames Landscape Strategy:

> It is now inconceivable to think of the Thames Landscape Strategy without Mavis's insight, scholarship and unstinting work. No request was ever too great and I have box files of her letters and investigations in her careful hand that must have been written between 5 and 7 am before her own day got going. I have worked with Mavis on everything from Strawberry Hill in Twickenham to Broad Street in Oxford. Always she has brought a clarity and depth of understanding that has given life to each place. More than anything else, Mavis has a unique ability to see landscape connections across history and cultures. The minute precision of her scholarship combined with the cultural breadth of her vision is very rare and very exciting.[11]

Another guest was Edward Fawcett. Mavis and Ted had become friends when Ted was director of the Architectural Association School of Architecture's course on the Conservation of Historic Landscape Parks and Gardens and Mavis was called to lecture for the students. Ted Fawcett's wife, Jane, formerly Hughes, was teaching building conservation at the Architectural Association School.

It had been at Bletchley Park, when Mavis and her husband Keith were there, that Jane had come to know Keith quite well. There was one occasion, in May 1941, when Jane had picked up a message – in German – on the main Luftwaffe Enigma and noticed the word 'Brest'. She and her fellow codebreakers had been briefed as to the whereabouts of the Germans' favourite new battleship, *Bismarck*, which rather than being in the Atlantic Ocean was believed to be moving in French waters. Quickly reading the message she noticed mention that the *Bismarck* was on its way to the French port, Brest. It was an outstanding vessel and had been involved in the Battle of Denmark Strait which had taken place the previous day and had been responsible for the loss of the British battleship, the *Hood*. Although having won this battle, it had been badly damaged and was now on the way to Brest to undergo repairs. Jane passed the transcript to Keith Batey, explaining that a Luftwaffe general had a son on the *Bismarck* and was enquiring about his safety. Keith immediately had the message forwarded to the Admiralty, which had previously thought the *Bismarck* to be in the Atlantic. The message was acted upon and the following day, as a direct response to the message from Bletchley Park, a Catalina flying boat tracked down the ship, which was consequently sunk by the Royal Navy on 27 May 1941.

On seeing Jane, once again the film *Sink the Bismarck*, that Mavis had seen with her son back in 1960, flashed through her mind. When at Bletchley Park Mavis had no idea that Jane and Keith had been involved with the incoming message concerning the *Bismarck*, as they had complied with the Official Secrets Act which imposed a prohibition on revealing any codebreaking activities.

After the party Jane and Mavis met up to have a chat about their time at Bletchley Park and discuss what they had since done. It is interesting to compare the post-war careers of Mavis and Jane Fawcett, née Hughes. They had come from very different backgrounds, and although they seldom met until later years they had similar and very successful careers after Bletchley Park. Like Mavis, Jane too had spent time in Zurich, where her parents had arranged for her to stay for six months so that she might learn to speak German; this they hoped would help her to get over the disappointment of not being able to fulfil her dream of becoming a ballet dancer. Jane returned to London for 'the season' and took her place with the young debutantes who were to be presented at court and, of course, this entailed accepting invitation after invitation to attend balls and parties, with the hope of meeting a young man offering the prospect of a suitable marriage. It could have been fun, but of course there were the chaperones. When Mavis found she had to return to London where war was looming, she soon decided that she should do something useful to help what had become known as 'the war effort'.

Surprisingly both young ladies found themselves working at Bletchley Park doing vital war work which secrecy made seem extremely exciting. Jane was sent to the decoding room where, along with the other girls, she worked hard on what she had been told was vital war work – and Mavis joined Dilly's department.

Jane was disappointed that there were no grand suites of offices, but she did not complain about the working conditions, which were genuinely appalling. The young ladies probably felt they had been rushed into this wartime situation but each decided they should accept the conditions. Mavis soon settled comfortably in her billet with a local family. Jane, however, was unhappy with her lodgings; although the owners of the house where she stayed were very kind, there was little about the house that could please her. She contacted her parents and it was fortunate that they were able to arrange for her to stay with some friends who lived in a grand country house near Bletchley Park – so life became much brighter for Jane, particularly when she was invited to house parties.

At this time Jane's beau, Ted Fawcett, was a Royal Naval officer, and Jane would hitch a ride to London to meet him in 'His Master's Voice' record shop in Oxford Street, but the meetings were often very short, with just time for a little cuddle in the listening booth and she then had to hitch a ride back to Bletchley Park. Mavis was more fortunate as Keith was around Bletchley Park until the time he went off to join the Fleet Air Arm.

When Jane left Bletchley Park at the end of the war in May 1945, she married Ted while training at The Royal Academy of Music to become a professional singer. For fifteen years, through to the early 1960s, she had a career as an opera singer, performing Scylla in Jean-Marie Leclair's *Scylla et Glaucus* and the Sorceress in Henry Purcell's *Dido and Aeneas;* she also did a considerable amount of recital work.

Jane's next job was as a secretary of the Victorian Society, which had been set up five years earlier to deal with the conservation of Victorian houses which were being swept away by the concrete high-rise of the late sixties.

Jane was offered a position by the society's director, Sir Nikolaus Pevsner, and was able to work from home using her own typewriter. Pevsner was involved in a campaign to save Britain's Victorian buildings. First it was the arch in front of Euston Station, and with that success behind them the Victorian Society moved on to the St Pancras locomotive shed and the station's Midland Grand Hotel. With the help of John Betjeman, and other celebrated and interested parties, after what seemed an endless length of time, the hotel was finally restored to its former glory.

While Jane was in liaison with John Betjeman in London, Mavis was probably thinking about him in Oxford whilst she was getting to know about the people and architectural history of her neighbourhood, the Dons' suburb, and delving into the history of the Victorian gardens there. Mavis had heard that a young undergraduate in the mid-1920s, a future Poet Laureate and great campaigner for Victorian conservation, when cycling along the North Oxford roads, would amusingly decorate his bicycle with 'Kant' painted on the handlebars and 'Marx' on the saddlebag. The garden walls were adorned with flowering shrubs, and when peeping over evergreen hedges he was moved to sing:

Belbroughton Road is bonny and pinkly bursts the spray
Of prunus and forsythia across the public way.

Like John Betjeman, the leafy roads of the dons' flowery garden suburb with its memories of Oxford family and donnish life – complete with campaigning – were as nostalgic for Mavis as the dreaming spires themselves.[12] North Oxford is a remarkably well-preserved area – one of the first conservation areas in the country to be championed by John Betjeman.

It is surprising that both Mavis and Jane should enjoy careers which involved campaigning for conservation, Mavis campaigning for the conservation of historic landscape, parks and gardens, and Jane for the conservation of historic buildings.

In 1976 Jane was appointed an MBE for her services to conservation and was elected a Fellow of the Royal Institute of British Architects, and, after gaining a post-graduate diploma in building conservation, she was appointed director of the building conservation department at the Architectural Association School of Architecture; she, too, became a successful author in her field, writing the definitive book *Historic Floors: Their History and Conservation.*

It was at the Architectural Association School of Architecture that she was tutor to Janie Price, the architect who led the recent conservation programme at Bletchley Park which preceded the streamlining of Bletchley as a museum and public information centre.

It is amazing that these two women, who hardly knew each other at Bletchley Park, should have both started out in Zurich, then worked as codebreakers at Bletchley, and in post-war conservation, and although their paths crossed now and again they did not really get to know each other until their later years.

CHAPTER NINETEEN
Literary Mavis

Literature was Mavis's first love, and literature was one of the interests she turned to when she found herself in North Oxford, with an almost grown-up family. It was when living at Nuneham Courtenay that Mavis discovered how much she enjoyed writing. In later life she remembered what a lovely thing it had been to find all this waiting for her. There were not only the gardens, but all the interesting people, long gone but now hiding in the shadows – and she would make excursions to seek out the places her garden heroes had once held dear. To imagine these people in their own setting was exciting, and she went out of her way to find the Three Pigeons Inn that Goldsmith had once frequented. Mavis had talked to a young graduate working on Thomas Hardy and found it difficult to understand how the young man could do this without ever having visited Hardy's house. A sense of place was very important to Mavis and part of the fun of research. She took an interest in the influence of the University of Oxford on the city's gardens through the centuries and learned that Pope had walked through Christ Church Meadows exactly where she liked to wander.

It was when first in Oxford that she became fascinated by *Alice in Wonderland* but of all children's stories, why *Alice*?

The author of the book was the Reverend Charles Lutwidge Dodgson (1832–1898), who in March 1856 adopted the pseudonym Lewis Carroll. He was a mathematician at Christ Church, a wordsmith who excelled at puns, and a creator of cyphers who invented and solved puzzles. These traits influenced his stories and inspired many people who had similar interests, so he became a particular favourite of cryptographers who worked for the Secret Service. Carroll was held in high regard by the cryptographers at Bletchley Park and could not have failed to have influenced Mavis. The eccentric and talented Dilly Knox admired Carroll's writing, and shared his sense of fun and 'magical thinking', sprinkling his conversation with quotations from Carroll's writing. Knox and his colleague Frank Birch, at the end of their World War I experiences with the Secret Service, wrote a parody on their office, Room 40, when they first became codebreakers. Their comical skit was *Alice in I.D. 25*, and with text by Birch, and poetry by Knox, it closely followed the pattern of Carroll's own *Alice in Wonderland*.

Carroll's Alice books, *Alice in Wonderland* (1865) and *Through the Looking Glass* (1871), have become classics. There were new adaptations of the books with which Carroll involved himself, sometimes contributing by not only giving permission for songs to be set to music, but adding an extra couplet, or supplying poetic riddles to magazines for the joy of creating games of logic. Alice appeared in advertisements; there were Alice dolls and Alice biscuit tins containing edible Alice biscuit characters. Alice gradually seeped into British culture and tradition.

Many of Bletchley Park's staff found themselves caricatured in the debut of *Alice in I.D. 25* when performed by codebreakers at the end of World War I, but little did they know that some of the characters would re-appear at Bletchley Park many years later.

Carroll had a lifelong love affair with the theatre and is said to have attended more than 400 plays. Nevertheless, as the theatre was thought by some to be a corrupt environment, he was always concerned that audiences should enjoy only that which was pure and good. He was in agreement with children acting professionally, even under twelve years of age, arguing that their wages were very important to many poor, struggling families, and Mavis no doubt shared these thoughts. Carroll had no objection to adaptations of *Alice in Wonderland* being performed on stage, and appeared to be unconcerned with royalties, but appreciated any thanks that he might receive.

So it would seem that he would not have objected to *Alice in I.D. 25,* the parody written by Frank Birch and his lifelong friend Dilly Knox, and would perhaps have been flattered if he knew how many other parodies were written. In 1902, *The Westminster Alice* appeared; Alice became a favourite with men in the trenches, *The Quartermaster in Wonderland* was enjoyed by the troops, and in the 1940s her popularity continued with *Adolf in Blunderland.*

At the end of World War I, *Alice in I.D. 25* was performed by the Secret Service as a pantomime – part of an in-house entertainment – and there were many references that would have been difficult for the general public to understand. Declared by Birch to be a private entertainment, presumably for the Secret Service only, it was put onto the secret list, however some copies were retained for private circulation.

In *Alice in Wonderland* the first character Alice meets is the White Rabbit, but in *I.D. 25* the rabbit disappears through an arch in the Admiralty Building and is sucked down a long communication tube accompanied by a shuttle full of gobbledegook messages. There is a tubist waiting to receive the messages, just as a tubist would be ready to receive batches of messages thirty years later at Bletchley Park.

The Victorian era was a time-dominated society which saw the introduction in 1847 of a standardised time system when new phrases such as 'behind the times', 'pass the time of day', 'not before time', 'all the time in the world' and 'time off' entered the English language. Carroll was obsessed by fixing time. When Mavis learned of this her thoughts must have returned to the day she first met Dilly Knox and he posed the question, 'Which way does the clock go round?'

In the Birch parody Captain James's hours are seven to ten and ten to seven; extraordinarily long hours it would seem, until it becomes apparent that the exact time of seven minutes to ten and ten minutes to seven are extremely short shifts.

And so the comparisons continue. A complicated selection of puns, puzzles and private jokes were aimed at other codebreakers, and when there is no answer a dead end is closed by a poem composed by Dilly Knox. Like Carroll, both Birch and Knox were masters of 'chopped logic', nonsense that seems to make sense – and their talents as wordsmiths in their work and their play cast them as geniuses.

Through Knox, who was addicted to Carrollian 'chopped logic', Mavis became familiar with Alice, and she also learned of *Alice in I.D. 25*. In 2007 a further edition was published[1] and Mavis wrote an introduction, *The Codebreaking Context*, and Edward Wakeling, another Bletchley Park codebreaker, also wrote an introduction, *The Carrollian Context*.

It had been Penelope Fitzgerald's intention to write an Oxford novel, but instead she wrote one about Cambridge set in Dilly's time there, but she always found Oxford and its history captivating, particularly the mid-Victorian period when Bishop Knox and Charles Dodgson, Lewis Carroll, author of *Alice in Wonderland*, were there. She remembered her grandfather, Bishop Knox, loved to enjoy the surrealist type jokes with the dons at Corpus: He knows a man whose feet are so large he has to put his trousers on over his head.

Penelope was writing her book *The Knox Brothers*[2] and it comes as no surprise that she was visiting Mavis at Oxford, as Mavis would be able to help her with her research. Penelope presented her with a copy of *Alice in I.D. 25* which Mavis treasured for the rest of her life. Knox's appearance was described in the text just as Mavis remembered him: 'Alice thought that he was the queerest bird she had ever seen. He was so long and lean and he had outgrown his clothes and his face was like a pang of hunger.'[3] Alice also mentioned that he kept his spectacles in his tobacco-pouch, just as Dilly did when Mavis had worked with him at Bletchley Park – and she had frequently spent time searching for them. Mavis thought it was a coincidence that she and Penelope should be sitting in her husband's rooms at Christ Church overlooking Deanery Garden, where the tabby cat of the real Alice, Alice Liddell, daughter of the Dean of Christchurch, often sat on the bough of the horse-chestnut tree which was still standing.

Mavis was writing a book on Lewis Carroll. 'I have always felt a bond with Dilly, who was for me Alice's White Knight, endearingly eccentric, and concerned for my welfare.'[4] She had become fascinated by the logic; she loved words and puzzles and was at home with Alice. She was very proud of *Alice in I.D. 25* and Alice was someone she frequently talked of in her old age.

When first arriving at Bletchley and meeting Dilly Knox in the Cottage, he handed her a pencil and told her to join in. There was no instruction, she had to think for herself, find connections within the codes and trust her own thinking; this became her habit. If we refer back to Mavis's early career as a codebreaker, it is possible to isolate some of the ways in which her writing was influenced by lessons learned at that time.

As she had searched and deciphered codes at Bletchley Park, when writing she delved into archives and satisfied her curiosity by revealing that which lay latent. Her scholarly methods became thorough, relying on original sources that she meticulously footnoted, and her books show examples of the links and connections she made.

The little book that Mavis was writing, *The World of Alice*, has been extremely popular with the tourist trade and has been republished numerous times. Mavis writes of the Reverend Charles Dodgson and his friendship with the Liddell family, how he came to write the Alice books, and his 'unique brand of fun-loving nonsense based on logic'.[5] Mavis tells how the story of *Alice's Adventures in Wonderland* had stemmed from the imagination of Dodgson who chose interesting features of the landscape and architecture in and around Oxford to set the scenes in his Alice books.

While at Bletchley, Mavis spent time searching for connections between items of information received in code, and in her Alice book she describes the links between Alice and Oxford: the brass firedogs in the hall at Christ Church may have inspired the illustrations of Alice portrayed with an elongated neck, 'which seemed to rise like a stalk'.[6] And there were links with the surrounding countryside, like the story of St Frideswide's Holy Well and how it became the *Treacle Well* at Binsey. Mavis's granddaughter, Rachel Alice, daughter of

Deborah, was baptised at St Frideswide's Church, and Mavis's book *The World of Alice* was dedicated to Eleanor, daughter of Elizabeth, Mavis's eldest daughter.

Mavis wrote a paper, *Alice's Adventures at Nuneham,* which was published for an Alice Exhibition at the National Society for the Prevention of Cruelty to Children Centenary Festival, held at Nuneham Courtenay in 1983, when a centenary fundraising appeal was launched. She was delighted to have the opportunity to write about Nuneham, particularly as it was an Alice tale, telling a story based on truth. The Harcourts' landscaped park at Nuneham had earlier been chosen as the setting for several chapters of *Alice Through the Looking Glass* (1871) and Mavis built her story around the cottages in Nuneham dingle and the Nuneham woodland.

There were links between the Harcourt and the Liddell families. William Harcourt, owner of Nuneham, was uncle of Augustus Vernon Harcourt of Christ Church, and one of Lewis Carroll's greatest friends, who gave him his stories to read before publication. The children of the Liddell family learned to row and were allowed to row upstream to Nuneham where they would be made welcome. The final link is sad – Alice's sister, Edith Liddell, later became engaged to Aubrey Harcourt of Nuneham but died before her wedding day.

This was at the beginning of Mavis's literary career, and she no doubt enjoyed the research which must have inspired her to delve into more serious history. Even though she was always busy with her three children, the evenings would usually find Mavis in the Bodleian Library where she would stay until closing time. Much of Mavis's writing at that time sprung from around Oxford, and her early work included some books and articles for the GHS journal, the journals of other learned societies and magazines, and sometimes she made contributions to other people's books. Some of Mavis's books will now be examined, and the first reveals her satisfaction with historical research and the erudition of her writing.

The Historic Gardens of Oxford and Cambridge (1989) was perhaps a natural progression from Mavis's previous book: *Oxford Gardens: The*

University's Influence on Garden History. 'It's where you are,' she would say 'I do what comes my way.' Mavis had no axe to grind in writing these books; they are born of her enthusiasm and convey her love of gardens and history and reveal her delight in historical research.

From the enormous amount of historical information made available by the universities, Mavis peeled back the many layers of the history of the garden quadrangles of Oxford and the courts of Cambridge, uncovering elements of the styles of bygone ages. Not only does she deal with the gardens individually, but relates them to intellectual movements and changing tastes in fashion. As she explains, she steers the reader through 'Renaissance ideas, Puritan good husbandry, the exuberance of the Restoration and baroque ideas of grandeur, classical philosophy, eighteenth-century taste, romanticism, Arts and Crafts principles and modernism'.[7] Mavis's broad knowledge enabled her to record garden history alongside social, political and technological developments, just as Amelia Amherst had done in her work on garden history. Amherst's knowledge was not acquired by formal study as there were probably no educational courses in garden history at that time – it was an academic subject which Mavis and the GHS were successfully establishing. Mavis's list of notes and references indicate this was an area which had previously been neglected, and Mavis extracted from the mass of material relevant information, which is presented as a coherent, orderly account revealing her thorough knowledge of the subject. The writer Julia Alvarez wrote: 'People think that writers write because they know things. We write because we want to find things out,'[8] and it was Mavis's meticulous research that gave her a good foundation for later writing. Her habitual use of primary sources remained her practice throughout her literary career.

Mavis's books are never a heavy read; she had a sense of humour and sometimes introduces an unexpected anecdote. She surprised her readers, writing that at the time of the Reformation, when Oxford became a garrison town, the grove of Trinity College was said to be the Daphne of the ladies and their gallants whose behaviour shocked some of the clerical dons. 'The ladies used to come to morning chapel "halfe dressed, like angels" and the President was heard to say to one of them, "Madam, your husband and father I bred up here, and I know your grandfather; I know you to be a gentlewoman, I will not say you are a whore; but gett you gonne for a very woman."[9]

Mavis had always had an interest in language and, when working at GC&CS and Bletchley Park, it became second nature for her to solve puzzles and iron out conundrums. In her later books, *Pope: The Poet and the Landscape*; *Arcadian Thames*; and *Jane Austen and the English Landscape,* she skilfully unravelled various words and terms which have changed their meanings over time.

Taste was one of the major preoccupations of Georgian England. It was an eighteenth-century cultural obsession along with architecture and/or horticulture and all things Graeco-Roman. It was the distinguishing mark of a polished citizen as learned by gentlemen on the Grand Tour. To be tasteless was to be vulgar. The Georgian period had been a fast-developing society, exploring issues of taste and feeling, fresh influences of literature, painting and poetry from abroad – new attitudes to society, and new ideas on nature and the environment were fast becoming accepted. Professional men such as doctors or preachers would be paid, it was acceptable for men to marry for, or even fight for, money but if a writer wrote for money he was said to have 'no taste':

Only gentlemen, it was asserted, understood about taste. The 'common herd' did not, could not. A hard-working, driven writer, paid for producing so many sheets a day, had no leisure to cultivate his taste. Real genius like real gentleman, would be above taking a fee.[10]

Mavis introduces her readers to a new vocabulary, that of the language of the gardens and landscapes of the eighteenth century, and the full connection is made. This may have been done for the benefit of those less familiar with the meaning of the vocabulary, but nevertheless her books remain of interest to professionals and academics. The term 'Picturesque' underwent a series of changes, and William Gilpin was the pioneer of the Picturesque Movement which reached its height towards the end of the eighteenth century. Gilpin popularised the wild scenery of the Wye Valley, which came to be defined as a particular type of scenery suitable for painting. In gardens the Picturesque was characterised by dramatic scenery, contrasts of texture and vegetation, and a sense of wildness giving an overgrown effect to the view. Humphry Repton devised a cosy version with flower gardens near the house, thinning trees to maximise the view of the house, and shrubberies in Regency gardens also became known as Picturesque. Mavis always took the opportunity in both her writing and teaching to clarify these terms and it is a feature that has become much appreciated.

Over the years Mavis had become a very proficient teacher, lecturer and tour guide and leader of tour groups. She visited primary schools to talk about *Alice in Wonderland*, lectured at various educational establishments and societies, including the Architectural Association, adult education colleges, the Workers Educational Society, the Jane Austen Society and many more venues. She was popular, and as well as frequently speaking at GHS events she was often requested to appear at public conferences, symposia and so on.

The Thames Connection Exhibition at the Royal Fine Art Commission in 1991 stimulated great interest in the area of the River Thames from Hampton to Kew. Two books sprung from the exhibition and the subsequent launch of *The Thames Landscape Strategy: Hampton to Kew*. The first book was *Arcadian Thames: The River and Landscape from Hampton to Kew*.[11] Mavis had strong opinions on some topics, particularly when fighting for conservation, but she was seldom an ardent activist, preferring a gentle approach, as this book shows. The aim of the book was, no doubt, to strengthen the following of the campaign, to broaden the interest, and influence an even wider audience.

The chapters written by colleagues of Mavis concentrate on landscape, natural history and historical background, each concerning a particular reach of the Thames. The history relating to the material in the exhibition is accompanied mainly by black and white prints and maps. Mavis's contribution is the introduction and six essays between chapters which describe places and people along the Thames in their eighteenth-century Arcadian setting. This perhaps appeals to a non-professional class who may more easily relate to social history presented on a domestic scale, rather than having to pore over the series of plans presented in the book, interesting though they are, but for some difficult to read.

Mavis describes a leisurely rural scene, of golf and gardens, flowers and follies; there were picnics and poetry, 'romantic shrubberies' and a 'romantic serpentine walk'; everything at Strawberry Hill was required to 'hang down somewhat poetical'.[12] Her style was to capture her audience and intoxicate them with a bygone age, so linking eighteenth-century text with the modern landscape. She brings an aura of grandeur to Twickenham, reaching out and connecting the scene with a painting by Claude Lorrain and casting the richness of one of his autumnal sunsets over the waterside. She suggests some of the views may be recaptured today, and it is noteworthy that this has recently been achieved at some Thameside villas.

In addition, there was a pamphlet written by Mavis, *The Arcadia in the City:"A Hill with a View"*, telling the historical story of this watery panorama from the days of Edward III who first built a royal palace there, at Sheen, and the continuous stream of royalty and then celebrity followed, including The Rolling Stones, and Benjamin Britten who produced his version of Purcell's *On the Brow of Richmond Hill* dedicated to the 'happy citizens of Richmond'. This was written at the height of the successful 1968 campaign to secure Richmond Hill as a protected conservation area. Needless to say the journey as described in *The Arcadia in the City: "A Hill with a View"* finishes with the celebrations of 2002 when the venture was complete.

The next book concerning the Thames Landscape Strategy is packed with information and celebrates *Indignation! The Campaign for Conservation*. It is divided into three parts and Mavis wrote the introduction and the first part on early campaigns; David Lambert, conservation officer for the GHS wrote on *Indignation Today;* and Kim Wilkie, the greatly admired landscape architect and urban designer, on *Indignation Tomorrow.*

Mavis's introduction describes how, 'The amenity movement and its campaigns for the sake of both the man-made and the natural environment has evolved through over a century of voluntary grassroots activity' and '... the passionate motivation of those pioneers who fought to save our green and pleasant land and to take heed of what they have to tell us about society, conservation and the environment'.[13] She went on to write the first part on *Ruskin, Morris and the Early Campaigners* and Ruskin's treatise *The Seven Lamps of Architecture.* Mavis was attracted by William Morris, John Ruskin, and Edward Burne-Jones whose life story Penelope had published in 1975, and it becomes clear that she and Penelope shared admiration for these heroes. *Indignation!* is a small book in which Mavis wrote succinctly and carefully, covering early Ruskinian origins and *The Seven Lamps of Architecture* and she was, no doubt, inspired by Penelope's biography of Edward Burne-Jones.

In summer 1996, on the occasion of Mavis's seventy-fifth birthday, Mavis and her old friend Edward Fawcett, whose wife had been a codebreaker with Mavis at Bletchley Park, were talking of old times – but looking to the future. "And what do you still wish to achieve?" asked Ted. "What about garden history?" "Well, there is my book on Jane Austen to be called *Jane Austen and the English Landscape,*" replied Mavis, knowing it would be appearing on the market any day soon. "I hope that as many people as possible will visit and love gardens, and that their history will become as much part of our lives as poetry or painting."[14] Mavis was looking forward, but it must have been the imminent publication of her book, which took place in October 1996, that was uppermost in her thoughts; she had been working on it for so long, but had frequently put it aside to attend to other pressing matters.

Many of Mavis's writings had been set in the Georgian era, which was her favourite historical period, and later Regency times. She had written an essay, *In Quest of Jane Austen's Mr Repton,* as early as 1977, and by the time she had written her Austen book she had become known as an unparalleled authority on both landscape and Jane Austen. She was a regular lecturer to Jane Austen Societies in Britain and had correspondence with other interested people around the world.

As the title of the book suggests, Mavis draws attention to the importance of the previously little considered landscape of the author's novels, enabling us to examine it in detail and see its half-hidden beauties and subtleties. Once again she writes of connections, this time between a much-loved writer and garden history, and our comprehension of Austen's books is enhanced.

Mavis introduces her readers to the Austen family and discusses the relationship between family members, unravelling the family tree and revealing Jane's opportunities to become acquainted with the estates of some of her family and their friends. The characters in the books are frequently inspired by relatives and friends, but they are fresh creations, or composite figures.

There is an examination of the part played by the landscape and garden settings, and Mavis explains that Austen was familiar with the countryside and the social scene around the areas in which she lived; the places she writes of are both real and imaginary, but always convincing. She shows that Austen often focused on the social context, describing the changes which were taking place, so making it clear that even when living a life of rural seclusion Austen was aware of new ideas and changing powers; she links this with her characters' changes in attitude and their reactions.

Austen's research for her books was thorough, Mavis points out. It becomes clear to the reader that she set her towns and villages geographically, using road books, almanacs, guides and books of engravings. Her place names were chosen with care and travelling distances between real places had to be correct. The fictitious estate Mansfield Park was said to be located four miles from Northampton, so other details had to be consistent, e.g. Edmund is ordained at Peterborough, in the correct diocese.

Mavis advises that Austen was well read in areas of importance to her source material. She was familiar with the writing, both poetry and prose, of Cowper, and admired his love of simple rural pleasures; Fanny Price, too, in Austen's *Mansfield Park*, was made a devotee. Dr Johnson was a favourite moral writer; she mentions Gilpin's *Tours* and Repton's *Red Books* and knew the works of Wordsworth, Scott, Byron, Goethe and other eminent writers, as well as popular contemporary novelists like Charlotte Smith and Maria Edgeworth.

Many incidents in Austen's novels set in Regency England take place outdoors, in the landscape park, garden, or countryside, and Mavis advises that each of the incidents are arranged in appropriate settings. When Fanny Price returned to Mansfield Park and the countryside, after her stay in Portsmouth, she sees Mansfield with Cowper's 'heart and eye', and 'liberty and freshness, fragrance and verdure'[15] came back into her life through the landscape that Austen had invested with verdant, symbolic promise, reflecting the prospects in Fanny's life.

In a similar way Mavis finds that Austen links the landscapes of other estates with the personalities of the characters involved with them. Pemberley, the estate of Mr Darcy, is important to the plot of *Pride and Prejudice*. Mr Darcy's aim is to win over the heroine, Elizabeth, who previously had a poor impression of him. To show him as a man of morals and good taste, Austen gives Pemberley Park a picturesque Gilpin landscape, and Elizabeth, upon seeing the beautiful grounds, is moved and changes her attitude towards him.

In *Jane Austen and the English Landscape* Mavis makes links and connections between landscape and people, an aspect of Austen's novels which had not been explored in such depth before. The book was a success, attracting a great deal of attention and leading to exciting events in Mavis's calendar when she was chosen to advise the American owners on the restoration of the Regency landscape of Austen's home, Chawton House, in Hampshire.

Mavis's memory was extremely clear, and in 2009 she published a biography of her team leader, Alfred Dillwyn Knox, a leading codebreaker at Bletchley Park, who had broken many of the variations of the Enigma cyphers during World War I, the Spanish Civil War and World War II. Mavis acknowledges that Dilly's close friends at Bletchley Park, including her husband, Keith, gave their assistance throughout, and first-hand accounts of his early life were available from his family, colleagues and friends.

After a brief summary on his personal life, and the chapter, 'The Making of a Codebreaker', the book goes on to record his years as a cryptographer. His work was complete when breaking the Enigma Abwehr variations, but unfortunately he died before his achievement enabled MI5 and MI6 to manipulate the intelligence the Germans were receiving through the Double Cross system ensuring the success of the D-Day landings.

One may ask why Mavis left it so late in her life to write this book? Secrecy was of absolute importance at Bletchley Park, and the release of information post war was restricted to a minimum of thirty years and then released sporadically. Details of her work at Bletchley were unavailable when Dillwyn Knox's obituary was written for *The Times* in 1943, and some information is still withheld. It is probable that Mavis had decided not to write at all, rather than inadvertently expose knowledge that was still secret. However, she gathered information over many years and delayed publication.

Mavis took the opportunity to include a useful chapter entitled 'Dilly's Girls' that allowed her to write about her own life at Bletchley Park. There are many quotes of her own which have been used time after time when she was being interviewed by various writers both before and after the publication of *Dilly* and, as often happens, the repetition of many anecdotes became a persistent habit during Mavis's old age.

Dilly: The Man Who Broke Enigmas is a worthwhile, detailed biography of a man who, in spite of being eccentric, was a genius; who regardless of extreme bad health gave himself to the task of solving the problems of various Enigma codes. Mavis became a very good friend to Dilly during her service at Bletchley Park; he had been her mentor, she knew him well, and she was the ideal person to write his biography, describing Dilly and his work in a sympathetic manner.

Reflecting on her career as a writer in January 2005, at the age of eighty-four, Mavis wrote to a friend:

I always feel it is getting to know the creators of gardens and landscapes, give or take their designers, is what matters. I have been singularly fortunate that practically all my owners have been romantically inclined. Of course, living in Nuneham for two years in the 1960s must be the most inspirational of all but others have come my way through conservation work...

CHAPTER TWENTY
Espionage and Cunning Schemes

In 1962, long after Mavis had left Bletchley Park, a new story erupted. Before her arrival at Bletchley Park she had been named as the accomplice of a couple of spies entering Kent, and now she was to be named as a spy gathering information from the Italians for Admiral Cunningham before the Battle of Matapan. Mavis never did become a spy but she found she had an extraordinary tale to tell about a glamorous spy known by the pseudonym Cynthia. Like all good spy stories it was one of intrigue and seduction.

Cynthia was plain, but she was tall and had beautiful blonde hair; her voice was soft and calm and she made intelligent conversation. She was attractive and had sex appeal, and knew how to use her charm. That is not say she was brazen – she was dignified, well-mannered and alluring. Cynthia was said to be a woman agent, a product of British intelligence and her expertise was unbelievable; willing to undertake tasks beyond the bounds of what was required of her – her bravado was limitless. She is said to have been…

… instrumental in obtaining the key to both the French and the Italian naval cyphers, which enabled the British Admiralty to read for the remainder of the war all the relevant cablegrams, radiograms and fleet-signals which were intercepted in code or cypher.[1]

Sir William Stephenson, the director of Britain's secret intelligence organisation in America during World War II, had his first meeting with Cynthia in late August 1941, in New York. They went for a walk along Madison Avenue where they read an announcement that a shooting incident had occurred in France threatening the life of Vice-Premier Pierre Laval. They bought a newspaper and then stopped at the hotel where Cynthia was living. Stephenson had recently recruited Cynthia to British Security Co-ordination (BSC), and in his biography of Stephenson, Montgomery Hyde makes it clear their meeting was only to discuss the Laval incident. Nothing more. Cynthia's alleged first major assignment was recorded in his book *The Quiet Canadian,* first published in 1962.

The beautiful blonde Cynthia made her debut in 1940-41 when she is said to have enchanted Admiral Alberto Lais, attaché in the Italian Embassy in Washington, with her soft, soothing voice and pillow talk and her intoxicating bodily charms. After a few weeks he imagined himself deeply in love and, enfeebled by passion, endeavouring to grant Cynthia's every wish to win her favours, he agreed to obtain the Italian naval cypher codebook used by Admiral Cunningham in the Italian defeat at Matapan – even though it meant working against the interests of his own country. Montgomery Hyde goes on to confirm that Admiral Lais kept his word. The codebooks were produced; photostatic copies were made and Stephenson arranged with experts in Washington to have them immediately despatched to London.

That could have been the end of the matter, but Cynthia and the besotted Admiral continued their dalliances and Cynthia was rewarded with other Axis plans, but it was all too good to last and Cynthia was eventually responsible for the enforced departure of Admiral Lais from the United States. When boarding a vessel to take him back to Italy, his wife and family were grouped at the quayside and Cynthia stood alone, some distance away, and then Lais spent his last minutes with Cynthia whilst the tearful family was ignored.[2]

Interest faded for a while but scandal came to the fore in Britain in 1974 when Frederick Winterbotham's book *The Ultra Secret* was published. There was an illustration of Bletchley Park on the cover, yet the Official Secrets ban had not been lifted. Inside the book were details of Dilly Knox having been the mastermind behind the Enigma affair. This pleased his girls, but to their dismay the Cottage was not mentioned; Dilly's rods were completely overlooked and the celebratory drink with Admiral Cunningham was forgotten. Matapan was credited with a Luftwaffe break in Hut 6, which was due to Winterbotham knowing only about air force intelligence. The Germans had always accused the Italians of having traitors amongst them and this was confirmed by Montgomery Hyde's book which told his story of Cynthia.

The Admiral's family was horrified by the book's contents and decided to take out a libel action, which in Italy was allowed to be made on behalf of the dead. The Italians were anxious for *The Ultra Secret* to be translated and published immediately in Italian. Dr Giulio Divita, fellow of Clare College, Cambridge, was commissioned to edit the manuscript and, as an historian, he dedicated himself to researching the material thoroughly. Winterbotham was not an historian, but Dr Divita had the ability to prove, without doubt, that the evidence was stacked against the Germans. Records were finally released in 1978 and evidence supported Dr Divita's research showing that it was undoubtedly Italian cyphers that had been broken.

Yet another book was being written by Ronald Lewin, who had seen the public records which by this time had been released, and his book *Ultra Goes to War*, published in 1978, was the first about Bletchley Park to be published since the release of the official records. It showed the part played by Dilly Knox's section in the Battle of Matapan, including information that had not been available to Winterbotham. It was now officially acknowledged that it was the Italian cyphers that had been broken.

The BBC took up this media opportunity and in 1980 ran a series of television programmes called *Spy!,* also publishing an accompanying book. This was another version of Cynthia's story, alleging that she had sent the codebooks enabling the signals to be deciphered to the Admiralty. After complaining to *The Times,* Dr Divita took his search further and traced the whereabouts of whom he thought was the real Bletchley Cynthia. To her amusement Mavis was almost, but not quite, named as the spy. 'I was sent a glowing account of the interview in an Italian news paper referring to me as an *"affascinante signora, il topo Penelope Keith"* in her *"bella casa di Oxford"*.[3]

Mavis was asked, if the actual Matapan Battle messages were brought from Rome, would she show them how they had been broken individually without a codebook? Mavis replied saying firmly that if they did have codebooks they would not have needed codebreakers, and that after forty years she could not be sure that she could remember. When Divita arranged for the Admiral in charge of naval history to visit Mavis, she explained the procedure and, when holding the message with the heading *SUPERMARINA* in her hand, without hesitation she immediately took up her old role as if back at work, even remembering that she was, at the time, wearing a green jumper. She then recalled that 'Margaret Rock and I had been able to read out enough of the rest of the message to ensure we had the right wheel position. It had been raining all day and was still pelting when I rushed it over to the machine room.'[4]

'My new Admiral friend drank the health of Dilly and his girls and he wrote a charming letter of thanks and, possibly with Cynthia in mind, he ended with a cautious note: "Hoping to be given the opportunity of meeting you again – on work matters."'[5] A libel action was brought by the son and nephew of the late Admiral Lais as they wanted to clear the Lais name, and in 1970 the Supreme Court in Milan came to its decision: evidence to clear Admiral Lais' name was not available but the author, H. Montgomery Hyde, was found guilty. The Italians were now satisfied that Lais could now be exonerated.

The story of the Battle of Matapan had lingered on – things became complicated and there was more excitement. Bletchley Park had heard about the various books Mavis had written and she was invited to write a brochure to accompany an exhibition to be held there. It was to be about author Ian Fleming's wartime years with the Naval Intelligence Division (NID) that had brought him into close contact with Bletchley Park, providing him with background, and motivating him to launch the many adventures of his fictitious hero, James Bond, 007. Mavis accepted the invitation, and in 2008 the little book, *From Bletchley with Love*, was published, accompanying the exhibition of the same name.

Having signed the Official Secrets Act many of the wild ideas of Ian Fleming out of necessity remained in embryonic stage for a long period, but his early musings led him to write several novels. Within their pages, action hero James Bond, 007, would battle against villains of all kinds: spies, agents and special forces, whose weapons of blackmail were nuclear bombs, space missiles or deadly viruses. It would eventually take a knowledgeable person to untangle the facts that had nurtured the fiction, so the person chosen was Mavis Batey.

Ian Fleming stayed true to Bletchley Park's security rules, but the exhibition uncovered the part of his career kept secret for thirty years.

A special day for Mavis was 24 July 2008 and she was excited – their Royal Highnesses the Prince of Wales and the Duchess of Cornwall officially opened the exhibition, 'From Bletchley with Love'. Also present were members of the Fleming and Rear Admiral John Godfrey's families and, of course, the writer of the accompanying book, Mavis Batey and her husband, Keith. Their Royal Highnesses were delighted when Mavis and Keith demonstrated an Abwehr Enigma machine and told them a little of its history.

We learn from Mavis's book, *From Bletchley with Love*, that when applying to join NID Ian Fleming, who had come from a banking family, had been a stockbroker, and was an expert linguist with impressive references. Nevertheless, it was his sense of adventure that appealed to Rear Admiral John Godfrey, Director of Naval Intelligence, who engaged Fleming as his personal assistant. Fleming's designation was NID 17F and he had confidential dealings with MI5 and MI6, which were responsible for espionage and counter-espionage, and also with Special Operations Executive, which controlled subversive activities and sabotage. Fleming would accompany Godfrey to meetings, and sometimes be called upon to attend important conferences alone as Godfrey's representative. Fleming was liaison officer with Bletchley Park, and Mavis wrote that about once a fortnight he would confer with

Dilly Knox. This was, of course, many years before the publication of Fleming's books and was carried out with customary Bletchley Park practice, without ceremony.

Bletchley Park's existence was still a secret when the early novels were written. Dilly had worked with Fleming since the early days, co-ordinating with Frank Birch. Godfrey and Fleming had a very successful partnership until 1943 when Godfrey transferred and became head of the Royal Indian Navy. As NID 17F Fleming remained in the same position, but then went on to serve under DNI Rear Admiral Edmund Rushbrooke, giving him the opportunity to become knowledgeable on information concerning espionage and counter-espionage, subversive activities and sabotage – excellent fodder for his fantasy Bond novels.

Godfrey always remained certain that he had made an excellent decision in choosing Fleming as his assistant. Fleming respected Godfrey and many years later when his novel, *On Her Majesty's Secret Service* (1963), was published his readers were never certain of the true identity of 'M', the person to whom the book was dedicated. A startling clue was revealed by Mavis in the book accompanying the exhibition. She pointed out that when the fictitious character James Bond made a visit to his boss at his home in Windsor Forest, he discovered the bell on his front door to be 'a clapper of the brass ship's bell of some former *HMS Repulse*, the last of whose lines, a battle-cruiser, had been 'M's' final sea-going appointment. Command of the battle-cruiser *Repulse* had indeed been Godfrey's last sea-going appointment'.[6] Godfrey was no doubt flattered that Fleming had chosen him as a model for 'M', although he was uncertain about being portrayed as such a ruthless character.

Mavis confirmed that the two men enjoyed a lifelong friendship and Fleming helped Godfrey to write his history of the Naval Intelligence Division. Fleming gained a great deal of inspiration for his James Bond novels, and it was no doubt in appreciation of his experiences when working as assistant to Rear Admiral John Godfrey, Director of Naval Intelligence, that he dedicated this novel to him, albeit under the pseudonym 'M'.

As liaison officer between NID and Bletchley Park in World War II, Ian Fleming's fortnightly visits to Dilly no doubt also provided inspiration for those mind-blowing schemes and awesome adventures of his fictional secret agent. Mavis reminds her readers that James Bond was the man who Ian Fleming would like to have been and, in some ways, Bond was a mirror image of the charismatic Fleming: a good-looking, tough bachelor with all-round athletic prowess; they were daredevils. However, as he was serving in the NID, with connections at Bletchley Park, and had knowledge of secret information, Fleming was forbidden to take part in any activity which might put him in danger of injury, or becoming the enemy's prisoner and open to interrogation. James Bond, the famous 007 of the thrillers, on the other hand, as a commander in Special Branch, would not have been allowed any communication with Bletchley Park, which was still a secret place when the first thrillers were written, but he was cast as an action hero.

In the brochure Mavis carefully and succinctly goes through some of the missions with which Fleming was involved. It was crucial that further loss of merchant shipping, bringing essential supplies so vital to Britain's existence, should be brought to a halt. The codebreakers, including Mavis, were working at full capacity to break the naval Enigma code which would make important information available. They needed the daily key settings from a German naval vessel in the Channel and Fleming played his part by producing his first Bond-type plan – a daring endeavour to obtain the 'pinches' – theft of original codebooks, or cypher material. It was a blood-thirsty, 'cunning scheme', given the name 'Operation Ruthless'. Much to the disappointment of all those involved, especially Alan Turing and Peter Twinn who were wrestling with the German Navy's Kriegsmarine machine, for various reasons, including adverse weather conditions, the exercise could not be undertaken. Mavis, always fond of a joke, reported that Frank Birch, who had showed his enthusiasm for the 'very ingenious plot', told Fleming that 'Turing and Twinn came to me like undertakers cheated of a nice corpse... all in a stew about the cancellation of *Ruthless*'.[7]

Fleming was undaunted by the cancellation and his attention soon turned to 'Goldeneye', set up to keep Spain under observation. Although his scheme was modified by the Foreign Office and became less intense, Fleming was proud of his involvement and gave the name 'Goldeneye' to his post-war home and personal paradise in Jamaica. James Bond came into being at 'Goldeneye', and Mavis points out that from that time forward, money and gold were a dominating thread through Fleming's writings: *Goldfinger*, *The Man with the Golden Gun*, blackmail and ransom demanded monetary reward, and 'Goldeneye' was the villain's weapon of mass destruction in the first Bond film starring Pierce Brosnan. The lust for gold, an innocent pursuit of many, appears in the colourful and fantastic Bond literature as a major quest, moving through the territories of villains, politicians and bankers, supported by crime, terrorism and warfare.

The Abwehr Enigma machine code was broken in December 1941. This was a major achievement, largely responsible for the success of the British Double Cross System which Godfrey had helped to set up. At Camp 020 on Ham Common, captured German agents were trained to operate as double agents deceiving their German Abwehr controllers with false information. Mavis explains that Fleming became intrigued by the work of double agents and Double Cross, and he had access to the most secret messages which were prefixed 00 in the filing system. We are told that his colleague, Patrick Beesly, in his book, *Very Special Admiral,* reveals that this was why James Bond was given the codename 007.

A great number of conspiratorial events took place and large amounts of money were withdrawn from banks in areas where spies were thick on the ground: 'Double-cross leaks and rumours were backed by tactical action through planting dummy tanks and pipelines, increased radio activity and other special means.'[8] Ian Fleming was present at the Trident discussions in Washington and, on this and many other occasions, he must have acquired a substantial amount of fuel for filling his thrillers which were to follow much later.

In 1941, a clandestine radio station was set up in the riding school at Woburn Abbey. Sefton Delmar, previously in charge of the broadcasting of insidious morale-destroying propaganda for the Political Warfare Executive (PWE), was appointed boss. The station, named 'Gustav Siegfried Eins', was designated to circulating rumours and smear campaigns about Nazi officials, an idea conceived by Godfrey to cause trouble between U-boat ratings and officers. Godfrey became co-ordinating chief and pounced upon the opportunity to appoint Fleming to ensure that an undercover naval intelligence would be 'an activity that had war-winning attributes'.[9] Godfrey then 'asked Ian Fleming to put the machinery in motion for creating a Naval Section 17z in collaboration with PWE'.[10] Delmar later became sure that Fleming found ideas for his spy thrillers from their black propaganda techniques when working with PWE.

Unlike Lord Haw-Haw's *Germany Calling*, which became a joke, Delmar's propaganda appeared to be transmitted to Germany for Germans. Once again, Mavis could not resist some humour and told her readers that the huge transmitter installed in Sussex was named *Aspidistra*, after Gracie Fields' popular song 'The Biggest Aspidistra in the World'.

Casino Royale, published in 1953, was the first novel Fleming wrote when staying in his tropical paradise, Goldeneye, and it was said to be recognised by Sefton Delmar, a close family friend of Fleming, as being modelled on his wartime experiences. However, Mavis points out that there were two variations to the true tale of the famous gambling incident that took place in the fictional *Casino Royale*. An account given by Delmar, said by him to be fact rather than fiction, names Fleming's target across the green baize in the casino at Estoril as a German spy, an Abwehr agent. Although unsuccessful, Fleming had set out to make a hole in Abwehr funds, but instead had lost a considerable amount of his own money. In the novel *Casino Royale*, James Bond retaliated by bankrupting the gangster Le Chiffre, named after the French translation of cypher, when playing *chemin de fer.*

In the second account, Godfrey claims that Fleming's opponent at the gaming table was a business man and not an Abwehr agent – and a certain Dusko Popov, a British double agent, claimed to be that person and went on to write his own story. Mavis wrote that it had been suggested that Godfrey and Fleming were checking on Popov's creditability as a double agent, and many other candidates also put themselves forward. Perhaps on this occasion, rather than endeavouring to solve the riddle herself, Mavis allowed the intriguing question to remain with readers to ponder, and kept the mystery flowing. Perhaps it should be remembered that after the D-Day landings, Fleming wrote: 'Everything I write has a precedent in truth', but the truth, as everyone else in the secret service business knew, could not begin to be revealed for thirty years, long after Fleming's death. [11]

During the final months of WWII, Fleming (James Bond, 007, was not involved!) founded a special spy commando unit, 30 Assault Unit, divided into different individual sections, with the motto, 'Attain by Surprise'. Their mission was to seize enemy intelligence from the front line. They were very successful and obtained the entire archive of the German Navy.

After Victory in Europe Ian Fleming worked with Godfrey, Mavis continuing briefly to cover their activities. When asked by Lord Kemsley to organise a Foreign News Service for his chain of newspapers, Fleming readily accepted as his contract included two months' holiday a year. In January 1946, his house, Goldeneye, that he had built in Jamaica was completed and every year he would spend two months there writing his novels. He visited Japan and his fascination with the country inspired his final book, *You Only Live Twice;* the title was taken from a quotation of a Japanese poet and written in 1964, the year of Fleming's death.

Within the pages of *From Bletchley with Love,* Mavis gives an exciting account of how Ian Fleming's daredevil schemes on the Bond novels develop and, cleverly, clearly deciphers the links between fact and fiction. Fleming, she tells the reader, did not have first-hand personal experience of dangerous exploits, but he knew many who had. During her codebreaking years at Bletchley, Mavis had little contact with Ian Fleming, but in her usual manner she delved deep into history and was very successful in producing a useful catalogue of events for the 'From Bletchley with Love' exhibition.

Years later, in the autumn of her life, Mavis's thoughts frequently returned to Bletchley Park, the codebreaking centre that had featured so strongly in her early life, and when asked by her friend Ted Fawcett if she would be writing another book, she jokingly replied that she thought it might be one about spies. This would surely confirm that she was impressed by James Bond, 007, and she did, indeed, have a short story to tell about Cynthia.

CHAPTER TWENTY-ONE

Back to Bletchley Park

Mavis joined the Veterans' Club and would sometimes attend their meetings and events; she never cut her ties.

As a codebreaker herself Mavis had always felt grateful to the three Polish codebreakers who had given their help in the days immediately before the outbreak of war in 1939 and she had written about this in her biography of Dillwyn Knox. Dilly had already broken both the Spanish and Italian Enigma cyphers, and the reconstruction of the Enigma machine used by the German armed forces was 'The key role of the Poles in ensuring the British breaks took place much earlier than they would otherwise have done',[1] and this is rightly celebrated at Bletchley Park.

Bletchley's Polish Memorial commemorates the work of the three Polish codebreakers, Marian Rejewski, Henryk Zygalski and Jerzy Rozycki, who had a meeting with Bletchley men in the Pyry Forest in 1939.

When Poland was invaded by the Germans, the three Polish men evacuated to France and then via Spain, Portugal and Gibraltar to Britain where they enlisted in the Polish Armed Forces and worked on solving low-grade German cyphers. Sadly, when travelling on an ocean liner, Jerzy Rozycki was drowned when it sank near the Balearic

Islands in January 1942, in circumstances which were unclear. After the war Rejewski was reunited with his family in Poland; Zygalski remained in the United Kingdom where he was happily married and worked until his retirement as a lecturer in mathematical statistics at the University of Surrey. He died in 1978 and was buried at Chichester Cemetery, West Sussex.

On 15 July 2011 a public memorial for veterans of Bletchley Park and its outstations was unveiled by Her Majesty Queen Elizabeth II at Bletchley Park National Codebreaking Station.

The memorial consists of two, eight-foot-high slabs of Caithness stone, interlinked at the top. This is to signify the mutual reliance of those who worked at Bletchley Park and those who intercepted enemy transmissions at the 'outstations'. One block displays the wording 'We also served' and the second has a sculpted list of twenty-five of around 300 outstations that existed around the world. A Morse code message is engraved on the back of the memorial and codebreaking worksheets are available to help visitors decipher the message.

The memorial was commissioned by the Bletchley Park Trust and GCHQ and designed and sculpted by the artist Charles Gurrey.

Mavis was grateful that this monument of remembrance had eventually been installed at Bletchley Park, but like many others she wished it had been erected before so many of the people remembered had already died. There was a general feeling that because so much had remained hidden due to the Official Secrets Act, many people had not been given the credit they deserved.

They had been overlooked.

At the end of the war each of the Bletchley Park codebreaking sections were given the task of writing its history, and these contributions were brought together by four authors as one document which became known to GCHQ as BBRT, taking the initials of each of the authors: Mavis Batey, Keith Batey, Margaret Rock and Peter Twinn. They worked together in Dilly's research section and then ISK – Intelligence Services Knox. Reports relating to the army, navy and air force had previously been released, but information relating to the German Secret Service was withheld. The original intention was that it should remain permanently classified as a secret government document and that it should not enter the public domain.

During a reunion held at Bletchley Park Mansion on 21 September 2011, the previously secret document, *Batey, Batey, Rock and Twinn,* was presented to Mavis – the only surviving author. Simon Greenish, Director of the Bletchley Park Trust, praised Mavis at the presentation, saying, 'Mavis is a national heroine. Her work was so advanced it is still relevant today,' and he went on to explain that this was the reason the documents had only just been declassified. Mavis was overwhelmed – no doubt wishing her husband, Keith, and their close colleagues could still be present.

As they had both signed the Official Secrets Act, Mavis and Keith had scarcely discussed their work at Bletchley Park, so to be able to read the complete contents of this historical document was especially poignant for Mavis. She was now able to discover just how clever her husband, Keith, who had died the previous year, had been, and she learned exactly what he had been working on during the war years.

Mavis's daughters were very glad to be able to read the document about their parents' work and thoughtfully, upon the death of their mother, lodged records with the Churchill Archives Centre, Cambridge. It was Mavis's wish that rather than the documents being on display in a glass case, she would like them to be in an archive and available to scholars and academicians.

When Mavis made return visits to Bletchley Park in later years, little remained of the original park. Visitors flock through the gates to visit the museum, but they come not only to see the huts where the Bletchley staff worked, to share the secrets of early codebreaking technology and the foundation of the computer industry, but also to admire the grounds, parts of which are gradually being reinstated.

Mavis would perhaps cast her mind back to the days of her first arrival at Bletchley Park when some areas of the garden were still tended, but gone were the rose gardens, the roses around the verandah, the maze, parts of the ha-ha and the greenhouses; although some of the stoves were removed from the greenhouses to the staff huts, proving to be useful in keeping the draughty offices warm during the cold winter months of the war years.

Mavis became interested in the history of the house and garden of Bletchley Park before it became the National Codes Centre. She learned the Victorian mansion was built in 1883 for the wealthy stockbroker, newspaper proprietor and Member of Parliament, Herbert Leon, later to become Sir Herbert Leon. The estate, set in the beautiful Buckinghamshire landscape, was once a mediaeval manor with a deer park. As with the personnel there in Mavis's time, Sir Herbert found its position could not have been better and he had a new private gate put in place to give easy access to the railway station. The tranquility of the peaceful landscape was retained by an additional screen of recently introduced American evergreen coniferous trees.

In Sir Leon's time forty gardeners were employed to take care of what, over the years, had become rough grazing ground, but was transformed into one of the foremost English gardens of its time, often attracting over 20,000 visitors on its August Bank Holiday open days.

Bletchley Park boasted all the features attributed to Victorian gardens of distinction: an eye-catching formal sunken garden of about an acre, with colourful carpet bedding surrounded by a belt of trees and shrubs. A lake of another acre, with steep banks, was partly overhung with trees, which Mavis remembered well for it was here that she and Keith would wander at break times to escape the over-crowded and smoky huts in which they worked; but always remaining alert and ready for the arrival of new messages. In the Leon family's garden there were several greenhouses filled with plants; there were walled gardens, an azalea garden, roses were abundant, spilling out of their own confined rose garden, and a maze and tennis courts. Special features were the American conifers and evergreen shrubs introduced to Britain in previous centuries.

When Sir Herbert Leon died in 1926 it became necessary to restrict the amount of money spent on the garden, and upon the death of his widow in 1937 Bletchley Park was offered for sale as a property with

581 acres of land. It was purchased by Mr Hubert Faulkner, a property developer, who set out to demolish the mansion and build a housing estate; he planned to live in a prime position in a house close by the lake.

Faulkner's property development was put in motion, but never came to fruition. In 1938, before demolition of the mansion had commenced, an offer was made by Admiral Sinclair, Chief of the Secret Intelligence Service, for the mansion and the land; Mr Faulkner reluctantly accepted the sum of £7,500. He must, however, have been very curious when a little later he was engaged to build a series of huts in the grounds. The gardens had practically disappeared, but war was looming and it was not long before the nation was told 'Careless talk costs lives'. Admiral Sinclair was careful to retain the lawns in front of the mansion; a thoughtful gesture, made to provide a comfortable country-house atmosphere still enjoyed by veterans and visitors.

Landscape historian Dr Sarah Rutherford, an advisor on the restoration of the grounds of Bletchley Park, pointed out that the site is recognised by English Heritage as the only surviving country house and park adapted for wartime intelligence use. Unlike many country houses this site became the property of the government so there was never the necessity to return it to public ownership. It was in very poor condition, in need of repair and refurbishment, and a decision was taken for a proposal to be put forward that would also include the landscape.

When Mavis heard of this she was delighted. She thought it wonderful that the house and grounds which became home to so many people during the war should be saved, *and* improved. She remembered the awful huts – smelly and stuffy after the men had been constantly smoking all day – but then how relaxing to take a quiet stroll around the lake.

To commemorate what Sir Winston Churchill called at the time of the D-Day landings, the 'Special Relationship' between Britain and America, and to celebrate the friendly partnership with the American codebreakers who worked at Bletchley Park, a permanent American Garden Trail was created supported by the Royal Horticultural Society. This was initiated by the Bletchley Park Trust and the GHS, and pushed forward by the enthusiasm and hard work of the doyenne of British garden historians, Mavis Batey, who advised the Trust on the project.

During her many years with the GHS Mavis had become extremely knowledgeable and was aware that an Anglo-American horticultural relationship had been enjoyed for over three centuries. Since the days of the early settlers, pioneering British explorers to North America had brought back plants, trees and shrubs never before seen in this part of the world, so were known as 'exotics' and 'curiosities'. In Britain, a thirst for knowledge and a desire to create beautiful gardens were fed by the discovery of the New World. This offered far-reaching opportunities and there has been an ever-increasing stream of these plants into the British Isles, and for many years there was a vogue for American gardens.

Mavis remembered the Americans who had worked beside them at Bletchley Park and thought how interesting it would be to have a new garden feature with American roots growing in British soil. Perhaps she was thinking how she and many others considered it was preferable to enhance the happiness and health of the living rather than build sad monuments in gloomy places. The two monuments already at Bletchley would now stand proud in what would be a splendid landscape and there would be a continuing and lasting friendship, through flowers and trees, marking the long association between Britain and North America. Such a strong horticultural link makes it appropriate for there to be an American Garden Trail growing the flowers, shrubs and trees emblematic of each of the United States of America. Mavis was happy with her idea for the American Garden Trail to follow the path around the perimeter of the lake.

As so often happens when a country expands industrially and agriculturally, towards the end of the nineteenth century the North American landscape began to suffer from the development taking place across the country. Many people became concerned about the environmental destruction caused by deforestation and land clearance for crops, cattle and industry. The North American people are proud of their natural landscape and there was a surge of interest in the environment, coupled with a desire to preserve local flora. It was, of course, gardeners who took the lead, and the Garden Club Movement, led by the Lexington Field and Garden Club, started to promote the adoption of horticultural state emblems in America.

A number of trees growing at Bletchley Park were planted at the time the mansion was built and, along with American trees donated by the Royal Horticultural Society, and rhododendrons given by Edmund de Rothschild, the extant trees have been included in the garden walk with many more donated by veterans from Bletchley Park codebreaking days. Mavis was delighted to receive a donation of rhododendrons and a beautiful tulip tree (*liriodendron tulipifera*) made by Mrs Wendy Osborne, her friend from the Alverstoke Crescent Garden, Gosport; and when the American Garden Trail later starred in the Bucks Garden Trust exhibit at the Hampton Court Garden Show, Wendy Osborne's choice of plants was featured.

The mighty redwood (*Sequoiadendron giganteum*), or wellingtonia, the state emblem for California State, which stands before the mansion and marks the beginning of the American Garden Trail, was planted in Victorian times by the Leon family, and according to Mavis the top of the tall *Sequoia* was used as a mast from which an aerial was slung to the radio room in a small tower on the roof of the mansion – Station X. 'It was soon realised that it was unwise to draw attention to Bletchley Park's secret listening activities and 'Y' wireless interception outstations were set up for the purpose in different parts of the country.'[2]

From the *Sequoia*, the trail leads to the lake where the planting is profuse: purple *fleur de lys* and the yellow flag iris (*Iris germanica*), for Tennessee, fringe the bank, where there are a number of American trees to be found. There is a sugar maple (*Acer saccharinum*) – the tree emblem for both Wisconsin and Vermont, and the northern red oak (*Quercus rubra*) – favourite of New Jersey. On the north bank is the swamp cypress (*Taxodium distichum*) – the tree emblem of Louisiana, and there are flower beds where carefully chosen groups of plants grow. There are Old World plants, taken to North America by the early settlers, and others that came across the Atlantic to

Britain and many have since become state flower emblems. Among them spiderwort *(Tradescantia virginiana)* and the autumn-flowering golden rod *(Solidago Canadensis)* – now the state flower emblems of Kentucky and Nebraska. The walk continues onward through the courtyard and back to the mansion, passing a multitude of botanical emblems, each with its own story to tell.[3]

On a spring day in the month of May 2004, Mavis paid a visit to Bletchley Park along with her friend Kim Wilkie, the world-renowned landscape architect, and David Jewell of the Royal Horticultural Society and they planted a number of emblem trees donated by the RHS. George Graham and Mary Sarre were two local garden designers who put in the hard landscaping and planted the floral plants in the lakeside beds, and continued their work when further stages of the garden trail were completed. They were also thoughtful in putting in some rabbit netting to keep out rabbits – also Canada geese – newcomers to the scene. The completion of the first stage of the trail was celebrated on 21 August 2004, a fun-filled day given the name USA Day when the American Garden Trail was inaugurated by Minister David T. Johnson, the chargé d'affaires at the American Embassy in London.

Everyone was in good spirits and the minister joined in the fun by pitching a ball for the local baseball team – on this occasion there was no discussion about the rules – and he went on to throw a pass for the American football team. The minister and his family appeared to enjoy all that was offered and kindly wrote a letter of appreciation of his family's day at Bletchley Park, commenting that the '*American Garden Trail* makes a living, growing reminder not just of how our countries worked together in the toughest days, but of our continued work to keep our citizens safe and free.'[4]

Mavis lived to see the American Garden Trail completed, and the project was signed off by her just a few months before her death on 12 November 2013.

Farewell

In 2009 Mavis and Keith moved to a retirement bungalow at Barlavington Manor, close to Petworth, West Sussex, where Mavis once led a GHS campaign to prevent a new road cutting across the estate. At first they had a bungalow and were happy there and later they transferred to an apartment which they enjoyed equally well. Mavis still had plenty of energy and one of the staff would sometimes take her out for a car-ride and stop at some place she found interesting.

On 28 August 2010 Keith died and soon after, no doubt still thinking of him, Mavis visited the Royal Aircraft Establishment, Farnborough, where Keith had once worked. Mavis was very interested and noticed a spelling error on one of the storyboards which she thought was an unforgivable error and quickly pointed this out. There was no fuss, it was corrected and she obviously felt pleased that she was still able to take control.

On Saturday 20 October 2012 Mavis attended the unveiling of a plaque dedicated to Dilly Knox on the village green at Naphill, near his home Courn's Wood House, Buckinghamshire. Mavis was pleased to find many Knox family members were in attendance and there were representatives from Bletchley Park, all of whom expressed their appreciation that the villagers had chosen to honour Dilly, and various donations covered the cost of the memorial and service. Mavis felt proud to have worked with Dilly, and made a contribution towards refreshments.

All was peaceful when returning home to the apartment at Barlavington Manor. Mavis had become fond of the view towards a woodland which reminded her of the Rhineland forest, 'my romantic *schoner, gruner Welt*' which she once loved, and now she could retire with her fond memories. Mavis had no fear and made it clear to her friends and family, in the last few weeks before her death, that she'd had a wonderful life and was ready to join Keith.

The funeral of Mavis took place in the afternoon of Wednesday 27 November 2013 and was attended by a great many relations, friends and colleagues. Her immediate family, Elizabeth, Christopher and Deborah, said they were very moved by the letters they had received, and these comments gave a summary of Mavis exactly as all her friends knew her:

> *Generous with her time and ideas*
> *In awe of the speed and clarity of her mind*
> *Very modest about her contributions*
> *It was always fascinating and fun to watch such a shrewd operator at work*
> and *Infectious laugh*

Her friend and colleague David Lambert said, 'She will remain a happy presence, one of those rare people who as Tolstoy said of Ruskin, "think with their hearts": endlessly kind and generous, always amused and wise, a lodestar to remind us of all that love.'

Yes, all give a true picture of Mavis, and a final comment could have come from her late husband and certainly her children:

Hard to keep up with.

Select Bibliography

Mavis Batey in conversation with Michael Smith http://aidopbpp.imboo. im/1736751-bletchley--park-extra-e28-mavisbatey

Mavis Batey: 'Down to Earth: An Oral History of British Horticulture', National Sound Archive, Interview recording: F15120-F15125

Interviewee: Mavis Batey; Interviewer: Louise Brodie Recording Date: 2003.02.19; 2003.03.10

Demobilisation memo, National Archives. Cited: Sinclair McKay, *The Secret Life of Bletchley Park* (London: Aurum, 2010) p. 282

BOOKS

Annan, Noel *Our Age: Portrait of a Generation* (London: Weidenfeld & Nicolson, 1990)

Austen, Jane *Pride and Prejudice*

Batey, Mavis *The Historic Gardens of Oxford and Cambridge* (London: Macmillan, 1989)

– *The World of Alice* (Andover, UK: Pitkin, 1998)

– et al, *Arcadian Thames* (London: Barn Elms, 1994)

– *Jane Austen and the English Landscape* (London: Barn Elms, 1996)

– *Alexander Pope: The Poet and the Landscape* (London: Barn Elms, 1999)

– *Dilly: The Man Who Broke Enigmas* (London: Biteback, 2010)

– *From Bletchley With Love* (Buckingham, UK: Bletchley Park Trust, 2008)

– et al, *Indignation Today! Indignation: The Campaign for Conservation* (London: Kit-Cat, 2000)

Bell, Oliver et al. eds. *The Diary of Virginia Woolf Vol V: 1936-1941* (London: Hogarth, 1984)

Birch, Frank et al. *Alice in I. D. 25*, compiled with introductions by Mavis Batey and

Edward Wakeling (Bedfordshire, UK: Aznet, 2007)

Brendon, Piers *Thomas Cook: 105 Years of Popular Tourism* (London: Secker & Warberg, 1991)

Briggs, Asa *Code Breaking in Bletchley Park* (London: Frontline Books, 2011)

Campbell, John *Roy Jenkins: A Well-Rounded Life* (London: Jonathan Cape, 2014)

Chalcraft, Anna and Judith Viscardi *Strawberry Hill: Horace Walpole's Gothic Castle* (London: Frances Lincoln, 2007)

Clarke, Norma *Brothers of the Quill: Oliver Goldsmith in Grub Street* (Cambridge, Massachusetts and London: Harvard University Press, 2016)

Cooper, Julie *Animals in War* (London: Heinemann, 1983)

Douglas-Fairhurst, Robert *The Story of Alice; Lewis Carroll and the Secret History of Wonderland* (London: Harvill Secker, 2015)

Dunmore, Helen H. *Exposure* (London: Penguin Books, 1995)

Elliott, Brent 'The Development and Present State of Garden History', occasional papers from the RHS, Lindley Library 9 (1912)

Erskine, Ralph and Michael Smith, eds. *Action this Day* (WW: Bantam Press, 2001)

Fitzgerald, Penelope *The Knox Brothers* (London: Macmillan, 1977 and New York: Alfred Knopf, 2014)

Forster, John *The Life and Adventures of Oliver Goldsmith*

Fry, Helen *The M Room: Secret Listeners who Bugged the Nazis in WW2 (London: Marrano, 2012)*

Gardiner, Juliet *The Animals' War* (London: Heineman, 1983)

Gardiner, Juliet *The Blitz: The British Under Attack* (London: Harper Press, 2011)

Gibson, Trish *Brenda Colvin: A Career in Landscape* (London: Frances Lincoln, 2011)

Hoskins, William G. *The Making of the English Landscape* (Penguin Books, 1975)

Lee, Celia and Paul Edward Strong, eds. *Women in War: From Home Front to Front Line* (South Yorkshire: Pen and Sword Military, 2012)

Lee, Hermione *Penelope Fitzgerald: A Life* (London: Chatto & Windus, 2013)

Lee, Hermione *Virginia Woolf* (London: Chatto & Windus, 1996)

Lownie, Andrew *Stalin's Englishman: The Lives of Guy Burgess* (London: Hodder & Stoughton, 2015)

Lycett, Andrew *Ian Fleming* (London: Weidenfeld and Nicholson, 1995)

Mason, William *The English Garden*

Masterman, J. C. *The Double Cross System: The War of 1939-1945* (Worldwide: Yale University Press, 1972)

McKay, Sinclair *The Secret Life of Bletchley Park: The WWII Codebreaking Centre and the Men and Women Who Worked There* (London: Aurum, 2010)

Minter, Sue *The Well-Connected Gardener* (Brighton, UK: Book Guild, 2010)

Montgomery Hyde, H. *The Quiet Canadian: The Secret Service Story of Sir William Stephenson* (London: Hamish Hamilton, 1962)

Oakley, Brian *The Bletchley Park War Diaries: July 1939-August 1945: Secret Intelligence of the Second World War*, 3.0 edn. (Wynne Press, 2011) (Security measures prohibited staff keeping diaries during the war.)

Prior, James *The Life of Oliver Goldsmith* (London: John Murray, 1837)

Quintana, Ricardo *Oliver Goldsmith: A Georgian Study* (New York: Macmillan, London: Collier Macmillan, 1967)

Rankin, Nicholas *Ian Fleming's Commandos* (London: Faber and Faber, 1950)

Sebag-Montefiore, Hugh *Enigma* (London: Weidenfeld & Nicholson, 2000)

Segrave, Elisa *The Girl from Station X* (London: Arum Press, 2013)

Seymour, Miranda *Noble Endeavours: The Life of Two Countries, England and Germany in Many Stories* (London: Simon & Schuster, 2013)

Sisman, Adam *Hugh Trevor-Roper: The Biography* (Weidenfeld & Nicholson, 2010)

Smith, Michael *Station X: The Codebreakers of Bletchley Park* (London: Channel 4 Books, 1998)

Taylor, J. A. *Bletchley Park's Secret Sisters* (Bedford, UK: The Book Castle, 2005)

Trumpington, Jean *Coming Up Trumps* (London: Macmillan, 2014)

Wardle, Ralph M. *Oliver Goldsmith* (Lawrence: University of Kansas Press, London: Constable, 1957)

Welchman, Gordon *The Hut Six Story* (Michigan: McGraw Hill Book Company, 1982)

JOURNALS, MAGAZINES, ON-LINE PUBLICTIONS, ETC.

Grice, Elizabeth 'Garden Campaigner Talks to Elizabeth Grice' *The Oldie, (January, 2013) 12

Haldane, Seán, 'Books for Burning', London Library Magazine, 23 (2014) 16—17

Sanecki, Kay N. 'Memories of the Founding of the Society', *The Garden History Society: Newsletter 15*

Subramaniam, Shula and Joel Greenberg, 'A Scrupulous Man', *Bletchley Park Magazine Issue 2* (Spring/Summer 2014) p. 10

Journals of The Garden History Society

Newsletters of The Garden History Society

Country Life

Hortus

The Bletchley Park Magazine

The Bucks Gardener

The Hardy Plants

http://www.telegraph.co.uk/news/pbituaries/military-obituaries/special-forces-obituaries/1044712/Mavis-Batey-obituary.html

The United States National Arboretum, State Trees and State Flowers Washington:

State Trees and Flowers http://www.isna.isda.gov/Gardens/collections/statetreeflower.html

Martin, Douglas, 'Mavis Batey, Allied Code Breaker in World War II, Dies at 92', *New York Times* (22 November 2013)

Jackson, Sarah 'Mavis Batey: From codebreaker to campaigner for historic parks and garden', Source: Personal interview with Mavis Batey, 24 January 2008 http://www.parksandgardens.org.

http://telegraph.co.uk/news/miltary/obituaries/special-forces-obituaries/1044712/MavisBatey-obituary.html

Books and Publications by Mavis Batey

BOOKS

Alexander Pope: The Poet and the Landscape (London: Barn Elms Publishing, 1996)

Alice's Adventures in Oxford (Andover, UK: Pitkin, 1980, 1994)

Dilly: The Man Who Broke Enigmas (London: Biteback, 2010)

From Bletchley with Love (Buckingham, UK: Bletchley Park Trust, 2008)

Jane Austen and the English Landscape (London: Barn Elms Publishing, 1999)

Oxford Gardens (Avebury, UK: 1982. 2nd ed. Aldershot, UK: Scolar, 1986)

Regency Gardens (Buckingham, UK: Shire, 1995)

The Adventures of Alice (London: Macmillan, 1993)

The Historic Gardens of Oxford and Cambridge (London: Macmillan, 1989)

Batey, Mavis and David Lambert *The English Garden Tour* (London: John Murray, 1989)

Batey, Mavis and Jan Woudstra *The Story of the Privy Garden at Hampton Court* (London: Barn Elms Publishing, 1995)

Batey, Mavis et al. *Arcadian Thames: The River and the Landscape from Hampton to Kew* (London: Barn Elms Publishing, 1994)

Batey, Mavis, et al. *Indignation! The Campaign for Conservation* (London: Kit-Cat, 2000)

Birch, Frank, et al. *Alice in ID 25* Compiled with Introductions by Mavis Batey and Edward Wakeling (Bedfordshire, UK: Aznet, 2007)

ARTICLES IN JOURNALS

'Alice's Wonderland Gardens', *Country Life* 170 (1981) pp. 1456-57

'Basing House Tudor Gardens', *Garden History* 15.2 (1987) pp. 94-109

'Brighton Pavilion Grounds', *Country Life* 175 (1984) pp. 1152-54

'Chawton House, Hants', *Country Life* 188 (1994) p. 74

'Edward Cooke', *Garden History* 6.1 (1978) pp. 18-24

'Evelyn Gardens in Surrey', *Garden History* 4.1 (1976) pp. 10-14

'Gertrude Jekyll and the Arts and Crafts Movement', *Gertrude Jekyll* ed. by
    M. Tooley (1884)

'Gilpin and the Schoolboy Picturesque', *Garden History* 2.2 (1974) pp. 24-26

'Guide to Nuneham Courtenay', (University of Oxford, 1970)

'History in Gardens', *Hortus* 1 (1987) pp. 33-40

'Horace Walpole as Modern Garden Historian', *Garden History* 19.I (1991)
    pp. 1-11

'In Quest of Jane Austen's "Mr Repton"', *Garden History* 5.1 (1977) pp. 19-20

'Jane Austen and the Picturesque', *The Picturesque* 5 (Winter 1993)

'Jane Austen at Stoneleigh Abbey', *Country Life* 160 (1976) pp. 1974-5

'Keats House, Hampstead', *Garden History* 3.4 (1975) pp. 35-39

'Landscape Gardens in Oxfordshire', *Of Oxfordshire Gardens* (Oxford
    Polytechnic Press, 1982)

'Landscaping of Amesbury, Wiltshire', *Country Life* 182 (1988) pp. 78-80

'Magdalen Meadows', *Garden History* 9.2 (1981) pp. 110-17

'Mount Edgcumbe, Cornwall', *Country Life* 183 (1989) pp. 214-217

'North Oxford Suburb', *Country Life* 167 (1980) pp. 888-90

'Nuneham Courtenay: An English Eighteenth-Century Deserted Village',
    Oxoniensia 33 (1968) pp. 108-24

'Oliver Goldsmith; an indictment of landscape gardening', *Furor Hortensis*
    ed. P. Willis (1974)

'Oxford Gardens' (Avebury, 1982, reissued Scolar, 1986)

'Recording Parks and Gardens', *The Threat to the Historic Rural Landscape*,
    eds. P. F. Brandon and R. N. Millman (1981)

'Shotover, Oxfordshire', *Country Life* 162 (1977) pp. 1912-14; 1978-79

'Some Restorations of Regency Flower Gardens', *The Hardy Plant* 17.2
    (1995) pp. 2-7

'Swiss Garden, Old Warden Bedfordshire', *Garden History* 3.4 (1975) pp. 40-43

'Taking Stock: The Garden History Society', *Hortus* 29 (Spring, 1994)
    pp. 82-87

'The Creation of Nuneham, Oxfordshire', *Country Life* 144 (1968), pp. 541-42; 640-42

'The High Phase of English Landscape Gardening', *British and American Gardens in the Eighteenth Century,* eds. Maccubbin and Martin (1984)

'The Landscaping of the Tamar Valley', *Association of Gardens Trust Journal* 1.1 (1996)

'The New Forest and the Picturesque', *Pleasure Grounds, the Garden and Landscapes of Hampshire* (1987)

'The Picturesque: An Overview', *Garden History* 22.2 (1994) pp. 121-32

'The Way to View Rousham by Kent's Gardener', *Garden History* II.2 (1983) pp. 125-32

'The Work of the Garden History Society', *The Garden* 104 (1979) pp. 402-405

'Two Romantic Picturesque Gardens', *Garden History* 22.2 (1994) pp. 197-205

'West Surrey – Gertrude Jekyll's Art', *Garden History* 2.2 (1974) pp. 12-23

'William Kent's Rousham', *Historic House* (Spring 1985) pp. 24-27

'William Mason', *Garden History* 1.2 (1973) pp. 11-25

Notes

An Introduction

1 Sarah Jackson, *Mavis Batey: from codebreaker to campaigner for historic parks and gardens*: Source: Interview 24 January 2008, http://www.parksandgardens. org [Accessed: 31 December, 2013]

2 Mavis Batey, *The World of Alice* (Andover, UK: Pitkin, 1998) p. 8

Chapter 1: *The Bliss of Growing Up*

1 Mavis Batey, *Down to Earth: An Oral History on British Horticulture* (London: National Sound Archive, 2003) F15120-5 Interviewer: Louise Brodie

2 ibid.

3 ibid.

4 Piers Brendon, *Thomas Cook: 105 Years of Popular Tourism* (London: Secker & Warburg, 1991) p. 276

5 Piers Brendon, ibid. p. 276

6 Miranda Seymour, *Noble Endeavours: The Life of Two Countries, England and Germany, in Many Stories* (London: Simon & Schuster, 2013) p. 319

7 Miranda Seymour, ibid. p. 319

8 Mavis Batey, *Dilly: The Man Who Broke Enigmas* (London: Biteback, 2010) p. 108

9 Sean Haldane, *Books for Burning*, London Library Magazine Spring 2014, p. 18

10 Mavis Batey, *Dilly: The Man who Broke Enigmas* (London: Biteback, 2010) p. 108

11 Cited: Andrew Lownie, *Stalin's Englishman: The Lives of Guy Burgess* (London: Hodder & Stoughton, 2015) p. 98

12 Hermione Lee, *Virginia Woolf* (London: Chatto & Windus, 1996) p. 664

13 Miranda Seymour, *Noble Endeavours: The Life of Two Countries, England and Germany, in Many Stories* (London: Simon & Schuster, 2013) p. 355

14 Mavis Batey, *Dilly: The Man who Broke Enigmas* (London: Biteback, 2010) p. 109

15 Mavis Batey, ibid. p. 109

16 Hugh Sebag-Montefiore, *Enigma: The Battle for the Code* (London: Cassell, 2001) p. 118

17 Juliet Gardiner, *The Blitz: The British Under Attack* (London: Harper Press, 2011) p. 52

18 Sinclair McKay, *The Secret Life of Bletchley Park: The WWII Codebreaking Centre and the Men and Women Who Worked There* (London: Aurum, 2010) p. 23

19 Sinclair McKay, ibid. p. 22

20 Sinclair McKay, ibid. p. 23

21 Michael Smith, *Station X: The Codebreakers of Bletchley Park* (London: Channel 4 Books, 1998) p. 37

22 Mavis Batey, *Dilly: The Man Who Broke Enigmas* (London: Biteback, 2010) p. 109

23 Mavis Batey, ibid. p. 110

24 Mavis Batey, op. cit. p. 110.

Chapter 2: Life at Bletchley Park

1 https/warandsecurity.com/2014/08/05/britain-cuts-german-cable-communications-5-august-1914

2 Penelope Fitzgerald, *The Knox Brothers: Edmund ('Evoe') 1881-1971, Dillwyn 1883-1943, Wilfred 1866-1950, Ronald 1888-1957* (London: Macmillan, 1977) p. 230

3 Miranda Seymour, *Noble Endeavours: The Life of Two Countries, England and Germany, in Many Stories* (London: Simon & Schuster, 2013) p. 411

4 Mavis Batey, *Dilly: The Man Who Broke Enigmas* (London: Backbite, 2010) p. 87

5 Mavis Batey, *Dilly: The Man Who Broke Enigmas* (London: Biteback, 2010) p. 110

6   Mavis Batey, ibid. p. 110

7   Michael Smith, *Station X: The Codebreakers of Bletchley Park* (London: Channel 4 Books, 1998) p. 38

8   Mavis Batey, *Dilly: The Man Who Broke Enigmas* (London: Biteback, 2010) p. 110

9   Michael Smith, op cit. p. 38.

10   Mavis Batey, op cit. p. 9

11   Michael Smith, *The Debs of Bletchley Park* (London: Aurum Press Ltd, 2015) p. 173

12   Sinclair McKay, *The Secret Life of Bletchley Park* (London: Aurum, 2011) p. 22

13   Jean Trumpington, *Coming up Trumps: A Memoir* (London: Macmillan, 2014) p. 42

14   Mavis Batey, *Dilly: The Man Who Broke Enigmas* (London: Biteback, 2010) p. 89

15   Max Hastings, *The Secret War: Spies, Codes and Guerrillas 1939-45* (London: William Collins, 2015) p. 73

16   Michael Smith, *Station X: The Codebreakers of Bletchley Park* (London: Channel 4 Books, 1998) p. 38

17   Sinclair McKay, *The Secret Life of Bletchley Park* (London: Aurum, 2010) p. 258

18   Penelope Fitzgerald, *The Knox Brothers* (London: Macmillan, 1977) p. 237

19   Sinclair McKay, *The Secret Life of Bletchley Park* (London: Aurum, 2010) p. 126

20   Sinclair McKay, *The Secret Life of Bletchley Park* (London: Aurum, 2010) p. 88

21   Jean Trumpington, *Coming up Trumps: A Memoir* (London: Macmillan, 2014) p. 42

22   Michael Smith, *Station X: The Codebreakers of Bletchley Park* (London: Channel 4 Books) p. 37

23   From a private memoir written by Mary Knight of Nailsea, Somerset, in 1999, and given to the writer by her daughter, after she had received an award from Bletchley Park on the occasion of her ninetieth birthday in July 2014

Chapter 3: Mavis Has Her First Big Break

1   Asa Briggs, *Secret Days: Code-Breaking in Bletchley Park* (London: Frontline Books, 2011) p. 127

2   Mavis Batey, *Dilly: The Man who Broke Enigmas* (London: Biteback, 2010) p. 112

3   Sinclair McKay, *The Secret Life of Bletchley Park* (London: Aurum Press, 2010) p. 44

4   Sinclair McKay, ibid. p. 43

5   Dr Brian Oakley, *The Bletchley Park War Diaries: July 1939-August 1945: Secret Intelligence of the Second World War* (Wynne Press, January 2011) 41/03A. p. 54 (Security measures prohibited staff keeping diaries during the war years)

6   Mavis Batey, *Dilly:The Man who Broke Enigmas* (London: Backbite, 2010) p. 116

7   Mavis Batey, 'Breaking Italian Enigma' in *Action This Day*, Eds. Ralph Erskine and Michael Smith (London, New York, Toronto, Sydney, Auckland: Bantam Press, 2001) p. 103

8   Mavis Batey, 'Breaking Italian Enigma' in *Action This Day*, Eds. Ralph Erskine and Michael Smith (London, New York, Toronto, Sydney, Auckland: Bantam Press, 2001) p. 103

9   Mavis Batey, 'Breaking Italian Enigma', in *Action This Day*, Eds. Ralph Erskine and Michael Smith (London, New York, Toronto, Sydney, Auckland: Bantam Press, 2001) p. 95

10 Mavis Batey, 'Breaking Italian Enigma', in *Action This Day,* Eds. Ralph Erskine and Michael Smith, p. 102

11 Mavis Batey, *Dilly: The Man Who Broke Enigmas* (London: Biteback, 2010) p. 115

12 Hermione Lee, *Penelope Fitzgerald: A Life* (London: Chatto & Windus, 2013) p. 13

13 Dr Brian Oakley, *The Bletchley Park War Diaries: July 1939-August 1945: Secret Intelligence of the Second World War* (Wynne Press, 2011) 40/11B p. 43

14 R. D. Foot, Obituary: Professor R. V. Jones. *Independent,* 19 December 1997

Chapter 4: *The Battle of Matapan, March 1941*

1   Mavis Batey, *Dilly: The Man who Broke Enigmas,* p. 116

2   Mavis Batey, ibid. p. 116

3   Mavis Batey, ibid. p. 117

4   Mavis Batey, ibid. p. 122

5   Sinclair, McKay, ibid. p. 131

6   Mavis Batey, p. 122

7   Jean Trumpington, *Coming up Trumps: A Memoir* (London: Macmillan, April 2014) p. 46

8   Hugh Sebag-Montefiore, *Enigma: The Battle for the Code* (London: Cassell Military Paperbacks) p. 125

9   Mavis Batey, *Dilly, The Man Who Broke Enigmas* (London: Biteback, 2010) p. 125

10 Mavis Batey, ibid. p. 118

11 Jean Trumpington, *Coming up Trumps: A Memoir* (London: Macmillan, April 2014) p. 44

12 Brian Oakley, *Bletchley Park War Diaries: July 1939-August 1945* (Wynne Press, 2011) 41/09B p. 67

13 Sinclair McKay, *The Secret Life of Bletchley Park* (London: Aurum, 2010) p. 159

Chapter 5: The Twenty Committee: Double Cross XX

1 Sinclair McKay, *The Secret Life of Bletchley Park* (London: Aurum Press, 2011) p. 125

2 John Masterman, *The Double Cross System* (World Wide: Yale University Press, 1972) p. 144

3 John Masterman ibid. p. 147

4 Mavis Batey, *Dilly The Man Who Broke Enigmas* (London: Biteback, 2010) p. 132

5 Mavis Batey, ibid. p. 135

6 Mavis Batey, ibid. p. 140

7 Mavis Batey, ibid. p. 137

8 Keith Batey, 'How Dilly Knox and His Girls Broke the Abwehr Enigma', in *Action This Day*, Eds. Ralph Erskine and Michael Smith (London, New York, Toronto, Sydney, Auckland: Bantam Press) p. 307

9 http://www.telegraph.co.uk/news/military-obituary/special-forces-obituaries/10447712/Mavis-Batey-obituary-html

10 Mavis Batey, *Dilly: The Man Who Broke Enigmas* (London: Biteback, 2010) p. 139

11 Mavis Batey, ibid. p. 139

12 Mavis Batey, *Letter from Dilly Knox to Valentine Vivian*, ibid. p. 141

13 http://www.thetimes.co.uk (London: Sept 10, 2010) News: p. 48

14 Dr Brian Oakley, *The Bletchley Park War Diaries: July 1939-August 1945*, 3rd edn (Wynne Press, 2011) 40 41/11B p. 71

Chapter 6: From Mutual Suspicion to Mutual Respect

1 Sinclair McKay, *The Secret Life of Bletchley Park* (London: Aurum, 2010) p. 204

2 Steven Budiansky, *Bletchley Park and the Special Relationship*, Eds. Michael Smith and Ralph Erskine *Action this Day* (London, New York: Bantam Press, 2001) p. 218

3   Brian Oakley, *The Bletchley Park War Diaries: July 1939-August 1945: Secret Intelligence and the Second World War* (Bletchley Park Trust, 2010) 44/12B p. 157

4   Mavis Batey, *Dilly: The Man Who Broke Enigmas* (London: Biteback, 2010) p. 215

5   Brian Oakley, *The Bletchley Park War Diaries:July 1939-August 1945: Secret Intelligence and the Second World War* (Bletchley Park Trust, 2010) 41/03B p. 55

6   Stephen Budiansky, *Bletchley Park and the Special Relationship* Eds. Michael Smith and Ralph Erskine *Action this Day* (London, New York, Toronto, Sydney and Auckland: Bantam Press, 2001) p. 213

7   ibid. p. 213

8   ibid. p. 213

9   Sinclair McKay, *The Secret Life of Bletchley Park* (London: Aurum, 2010) p. 169

10 Mavis Batey, *Dilly: The Man Who Broke Enigmas* (London: Biteback, 2010) p. 164

11 Mavis Batey, ibid. p. 164

12 Mavis Batey, ibid. p. 164

13 Mavis Batey, ibid. p. 164

14 Sinclair McKay, *The Secret Life of Bletchley Park* (London: Aurum, 2010) p. 208

15 Derek Taunt, *Hut 6 From the Inside,* Eds. Michael Smith and Ralph Erskine, *Action This Day* (London, New York, Toronto, Sydney, Auckland: Bantam Press, 2001) p. 89

16 Ibid. p. 89

17 Mavis Batey, op. cit. p. 164.

18 Michael Smith, *Station X: The Codebreakers of Bletchley Park* (London: Channel 4 Books, 1998) p. 133

19 Sinclair McKay, *The Secret Life of Bletchley Park* (London: Aurum, 2010) p. 302

20 Sinclair Mackay, ibid. p. 302

21 Sinclair Mackay, ibid. p. 302

22 Sinclair McKay, *The Secret Life of Bletchley Park* (London: Aurum, 2010) p. 195

23 Hugh Sebag-Montefiore, *Enigma: The Battle For The Code* (London: Cassell, 2004) p. 119

24 Sinclair Mackay, *The Secret Life of Bletchley Park* (London: Aurum, 2010) p. 196

Chapter 7: D-Day and Victory in Europe

1   Brian Oakley, *The Bletchley Park War Diaries 1939-45* (London: Wynne Press, 2011) 40/10A p. 40

2   Brian Oakley, *The Bletchley Park War Diaries 1939-45* (London: Wynne Press, 2011) 40/10A p. 40

3   Juliet Gardiner, *The Blitz: The British Under Attack* (Great Britain: Harper Press, 2010) p. 285

4   Sinclair McKay, *The Secret Life of Bletchley Park* (London: Aurum Press, 2010) p. 275

5   Sinclair McKay, ibid. p. 275

6   Sinclair McKay, ibid. p. 274

7   Dr Brian Oakley, *The Bletchley Park War Diaries: July 1939-August 1945* (London: Wynne Press, 2011) 44/12A p. 156

8   Mavis Batey, *Dilly: The Man Who Broke Enigmas* (London: Biteback, 2010) p. 156

9   John Masterman, *The Double Cross System* (World Wide: Yale University Press, 1972) p. 146

10 Dr David Kenyon, 'All Ears on D-Day', *Bletchley Park Magazine 7* (Autumn 2016) pp. 28-35

11 *Women in War*, eds. Celia Lee and Edward Strong (Barnsley: Pen & Sword Military, 2012), p.103.

12 Mavis Batey, *Dilly: The Man Who Broke Enigmas* (London: Biteback, 2010) p. 111

13 Dr David Kenyon, 'All Ears on D-Day', *Bletchley Park Magazine 7*, p. 35

14 Dr Brian Oakley, *The Bletchley Park War Diaries: July 1939-August 1945* (London: Wynne Press, 2011) 45/05A p. 170

15 Dr Brian Oakley, ibid. 45/05A p. 170

16 *Action This Day*, Eds. Michael Smith and Ralph Erskine: 'An Undervalued Effort: How the British Broke Japan's Codes' (London: Bantam Press, 2001) p. 149

17 National Archives: Demobilisation memo. Cited: Sinclair McKay, *The Secret Life of Bletchley Park* (London: Aurum, 2010) pp. 281, 282

Chapter 8: Post-War Life

1   Shula Subramaniam and Joel Greenberg: 'A Scrupulous Man' *Bletchley Park Magazine*, Issue 2, Spring/Summer 2014 p. 1

2 Sinclair McKay, *The Secret Life of Bletchley Park* (London: Aurum, 2010) p. 309

3 Sinclair McKay, *The Secret Life of Bletchley Park* (London: Aurum, 2010) p. 313

4 Sinclair McKay, *The Secret Life of Bletchley Park* (London: Aurum, 2010) p. 290

5 Sinclair McKay, *The Secret Life of Bletchley Park* (London: Aurum, 2010) p. 290

6 Mavis Batey, 'Down to Earth: An Oral History of British Horticulture' (London: National Sound Archive, 2003) F15120-5 Interviewer: Louise Brodie

7 Mavis Batey, ibid.

Chapter 9: Return to England

1 Michael Smith, *Station X: The Codebreakers of Bletchley Park* (London: Channel 4 Books, 1998) p. 59

2 Elizabeth Grice, 'Garden Campaigner Talks to Mavis Batey' (*The Oldie*, January 2013) p. 12

3 Mavis Batey, 'Down to Earth: An Oral History of British Horticulture' (London: National Sound Archive, 2003) F15120-5 Interviewer: Louise Brodie

4 W. G. Hoskins, *The Making of the English Landscape* (London: Pelican Books, 1975) p. 303

5 Mavis Batey, 'Down to Earth: An Oral History of British Horticulture' (London: National Sound Archive, 2003) F15120-5 Interviewer: Louise Brodie

6 Mavis Batey, ibid.

7 *The Oxford Times* (20 October 2013)

8 Mavis Batey, 'Down to Earth: An Oral History of British Horticulture' (London: National Sound Archive, 2003) F15120-5 Interviewer: Louise Brodie

9 Mavis Batey, ibid.

Chapter 10: Nuneham Courtenay

1 Oxford University Register of Estates, etc. (Ref: UC 7/2)

2 Elizabeth Grice, 'Gardener Campaigner Talks to Elizabeth Grice', *The Oldie* (London: January, 2013) p. 12

3 Mavis Batey, *Dilly: The Man Who Bbroke Enigmas* (London: Biteback, 2010) p. 160

4 Mavis Batey, ibid. p. 160

5 Mavis Batey, 'Elitism For All', *The Garden History Society: Newsletter 67* (Spring 2003) p. 2

6   Norman Scarfe, *Innocent Espionage: The La Rochefoucauld Brothers' Tour of England in 1795* (London: Boydell & Brewer, 1995) see *The Garden History Society: Newsletter 44* (Summer 1995) p. 24

7   Mavis Batey, 'Down to Earth: An Oral History of British Horticulture' (London: National Sound Archive 2003) F15120-5 Interviewer: Louise Brodie

8   Mavis Batey, ibid.

9   Jackson's Oxford Journal, 17 February 1769

10   R. S. Crane, *New Essays by Oliver Goldsmith* (Chicago: 1927) p. 116

11   Oliver Goldsmith, *The Revolution of Low Life,* cited by Mavis Batey, *Nuneham Courtenay; An Oxfordshire Deserted Village,* p. 120

12   R. S. Crane, *The Revolution in Low Life, New Essays by Oliver Goldsmith* (Chicago, 1927)

13   Ralph M. Wardle, *Oliver Goldsmith* (Lawrence: University of Kansas Press) (London: Constable,1957) p. 204

14   Mavis Batey, *Oxoniensia: The Journal of the Oxfordshire Architectural and Historical Society, 1968* Vol 33 and various other magazines.

15   Mavis Batey, *The Garden History Society: Newsletter 15* (Autumn 1985) p. 3

16   Mavis Batey, ibid.

Chapter 11: Mavis Joins the Garden History Society

1   E. Graham, *Gardening in Wartime* (London: Peter Davis, 1940)

2   Gordon Honeycombe, *Selfridges: Seventy-five Years 1909-1984: The Story of the Store* (London: Park Lane Press, 1984)

3   Percy Cane, 'Post-war Gardens', *Journal of the Royal Society of Arts* (25 December 1942) p. 46

4   Brent Elliott, 'The Development and Present State of Garden History', *Occasional Papers from the RHS Lindley Library,* 9 (2012) 3-94 p. 23

5   Sue Minter, *The Well-connected Gardener: A Biography of Alicia Amherst, Founder of Garden History* (Brighton, UK: Book Guild, 2010) p. 28

6   Tim Richardson, (ed) *Timeline: 50 years of the GHS; Kay Sanecki, The Early Days, GHS at 50* (Summer 2015)

7   Kay Sanecki, From a recently discovered news sheet. Untitled. *c.*1997

8   Kate Tiller, 'Garden History at Oxford', *Garden History,* 24:1 (1996) pp. 146-147

9   Mavis Batey, *The Garden History Society: Newsletter 18* (Autumn 1986) p. 3

10   W. I. Corlett, *The Garden History Society: Newsletter 16* (Spring 1986) p. 11

11 Private letter, 30 January 2005

12 Mavis Batey, 'Down to Earth: An Oral History of British Horticulture' : F15120-5 (London: National Sound Archive, 2003)

13 Sarah Jackson, 'Mavis Batey: From Codebreaker to Campaigner for Historic Parks and Gardens, Http://.parksandgardens.org/learning/explore/175-contemporary-profiles/335-mavis-batey?showall&start=1 [accessed:12 December 2013]

14 *The Garden History Society: Newsletter 13* (Spring, 1985) p. 12

15 Kate Tiller, 'Garden History at Oxford', *The Journal of Garden History* (1996) 24:1 p. 147

16 Mavis Batey, 'The Garden History Society and the Conservation of Gardens', *c.*1989 Reproduced: *GHS Newsletter 93* (Spring 2014)

17 Mavis Batey, 'Down to Earth: An Oral History of British Horticulture': F15120-5 (London: National Sound archive, 2003)

18 Mavis Batey, ibid.

19 Mavis Batey, 'Down to Earth: An Oral History of British Horticulture': F16120-5 (London: National Sound Årchive, 2003)

20 Mavis Batey, David Lambert and Kim Wilkie, *Indignation: The Campaign for Conservation* (London: Kit-Cat Books, 2000) p. 54

21 Mavis Batey, 'The Restoration of the Garden of Keats House, Hampstead', *The Journal of Garden History* (1975), 3:4 p. 37

22 Mavis Batey, ibid. p. 39

Chapter 12: Life in the Oxford Dons' Suburb

1 Private correspondence

2 Helen Turner, 'Rara Mavis: an Ultra good code-cracker', *The Oxford Times*, Friday, December 15, 1978

3 Private correspondence

4 Hermione Lee, *Penelope Fitzgerald, A Life* (New York: Alfred A. Knope, 2014) p. 214

Chapter 13: Mavis Becomes a Campaigner for Conservation

1[i] Kay N. Sanecki, 'Memories of the Founding of the Society', *GHS Newsletter: No. 15* (Autumn 1985) p. 13

2 Tim Richardson, 'Time-line: 50 years of the GHS 'The GHS at 50', *GHS News*

(Summer 2015) p. 10

3 Dominic Cole, 'Mavis Batey, MBE', *GHS News No. 93* (Spring 2014) p. 12

4 Kay N. Sanecki, 'Memories of the Founding of the Society', *GHS Newsletter: No. 15* (Autumn 1985) p. 13

5 Mavis Batey cited: Tim Richardson, 'The Garden History Society Time-line, 1965-2005', *GHS News No. 76* (Winter 2005)

6 Sarah Jackson, 'Mavis Batey: From Codebreaker to Campaigner for Historic Parks and Gardens' http://www.parksandgardens.org/learning/explore/175 contemmporaryprofiles/335-mavis-batey?showal&start=1 [Accessed: 12 December 2013]

7 John Campbell, *Roy Jenkins: A Well-Rounded Life* (London: Jonathan Cape, 2014) p. 736 Note 238. Extract from *Evening Standard* n.d.

8 Campbell, ibid. p. 45

9 Andrew S. Crines and Kevin Hickson, 'Harold Wilson: The Unprincipled Prime Minister, Patrick Diamond' *(Times Literary Supplement*, 29 July 2016) p. 31

10 Sarah Jackson, ibid. [Accessed: 12 December 2013]

11 Margaret Campbell-Culver, 'Mount Edgcumbe', *Garden History*, 24:1 (1996) pp. 8-9

12 Cited: David Lambert, 'Indignation Today', *Indignation! The Campaign for Conservation*, Mavis Batey, David Lambert, Kim Wilkie (London: Kit-Cat Books, 2000) p. 35

13 Sarah Jackson, 'Mavis Batey: From Codebreaker to Campaigner for Historic Parks and Gardens' [Accessed: 12 December 2013] http://www.parksandgardens.org/ learning/explore/175-contemporary-profiles/335-mavis-batey

14 Arthur Jones, *Britain's Heritage: The Creation of the National Heritage Memorial Fund* (London: Weidenfeld & Nicholson, 1986) Cited: Keith Grieves and Jennifer White, *Garden History* 42:Supl 2014 p. 30

15 Kay N. Sanecki, 'Memories of the Founding of the Society', *GHS Newsletter: No.15* (Autumn 1985) p. 13

Chapter 14: The Garden History Society Spreads Its Wings

1 Michael Symes, *Garden History Society: Newsletter 13* (Spring 1985) p. 7

2 A letter from Dmitri Shvidkovsky to Mavis Batey, cited. *Garden History Society: Newsletter 21* (Autumn 1987) p. 6

3 A letter from Dmitri Shvidkovsky to Mavis Batey, ibid.

4 ibid.

5   John Anthony, *Garden History Society: Newsletter 21* (Autumn 1987) pp. 9-12

6   'Visit to Russia, 15-26 September 1989', *Garden History Society: Newsletter 28* (Spring 1990) p. 9

7   Mavis Batey, 'Review of the Conference: The English Garden Overseas: Eastern Europe', *Garden History Society: Newsletter 33* (Winter 1991) p. 10

8   Mavis Batey, 'The English Garden Overseas: Eastern Europe', *Garden History Society: Newsletter 33/34* (Winter-Spring 1991-2) p. 11

9   Mavis Batey, 'Down to Earth: An Oral History of British Horticulture' F15120-5 (London: National Sound Archive, 2003)

Chapter 15: A New Home: Living on the South Coast

1   Mavis Batey, 'Down to Earth: An Oral History of British Horticulture' (London: National Sound Archive, 2003) F15120-5 Interviewer: Louise Brodie

2   Noel Annan, *Our Age: Portrait of a Generation* (London: Weidenfeld and Nicholson,1990) p. 165

3   ibid.p. 56

4   ibid. p. 33

5   Mavis Batey, 'Down to Earth: An Oral History of British Horticulture' (London: National Sound Archive, 2003) F15120 Interviewer: Louise Brodie

6   John Sales, 'Garden Restoration Past and Present', *Journal of the Garden History Society* (1995) 23.1, p. 5

7   Mavis Batey, 'Down to Earth: An Oral History of British Horticulture' (London: National Sound Archive, 2003) F15120-5 Interviewer: Louse Brodie

8   Mavis Batey, ibid.

9   Juliet Gardiner, *Animals at War* (London: Heinemann, 1983) p. 80

10 Mavis Batey in conversation with Michael Smith, httplausioiboo/1736751-bletchley-park-extra:e28-mavisbatey

11 Mavis Batey, 'Down to Earth: An Oral History of British Horticulture' (London: National Sound Archive, 2003) F15120-5 Interviewer: Louise Brodie

12 Mavis Batey, op. cit.

Chapter 16: Two Regency Gardens

1   Travis Elborough, editor *Our History of the 20th Century* (London: Michael O'Mara, 2017) Cited: Review: Libby Purvis, *Times Literary Supplement*

(14.11.2017) p. 27

2   Wendy Osborne, 'The Bletchley Codebreaker Who Came To Tea', *Daily Telegraph*,
     18 November 2013

3   Wendy visited Hazel

4   Correspondence between Wendy Osborne and the author

Chapter 17: Thames Landscape Strategy: Hampton to Kew and The Garden at Strawberry Hill House

1   Mavis Batey, Letter to Jane Crawley, 30 January 2005

2   Kim Wilkie, *Mavis Batey: The Genius of the Scene at Ninety*, ed. Charles Boot
     (1 June 2001)

3   Mavis Batey, 'Down to Earth: An Oral History of British Horticulture' (London:
     National Sound Archive, 2003) F15120-5 Interviewer: Louise Brodie

4   Mavis Batey, 'Revisiting Strawberry Hill' speech at Strawberry Hill at the launch
     of the Restoration Appeal by the World Monuments Fund, 12 July 2000

5   Fred Karno (1866-1941) was an English theatre impresario and slapstick
     comedian of music-hall fame. He purchased Tagg's Island on the River Thames
     and replaced the existing hotel with his newly built *Karsino*.

6   David Lambert, 9 May 2016

7   *Garden History Society: Newsletter 42* (Winter 1994)

8   Mavis's younger daughter in conversation with the writer

Chapter 18: Film, Theatre and Friends

1   Mavis Batey, 'As Seen on TV', *Garden History Society: Newsletter 46* (Spring
     1996) p. 2

2   Mavis Batey, ibid.

3   *Daily Telegraph* 'Kate was fine – if a little scruffy', 4 October 2001, p. 25

4   *Daily Telegraph*, ibid.

5   *Daily Telegraph*, ibid.

6   *Daily Telegraph*, ibid.

7   Doug Pinchin, private correspondence

8   Ibid.

9   Ibid.

10   Ibid.

11 Ed. Charles Boot, Kim Wilkie, 'Mavis Batey MBE – The Genius of the Scene at 90', *Garden History Society Newsletter 87* (Spring 2011)

12 The family's life in North Oxford is partly taken from a private paper of Mavis Batey and memories shared with the author by her daughters

Chapter 19: Literary Mavis

1   An original copy of *Alice in ID25* can be found among the papers of Alexander Guthrie Denniston. The Denniston Archive is housed at the Churchill College Archive Centre, Churchill College, Cambridge (Ref. DENN 3/3).

2   Penelope Fitzgerald, *The Knox Brothers: Edmund ('Evoe') 1881-1971, Dillwyn 1883-1943, Wilfred 1866-1950, Ronald 1888-1957* (London: Macmillan, 1977)

3   Frank Birch, Dilly Knox, *Alice in ID25*, compiled with introductions by Mavis Batey and Edward Wakeling (Bedfordshire: UK: Aznet, 2007) p. 43

4   Mavis Batey, *Dilly, The Man Who Broke Enigmas* (London: Biteback, 2010) p. 111

5   Mavis Batey, *The World of Alice* (Hampshire UK: Pitkin Books, 2009) p. 8

6   Mavis Batey, ibid. p. 9

7   Mavis Batey, *The Historic Gardens of Oxford and Cambridge* (London: Macmillan, 1989) p. 13

8   Julia Alvarez, 'Fixed Facts and Creative Freedom in the Biographical Novel', in *Truthful Fictions: Conversations with American Biographical Novelists*, ed. by Michael Lackey (London: Bloomsbury, 2014) p. 30

9   Mavis Batey, *The Historic Gardens of Oxford and Cambridge* (London: Macmillan, 1989) p. 68

10 James Ralph, *The Case of Authors by Profession or Trade, Stated with Regard to Booksellers, the Stage and the Public* (London: Griffiths, 1758) Cited: Norma Clarke, *Brothers of the Quill, Oliver Goldsmith in Grub Street* (Cambridge, Massachusetts and London: Harvard University Press, 2016) p. 73

11 Mavis Batey, *Arcadian Thames: The River and Landscape from Hampton to Kew* (London: Barn Elms, 1994)

12 Mavis Batey, 'Horace Walpole and the Landscaping of Strawberry Hill', *Arcadian Thames: The River Landscape from Hampton to Kew* (London: Barn Elms, 1994) p. 63

13 Mavis Batey, 'Introduction': *Indignation! The Campaign for Conservation*, Mavis Batey, Kim Wilkie, David Lambert (London: Kit-Cat Books, 2000) p. 7

14 Edward Fawcett, 'The Genius of the Scene', *Garden History 24.1* (1996) p. 1

15   Mavis Batey, *Jane Austen and the English Landscape* (London: Barn Elms, 1996) p. 22

Chapter 20: Espionage and Cunning Schemes

1   H. Montgomery Hyde, *The Quiet Canadian: The Secret Service Story of Sir William Stephenson* (London: Hamish Hamilton, 1962) p. 105

2   H. Montgomery Hyde, *The Quiet Canadian: The Secret Service Story of Sir William Stephenson* (London: Hamish Hamilton, 1962) p. 108

3   Mavis Batey, *Dilly: The Man Who Broke Enigmas* (London: Biteback, 2010) p. 130

4   'Mavis Batey Breaking Italian Naval Enigma' in *Action This Day*, ed. by Ralph Erskine and Michael Smith (WW: Bantam Press, 2001) pp. 108,109

5   Mavis Batey, op. cit. p. 130

6   Mavis Batey, *From Bletchley with Love: Ian Fleming's wartime years with Naval Intelligence which brought him into close contact with Bletchley Park providing the background for his Bond novels* (Milton Keynes: Bletchley Park Trust, 2008) p. 7

7   Mavis Batey, *Dilly: The Man Who Broke Enigmas* (London: Biteback, 2009) p. 113

8   Mavis Batey, *From Bletchley with Love* (Milton Keynes: Bletchley Park Trust, 2008) p. 21

9   Mavis Batey, ibid. p. 24

10   Mavis Batey, ibid. p. 25

11   Mavis Batey, ibid. p. 23

Chapter 21: Back to Bletchley Park

1   Michael Smith, 'Bletchley Park Mythbusters', *Bletchley Park Magazine*, 2016, No. 6 p. 9

2   Mavis Batey, 'Reviving the Gardens at Bletchley Park', *The Bucks Gardener, Buckinghamshire Gardens Trust Newsletter* (Spring 2004) pp. 2-3

3   Jean Stone, *The American Spirit in the English Garden* (Suffolk, England: Garden Art Press, 2015) pp. 91-97

4   Inauguration of American Garden Trail, *Friends of Bletchley Park Newsletter* (Winter 2004)

INDEX